MACROECONOMICS FOR AFRICA

Studies in the Economics of Africa

Editor: I. LIVINGSTONE

Money and Credit in Developing Africa
ERIC L. FURNESS

Development Economics in Action
TONY KILLICK

Economics for Eastern Africa
I. LIVINGSTONE and H. W. ORD

Stabilization Policy in an African Setting
J. R. KING

Papers on the Political Economy of Tanzania
K. KIM, R. MABELE and M. SCHULTHEIS (Eds)

Essentials of Demographic Analysis for Africa
G. M. K. KPEDEKPO

Agricultural Economics for Tropical Africa
I. LIVINGSTON and H. W. ORD

Papers on the Economy of Botswana
CHARLES HARVEY (Ed.)

Industry and Accumulation in Africa
MARTIN FRANSMAN (Ed.)

Papers on the Kenyan Economy
TONY KILLICK (Ed.)

Macroeconomics for Africa

The elementary theory of the working of present-day African economies, illustrated by examples taken mainly from the economy of Zambia

CHARLES HARVEY

Fellow of Institute of Development Studies, University of Sussex
Formerly Senior Lecturer in Economics, University of Zambia

H·E·B

LONDON
HEINEMANN
NAIROBI · IBADAN

Heinemann Educational Books Ltd
22 Bedford Square, London WC1B 3HH
P.M.B. 5205, Ibadan · P.O. Box 45314, Nairobi

EDINBURGH MELBOURNE AUCKLAND
HONG KONG SINGAPORE KUALA LUMPUR
NEW DELHI KINGSTON PORT OF SPAIN

ISBN 0 435 97201 4

First published 1977
Reprinted 1979, 1981, 1983

Printed and bound in Great Britain by
Biddles Ltd, Guildford and King's Lynn

Contents

List of Tables

List of Figures

Preface

All good macroeconomic textbooks are set in the context of a particular economy. It is almost impossible to discuss the measurement of national income or the workings of the monetary system, for example, without reference to particular national income figures and monetary institutions. This alone makes it difficult to teach macroeconomics in anglophone Africa using British or American textbooks. The student is forced to read and learn a great deal about the British or American economy in order to understand the text; and the teacher must spend a great deal of time explaining the differences between Western and African conditions. *Some* comparison of this sort is probably valuable, but a little goes a long way.

However, much more serious problems are created by using Western textbooks. Basically, they deal extensively with problems of little or no relevance to Africa, and discuss very little or ignore completely problems which are of very great if not fundamental importance in Africa. To some extent this is merely a matter of balance – the need is for less about industry, more about agriculture and the export sector. From an African point of view too much attention is given in Western texts to domestic profit-seeking investment as a source of fluctuations in national income, whereas in Africa export prices, foreign investment, fluctuations in agricultural supply are often more important.

To some extent, though, it is more than a matter of balance. The structure of African economies is so fundamentally different in some respects from the structure of, say, the British economy, that parts of established theory simply do not apply and may indeed be positively misleading.

For example, the emphases on the relationship between savings and investment, on liquidity preference, on the interest rate as a determinant of investment, all depend on the existence of well-developed capital markets and a variety of financial intermediaries which do not exist in African economies. There are thus a series of links, in the basic macroeconomic model of Western texts, which do not exist in African conditions.

A second example: rising demand for manufactured products would, according to Western theory, induce investment in increased production facilities. In Africa it is more likely to induce increases in imported inputs and in profits sent out of the country, if manufacturing is foreign-owned.

These criticisms are relatively easy to make. The problems lie in deciding how to handle them in a textbook. There are three rough categories.

(1) Situations where the student can usefully learn existing theory, for example how to measure national income in the modern sector, but must also learn additional material, in this example how to measure and compare subsistence income. This results in very long chapters.

(2) Situations where the basic type of analysis is useful, but must be applied to African situations which do not occur in industrialized economies and are thus not treated in Western textbooks – for example national income analysis applied to the doubling of export prices over a very short period.

(3) Situations where 'Western' theory is thoroughly inappropriate and the text must really start from scratch with a new approach, in order to avoid a major learning and teaching effort for the acquisition of misleading theories – for example investment theory. Existing theory must of course be mentioned in these cases, but preferably in a very minor way at the end, when more appropriate ideas have already been thoroughly discussed.

Clearly the last category is hardest to handle. It can be very damaging if a student starts off with the wrong set of ideas. At the same time it may be unfair to put a new approach into something called a textbook. This problem is made worse by the fact that new theories are often hard to test, because official statistics are collected to serve old-established theories. On the whole I have been slightly cautious. It is to be hoped that future texts will be able to be more adventurous as more research results become available.

The book is based on a second-year course in macroeconomics which I taught for four years at the University of Zambia. Although other African economies are mentioned in making comparisons and in using research results, the book is based to a considerable extent on the Zambian economy. It seemed much better to rethink macroeconomic theory from a relatively thorough knowledge of one economy than to try and do so from a more superficial knowledge of several. After all it was the indiscriminate application of 'English' theory to African economies, without making clear that industrialized economies are a very 'special case'[1] with their own (usually unstated) sets of assumptions, that caused all the trouble in the first place. Clearly I did not want to fall into the same trap. However, if Zambia is something of a special case in Africa, I am confident that it will be much easier to adapt the analysis of this book to the conditions of, say, Malawi or Nigeria than to adapt the analysis of a typical Western text. In short, this book is written with English-speaking African students in mind; the use of a mainly Zambian context will have reduced the analytical errors. Teachers both in

Zambia and elsewhere will in any case use local and/or updated material for their own teaching.

The choice of subject matter is fairly conventional. The book covers the 'usual' macroeconomic topics except that trade cycle theory is excluded. I have assumed that students have done an elementary introductory course in economics, although the book could probably be read with only a little difficulty by a beginner. A knowledge of simple algebra and graphs is also assumed – without it no student can pretend to even a remotely serious study of the subject.[2] It has also been assumed that university economics courses go on to cover important subjects in greater depth in the third (and fourth) years – this one book cannot cover everything.

NOTES

[1] The reference is to Dudley Seers, 'The Limitations of the Special Case', *Bulletin of the Oxford Institute of Economics and Statistics*, May 1973, reprinted in K. Martin and J. Knapp (eds.), *The Teaching of Development Economics*, London, Frank Cass, 1967.

[2] See my article 'Mathematics and the teaching of economics' in I. Livingstone *et al.* (eds.), *The teaching of economics in Africa*, London, Chatto and Windus for Sussex University Press, 1973.

Acknowledgements

The original encouragement to write the book came from correspondence students at the University of Zambia for whom I first wrote up my lectures. Colleagues who gave tutorials in the course, especially Tom Warke, supplied valuable feedback and criticism. Robert Baker and James Fry, who have taught the course more recently, also provided helpful comments; Percy Selwyn, Alex Tweedie and Dudley Seers read some chapters with great care, and Reg Green read nearly all of it, covering the draft in blunt-pencilled, pointed comments. Christine Smith agreed to act as a student guinea-pig, in the absence of a class taking the course, and also did some work on Zambian figures for the book; her work was both helpful and encouraging. Sue Humphrey typed all of it more than once, drew most of the graphs and never looked more than slightly disapproving. Patience Nyadza typed the index quickly and efficiently. Finally, my wife, by virtually never mentioning it, enabled me to forget it when I was at home.

CHARLES HARVEY
Institute of Development Studies at the University of Sussex

1 *Introduction*

1 THE DIFFERENCE BETWEEN MACROECONOMICS AND MICROECONOMICS

The distinction between macroeconomics and microeconomics is more than just a casual and convenient division of economics into two parts. Macroeconomics is the study of large aggregates (*makros* is the Greek word for large) such as national income, aggregate demand and supply, aggregate consumption and investment. Because these aggregates are large in relation to the national economy, a change in one aggregate tends to affect all the others.

For example, if wages rise, wage-earners will spend more. This in turn will increase the demand for goods and services, which will increase employment, profits, imports and possibly prices. As a result, tax revenue will increase and government may decide to spend more; wages may rise further as a result of increasing demand for labour or as a result of trade union activity to get higher wages to offset price rises. Thus in macroeconomic analysis it is important to take account of the effect of changes in one variable on all the other variables; and to take account of 'feedback', that is that a change in one variable may eventually feed back on to that variable itself. In the example given, a change in wages affected not only a number of other macroeconomic variables, but also fed back in the form of further changes in wages.

Microeconomics, on the other hand, is the study of small individual parts of the economy (*mikros* is the Greek word for small) where it is reasonable to assume that there is no feedback. For example if there is an increase in the wages of people making shoes, the cost of shoe-making increases and the price of shoes may go up or the profits of shoe-making firms may go down, or both. But it is reasonable to assume that the increased incomes of the shoe-workers do not cause a significant increase in the demand for shoes, because the shoe-workers are a very small proportion of the total number of people who buy shoes. In addition, any increase in the price of shoes has a negligible effect on the general price level and is not likely, therefore, to cause the shoe-workers to demand further wage increases. In other words it is reasonable to assume, in studying a small, microeconomic sector of the economy, that there are no feedback effects.

Another way of putting the distinction between microeconomics and macroeconomics is to say that in microeconomics one can assume 'ceteris paribus' (which is Latin for 'other things being equal'). This means that one analyses a small sector of the economy on the assumption that changes in that sector are too small to affect the rest of the economy. One can therefore assume all other factors unchanged (or 'equal'). In macroeconomics it is normally quite wrong to assume 'ceteris paribus' – indeed the main purpose of macroeconomic analysis is to examine how 'other things' change in response to each other.

The three main macroeconomic aggregates are demand, supply and income. If total demand increases, total supply will increase or prices will increase. In either case, income rises. If income rises then people with increased incomes will try and demand more goods and services, that is, demand increases again. There is thus a continuous flow of causation:

DEMAND→SUPPLY AND PRICES→INCOME→DEMAND etc.

Again pointing out the important difference between macro and micro, in microeconomics the same flow of causation looks like this:

DEMAND FOR SHOES→SUPPLY OF SHOES AND PRICE OF SHOES→ INCOMES OF SHOE-MAKERS

but the incomes of shoe-makers do *not* significantly affect the demand for shoes, so that the chain of causation is broken and there is no feedback effect.

Deciding which is a macro and which a microeconomic variable is not always easy; furthermore there is some variation from country to country. For example, the price of copper is clearly a microeconomic variable in most countries. In Zambia, it is equally clearly a macroeconomic variable, since copper accounts for about half of national income,[1] at times more than half of government revenue, more than 90% of exports. Similarly, in a rich country like the USA, the price of any one foodstuff is very much a microeconomic variable. Americans are mostly rich enough to enjoy a varied diet and to spend quite a small proportion of their incomes on food. In poor countries the staple food is such an important part of the diet of the urban and rural poor, and such an important part of the income of the rural poor, that anything affecting its production and price is probably best treated as a macroeconomic factor. Thus in Zambia, the prices paid to farmers for maize and the price paid by consumers for maize meal are macroeconomic variables; indeed they are determined by government, with a large subsidy to the consumer, precisely because of their great importance to the majority of the population.

2 THE CIRCULAR FLOW OF INCOME

The flow of money from demand to supply and prices, and back into people's pockets as income, is often called the 'circular flow of income'. Because the income being discussed is aggregate income in the whole economy, or national income, macroeconomics is often called 'national income analysis'.

There are three main 'leakages' out of the circular flow of income. The demand for goods and services is not *all* satisfied by production within the economy – some demand is met by imports. Buying imports increases the incomes of foreigners. For a small country like Zambia, the amount of income created for foreigners by an increase in Zambian imports is highly unlikely to cause a noticeable increase in the demand for Zambian exports. In other words there are negligible feedback effects from an increase in Zambian imports, so that imports are a leakage out of the circular flow of income. For most countries in fact it is true that their demand for imports is so small in relation to world trade that it is reasonable to assume 'ceteris paribus', or no feedback effects from an increase in imports. Only in the case of Britain in the nineteenth century, when two thirds of international trade was British, or the USA in the twentieth century (and perhaps Japan in the last part of the twentieth century), would it be necessary to investigate the feedback effects on the demand for exports, of an increase in imports. The flow of causation now looks like this:

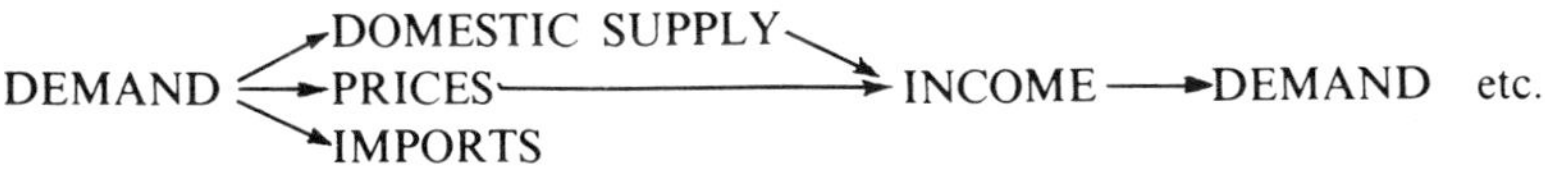

The second main leakage arises because not all increases in income result immediately in increased spending. Savings also increase. If people whose incomes increase bury money in the ground, or keep it under the bed, or deposit money in a bank or a building society or the Post Office, then demand remains unaffected by the amount of money that is saved, *provided that* the savings institutions do not immediately lend the money, for spending by someone else. If, say, the bank in which savings are deposited lends the money to people to buy cars, to businesses to buy new equipment and to the government to spend more than it has received in taxes, then the savings leakage from the circular flow of income is offset by a new injection into demand caused by spending out of borrowed money. The flow of causation now looks like this:

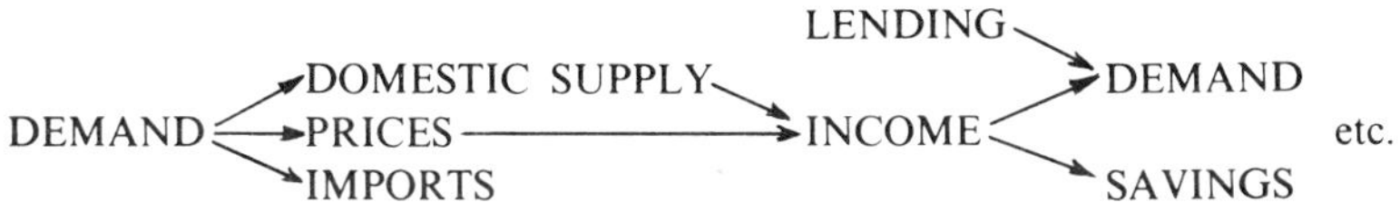

The third main leakage is taxation. If income increases, people usually find themselves paying more tax. In Zambia, income tax affects only the highly paid – only about one in six of people in employment paid any income tax in 1970, and the proportion has increased only slightly since then. But nearly all wage earners pay Personal Levy which increases with income; and all wage earners pay National Provident Fund (NPF) contributions which also increase with income. Contributions to the NPF are not a tax because they are returnable to the contributor at some time in the future – they are really a form of compulsory saving. The macroeconomic effect is the same as an income tax, however, precisely because the contributions are compulsory. Companies also pay increased tax if their profits increase. In addition to taxes on income, the government receives more revenue from increased spending. Cigarettes and alcoholic drinks are taxed, so that if, as is very likely, people spend part of increases in income on cigarettes and beer, some of the money leaks out of the circular flow of income to the government, rather than increasing the incomes of bar-owners and the people who make cigarettes and brew beer. A wide range of imported consumer goods are also taxed, so that money spent on imports, especially luxury imports like big cars which carry exceptionally high tax rates, causes a flow of income to the government as well as to foreign manufacturers.

Now obviously if government promptly spends every increase in its revenue from taxes then tax is not really a leakage from the circular flow of income. In practice, the connection between tax receipts and spending by government is not very close *in the short term*. The government's spending plans cannot usually be changed quickly in response to changes in tax receipts – civil servants' salaries, for example, which are a large part of government spending, are normally only changed as a result of a fairly lengthy review procedure, and the number of civil servants employed changes fairly slowly too. In the long term, tax revenue is a very important determinant of government spending, although even in the long term there are other determining factors, such as aid receipts and government borrowing.

Allowing for the existence of government alters the flow of causation to look like this:

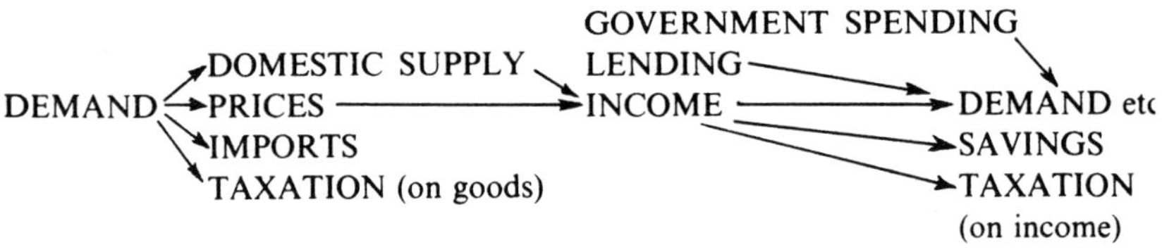

Government spending is shown as an independent factor affecting demand, to indicate that it is not directly affected in the short term by changes in tax revenue, and that it can increase quite independently of tax revenue, through government borrowing for example.

The final addition to demand comes from exports. In Zambia this is in many ways the most important since so much of the economy depends on the copper mining sector, and on the price of copper. The copper price is determined by supply and demand in the world market, so that it is almost wholly independent of the Zambian economy. Although Zambia is a major producer of copper, accounting for about 12% of world production, this share is not large enough for Zambian events to have more than a very small short-term impact on the copper price. This is in sharp contrast to countries which export manufactured goods, where domestic events, for example rising costs, affect the demand for exports via changes in export prices. The final version of the circular flow of income now looks like this:

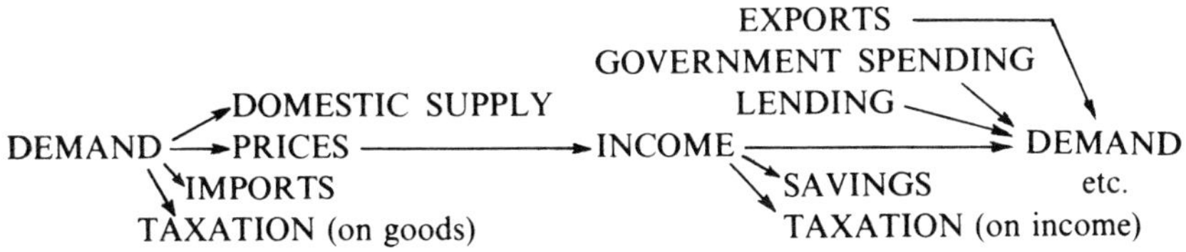

3 THE MAIN MACROECONOMIC AGGREGATES

The above formulation yields most of the main components of demand and supply. Demand is made up of:

(1) Consumer demand (consumption) – that is, the demand for food, clothing and other day-to-day necessities by individuals, paid for mainly out of income.
(2) Investment demand – that is, the demand for long-lasting goods such as buildings and machinery, roads and dams, paid for mainly out of savings and borrowing.
(3) Government demand – that is, spending by government in providing services such as defence and education, paid for mainly out of taxes.
(4) Export demand – that is, in Zambia, the demand for copper by foreign buyers.

Supply is split into only two main components, namely

(1) Domestic (home) production.
(2) Imports.

The subdivisions of demand are used because the factors influencing consumption, investment, government spending and export demand are clearly very different. The subdivisions of supply are used because domestic production generates domestic income, whereas imports generate income for foreigners. Clearly the two types of supply have quite different feedback effects.

Further subdivisions of demand and supply are frequently used: for example, small farmers and urban wage earners tend to have different consumption habits, so it is useful to treat them separately sometimes. Investment can usefully be subdivided into investment by individuals (mainly in housing) and investment by firms (mainly in productive buildings and machinery). Firms can be subdivided further into large and small, or locally owned and foreign-owned. For the moment, however, the analysis will be mainly confined to the four main subdivisions of demand and the two of supply.

Because of the different economic objectives of individuals and companies, income can also be usefully subdivided into business income (profits) and individual income (wages and salaries). The income earned by self-employed people – farmers, small traders and professional people like doctors and lawyers – is rather difficult to classify, since such people behave with a mixture of individual motives. For example, savings out of business profits are usually much higher than savings out of wages and salaries; savings out of farmers' incomes are usually somewhere in between, probably because farmers are both individual consumers and businessmen at one and the same time.

The subdivisions of demand, supply and income, and the variables which may be of interest because of the particular structure of the Zambian economy like the maize and copper prices, are not the only important macroeconomic variables. From the diagrams of the circular flow of income it is clear that anything affecting the general level of prices must also be important; that wages, and therefore unions and the labour market, are very important in determining individual incomes; and that all the factors affecting the amount of spending out of borrowed money, such as interest rates and the supply of money, must also be studied.

4 AGGREGATES AND LARGE NUMBERS – AN ADVANTAGE OF MACROECONOMICS

One further point should be made about working with economic aggregates. An aggregate such as consumption is made up of the consumption spending of a very large number of individuals. It is likely therefore that the sort of random factors which can affect microeconomic decisions will cancel out. For example, the spending of an individual will be the result not only of his income, savings and borrowing ability, but also of special factors such as the birth of a son, the death of a relative, the prospect of losing his job. These special factors would make it very difficult to forecast an individual's spending in any particular year. But when the spending of large numbers of people is aggregated, most of these special factors cancel out. One man spends more because of a funeral, another spends less because he is ill. Furthermore, deaths, births, marriages, illnesses all tend to be much the same from year to year unless some 'macroevent' occurs, universal enough to affect large numbers of people, such as a drought or an epidemic. It is thus probable that changes in aggregates can be analysed without having to pay attention to random personal events. The tendency for random events to offset each other if the numbers involved are very large is sometimes called the 'law of large numbers'.

Another advantage of macroeconomics is that while any particular individual may be able to get credit from his friends, not everyone can since someone must be doing the lending. In fact such private lending and borrowing must by definition cancel out over the community as a whole, so that spending out of borrowed funds can be analysed in terms of institutional credit, from banks and other financial institutions, while ignoring interpersonal loans. Similarly, while an individual farmer can always increase his holding of land, and an individual employer can get more skilled labour, all farmers and all employers cannot get more land and more skilled labour at the same time unless there is a spare supply of these resources.

Not all macroeconomic aggregates are subject to the so-called law of large numbers, however. Investment, especially in a small economy, is made up of a relatively small number of large projects. This is especially true of many government investments, which are undertaken by government partly because they are so large, as for instance in Zambia the Kafue and Kariba hydroelectric schemes and the Tanzam railway. Similarly, the Zambian mining sector dominates the economy and is run by only two major private groups, in conjunction with the government. In considering mining investment it is thus very necessary to take account of 'special' events as well as more usual economic factors such as profitability; and because mining is so large in relation to the economy, the same events must be taken account of in analysing aggregate investment.

Government's current expenditure, and to a lesser extent capital expenditure, shows characteristics of both sorts. The total is made up of a large number of relatively small amounts, and changes are the result both of large numbers of individual decisions, and of general economic factors such as the growth of the economy. So government spending can be analysed to *some* extent in the same way as economic aggregates like consumption and imports. But at the same time a single decision, for example to raise civil servants' salaries or to build Mulungushi Hall in a few months, can have a significant effect on the figures for total spending.

5 CONCLUSION

The absolutely vital thing to grasp from this chapter is the way that changes in aggregate demand and supply cannot be analysed without taking account of feedback. Most fundamentally, feedback occurs through changes in income. The detailed *way* in which feedback occurs depends on the ability of the home economy to increase its output in competition with imports, on how much prices rise, on the tax system, and so on. Each of the key macroeconomic variables will be discussed in detail in subsequent chapters, but students will find those chapters easier to follow if they think of all the implications of a statement such as: 'Every price rise is an increase in someone's income.'

It is also important to remember that although subsistence production is very little affected *directly* by changes in the macroeconomy, there is some indirect influence. Production for own consumption and investment normally uses few if any purchased inputs, and by definition the output is not sold. But relatively few farmers have no monetary dealings at all; and as regards their subsistence activities they *do* have alternatives. They can produce for the market, they can migrate to town in search of a job, or they can seek employment locally with other farmers or in non-agricultural work. Migration is a particularly important possibility in Zambia with its large proportion (for Africa) of people in towns. So changes in employment opportunities and cash wages on the one hand, and in opportunities to earn a cash income from farming on the other hand, do have some influence on subsistence farmers and their families and even, indirectly, on their subsistence activities.

NOTE

[1] This is a deliberately vague statement: the next chapter goes into the definition of national income in greater detail, and discusses just how to measure the contribution of copper.

2 *Measuring National Income I*

1 INTRODUCTION

If two people live in similar sorts of houses in the same town, earn their living by going out to work, spend their incomes in similar sorts of ways in the same group of shops, have roughly equal access to the same range of publicly provided services like health care, education for their children and the protection of the law, then it is reasonable to compare their economic well-being by comparing their money incomes or the spending of their money incomes. If two people live totally different lives, one of them being an urban wage earner, another a small farmer living in a village, producing mainly for his own consumption and using money irregularly and for only a minor part of his needs, then it is not really very reasonable to compare their economic well-being by means of monetary measures, even with adequate data.

The majority of people in Africa still live in villages and depend, for satisfying their basic needs, on consumption of their own production – although the use of money is increasing. Yet figures are published claiming to show, in money terms, the incomes of small farmers, and these figures are added to other forms of income in order to reach a figure for national income. National income figures are used to compare the economic achievements of different nations, and of nations over time. There is tremendous pressure on governments to produce national income figures, and if governments do not produce the figures other private people and organizations do; the figures are then used for all sorts of purposes whether or not they are published with suitable warnings about their unreliability and lack of comparability. It is very important therefore to know how national income estimates are compiled, how accurate are the component parts of the total, and just what it is that a figure for national income, even if based on accurate facts, really does measure.

The distinction between estimate and fact is very important. Some parts of the national income accounts can reasonably be said to be fact: in Zambia, for example, statistics relating to copper production tend to be reliable because provided by a small number of large, well-organized companies. Other parts, however, are based on partial information like surveys, from which only estimates of the whole can be deduced. Or they are based on complete but unreliable information: for example foreign payments are recorded by large numbers of bank clerks who may not fully understand the categories used by the statisticians and who have relatively little motive to provide an accurate breakdown of the figures. Because all national accounts are combinations of facts (of varying degrees of reliability), estimates and guesses, the total should always be described as an estimate.

The whole process of measuring national income was developed in industrialized economies, so the concepts and techniques are better suited to measuring income in the modern than in the rural sector of African economies. Even in the modern sector, though, and in its relations with the rural sector, some problems arise. The first priority then is to show how national income is estimated in a modern economy, or sector of an economy, and then to discuss how these methods are applied elsewhere.

2 MEASURING GROSS DOMESTIC PRODUCT IN THE MODERN SECTOR: THE PRODUCT METHOD

'National income' is the term normally used in conversation to mean the total of goods and services produced in a year in a particular country. A more precise term is 'Gross Domestic Product' or GDP. GDP can be measured in three different ways, by adding up production, income or expenditure.

In adding up the *production* of each sector of the economy it is most important to avoid double-counting. Products which are bought by other producers ('intermediate' products) would be double-counted if the total sales of all producers were added together. So the concept of 'value added' is used. Each producer buys certain inputs and adds value to them before selling his production. For example, a shoe manufacturer buys leather and rubber and shoelaces which he manufactures into shoes. His value added is the value of the shoes minus the cost of what he buys from other producers. A very simple account for a shoe firm might be as in Table 2.1.

TABLE 2.1
Receipts and payments of a manufacturer

Payments	*K'000*	*Receipts*	*K'000*
Purchase of leather	35	Sale of shoes	100
Purchase of rubber	5		
Purchase of shoelaces	5		
Rent	5		
Wages and salaries	35		
Gross Profit	15		
	100		100

The value added in this case is the value of sales less the cost of intermediate goods. If the cost of leather, rubber and shoelaces is not deducted from the value of sales then the production of the leather tannery, the rubber processing firm and the shoelaces produced by a textile firm, would all be counted twice. If any of these intermediate inputs has been imported it is obviously important not to count them as part of national product. Furthermore, if part of the profit is sent abroad to foreign shareholders then it is of no value to the local economy.[1] In underdeveloped countries it is quite common for a foreign-owned company to be set up to assemble imported components; in such cases the sales may be very high, but the local value added and thus the benefit to the country may be very small. For example, the new motor car assembly plant at Livingstone will use mainly imported components, so that the value added locally consists almost entirely of the value of the labour used in assembling the imported components, plus that part of the profit which is kept in the country. The long-term value of such a project depends greatly on whether the factory stimulates local production of motor car components which are at present imported.

Value added in the case illustrated by Table 2.1 is total sales (K100,000)[2] minus purchases of intermediate goods (K45,000), which is K55,000 (assuming the firm is locally owned and the profits are not sent abroad).

The concept of value added leads directly to the concept of income. Value added in this example is made up of payments to land (rent K5,000), labour (wages and salaries K35,000) and capital (profit K15,000). Land, labour and capital are the three classical factors of production. Payments to these factors are rent, wages and salaries, and profits, which are the three types of income. From this you should be able to see why total output is equal to total income. The value added by each business is the contribution of that business to total output, and *also* consists of incomes which are payments to the factors of production.[3]

A problem arises if the firm produces some shoes which, at the end of the year, it has not yet sold. Perhaps demand for the firm's shoes has fallen off; or perhaps the firm expects a big upsurge in demand quite soon, and wants to be able to supply it quickly, before its rivals. Whatever the reason, an addition to stocks is treated as an addition to output – above all, the shoes are there, and having been produced during the year are part of that year's total output.[4] As far as value added is concerned the addition to stocks is treated as though the firm had sold the shoes to itself. Suppose then that the shoe firm had added to stocks of finished shoes by K20,000, in addition to sales of K100,000. The account would then be as in Table 2.2.

You will notice that gross profit has gone up, although actual cash sales are unchanged; that is, the calculation of profit assumes that an addition to stocks is as good as a sale. It is not of course. If the stock

TABLE 2.2
Receipts and payments of a shoe manufacturer (including unsold stock)

Payments	*K'000*	*Receipts*	*K'000*
Purchase of leather	42	Sales of shoes	100
Purchase of rubber	6	Addition to stocks of finished shoes	20
Purchase of shoelaces	6		
Rent	5		
Wages and salaries	42		
Gross profit	19		
	120		120

eventually proves unsaleable, the firm would find that it had in fact made no profit. There is a moral to this, which is to beware of buying a business whose profits are represented by additions to stocks rather than by cash. The actual valuation of stocks and work in progress is obviously difficult, cautious firms tending to value them at cost, that is allowing nothing for the firm's profit margin, even if this understates their true value.

Gross profit is put down in the accounts as a 'payment'. It is, in a way, since conceptually profit is considered as a payment to owners of the business, that is, as a payment to capital as a factor of production. The other reason for showing profit as a payment is that there is an accounting convention that both sides of an account must add up to the same figure. Profit is described in the accounts as 'gross' profit because nothing has been deducted from the accounts for the depreciation of capital goods – buildings and long-lasting machinery.

Because capital goods are those which last a long time it is normal business practice to account for them over their estimated useful life. That is, gross profit is reduced each year by an estimated amount, called depreciation, which is that year's share of the cost of capital goods used up in production. Because it is only an estimate, influenced by many factors and estimated differently from firm to firm, national accounts are normally calculated gross of depreciation.[5] That is why the word 'Gross' is included in GDP. An estimate for depreciation of capital assets for the country as a whole is then subtracted from the GNP to arrive at *Net* National Product.

The basic components of GDP are thus the amounts of value added by each sector of industry. This method of calculating GNP has the additional advantage of indicating the relative size of each sector's contribution to GDP, and changes in relative size over time. 'Industry' in this context means not only manufacturing industry, but mining, construction, transport, agriculture, telephone and Post Office services, the services provided by retail and wholesale traders, electricity and water services, insurance, banking, and so on. The provision of services is as much a part of production as the production of physical commodities. The value added by a retailer, for example, is the total of sales less the cost of buying his stock and less the cost of other inputs bought from other sectors of industry such as electricity. In the case of the one-man business, value added consists of rent (if any) plus the profits of the business – these profits being of course the income of the trader. Many people misunderstand the service provided by traders, seeing them simply as people who make an easy profit out of their less fortunate fellows. But by keeping stocks of goods available in convenient places and at convenient times, and by selling goods in conveniently small quantities ('breaking bulk') traders perform a service as essential as the original production of the goods by farmers, miners and manufacturers.

The official Zambian figures for GDP in 1970 are shown in Table 2.3, with the contribution of each sector of the economy indicated separately.

TABLE 2.3
Zambian GDP by economic sector at current prices, 1970

	K mn
Agriculture, forestry and fishing:	
commercial output	27
subsistence output	64
Mining and quarrying	437
Manufacturing	91
Electricity, gas and water	15
Construction	82
Wholesale and retail trade	113
Hotels and restaurants	11
Transport, communications and storage	56
Financial institutions and insurance	41
Real estate	40
Business services	17
Public administration and defence	63
Education	40
Health	13
Other services	12
GDP	1122

3 MEASURING GDP IN THE MODERN SECTOR: THE INCOME METHOD

As already explained, value added is precisely equal to the various forms of income. It is thus possible to calculate GDP by adding up income, rather than by adding up production. The main sources of income are:

wages and salaries
profits
self-employment income
rent

The profits of companies owned by governments, like electricity companies and railways, are sometimes called 'surpluses' – presumably because of a general political attitude to nationalized industries. Firms are usually nationalized by left-of-centre governments who have a certain dislike of the profit motive, so that if nationalized firms continue to make profits it may be tactful to call them surpluses.

In the Zambian national accounts only three types of income are distinguished:

TABLE 2.4

GDP by type of income, 1970

	K mn
Wages and salaries	468
Operating surplus: rural household consumption of own products	64
other	468
Depreciation ('Consumption of fixed capital')	122
GDP	1122

Source: National Accounts 1970, Table 7.

In the Zambian accounts the item 'operating surplus' includes rent, imputed income from owner-occupied property, self-employment income and of course the profits of companies (net of depreciation). By far the most important component of the operating surplus is the profit from copper mining (K279 mn in 1970).

Self-employment income is presumably included in 'operating surplus' on the grounds that the self-employed are running their own businesses. Their incomes are therefore the 'profits' of these businesses and so are included in 'operating surplus'. That may be quite a good way of describing the one-man trading business which is providing essentially the same service as the large trading company with hundreds of employees. But it is stretching the definition to include 'rural household consumption of own products' which is mainly the subsistence income of small-scale farmers whose lives are not 'businesslike' at all. No doubt that is why this item is shown separately.

4 MEASURING GDP IN THE MODERN SECTOR: THE EXPENDITURE METHOD

Since every sale of goods or services involves both a seller and a buyer, it should be obvious that GDP can also be calculated by adding together all forms of spending in the economy – *provided that* purchases of intermediate goods and services are excluded. Intermediate purchases are the goods and services bought by businesses and used up in production. It is necessary to exclude intermediate purchases in calculating national expenditure in order to avoid double-counting. In exactly the same way, value added had to be used rather than gross sales when calculating national output. So there are two main components of national expenditure: consumption and investment.

Personal consumption consists of people buying goods and services for their personal use: food, clothing, furniture, bus trips, haircuts, etc. Although some of these things may not be used up (consumed) immediately, all purchases by individuals are counted as consumption, except houses which are treated as investment. The other item in consumption is government current spending.

Investment includes spending by businesses and governments on items such as buildings and machinery, the development of new mines and the improvement of land, which are not immediately used up in production. The amount of investment goods estimated to have been used up in production is called consumption of fixed capital, or depreciation, and can be deducted to give Net Domestic Product (or Expenditure). As has already been explained estimates of depreciation contain a great deal of guesswork.

As when calculating value added, additions to stocks must be included, since it is assumed that businesses buy additions to stocks from themselves. The point is that an addition to stocks of goods is a form of production which is not immediately consumed, and is thus a second form of investment. In the simplest case, a subsistence farmer who produces more than he consumes and stores the surplus is investing for the future. In the modern sector as well, some part of investment usually consists of an addition to stocks. This item can be negative if stocks are reduced, as happened in Zambia in 1964 (probably for political reasons, as the mainly foreign-owned business sector was nervous of the prospect of political independence) and in 1969 and 1970 when the mining industry sold off accumulated stocks.

In order to distinguish between these two types of investment the first is called 'Gross Fixed Capital Formation' in the national income accounts, the second is called 'Net Change in Stocks'. In fact Gross Fixed Capital Formation is not all 'fixed' in the literal sense, since it includes, for example, investment in earth-moving equipment by construction firms, and in lorries for shifting copper ore by the mines.

The other form of investment which must be included is the difference between exports and imports. If, as has often been the case since Independence, Zambia's exports are worth more than the cost of imports, then the difference is a form of investment in foreign assets. Zambia receives foreign exchange for exports and has to pay foreign exchange for imports (since the country's foreign suppliers do not want to be paid in Kwacha). If exports are greater than imports Zambia's foreign exchange reserves will rise (or foreign borrowing can be repaid) so that net foreign assets are greater. This is a form of investment, since foreign assets are available to buy imports in future years – just as an addition to stocks can be used in the future. Naturally, investment abroad can, like the net change in stocks, be negative as well as positive.

National expenditure at market prices is shown in Table 2.5.

TABLE 2.5
GDP by categories of expenditure, 1970

		K mn
Private consumption	458	
Government consumption	198	
Total consumption		656
Gross Fixed Capital Formation	327	
Net change in stocks	−13	
Net export of goods and services	215	
Total investment		529
Total Expenditure on Gross Domestic Product		1185

Source: *Monthly Digest of Statistics.*

Now Table 2.5 shows total expenditure on GDP to be different (K1,185 mn) from GDP as calculated earlier by the product and income methods – yet all three methods should give the same result. The reason for the difference is that when consumers buy cigarettes or beer, for example, the market price includes a large amount of tax, which of course ends up with the government. The producer only receives the amount *net* of tax (that is, after payment of tax to the government); out of this he is able to pay the factors of production, namely wages and profits. Table 2.5 therefore shows expenditure at market prices whereas Tables 2.3 and 2.4 showed GDP at 'factor cost'. This distinction is further discussed in Section 6, p. 22.

5 SUBSISTENCE FARMING

Subsistence output is, by definition, not bought and sold. It creates two problems therefore for the national income statistician, the first conceptual and the second practical. It is difficult to decide conceptually what activities of the subsistence farmer and his family should be included in national income and at what prices they should be valued. From the practical point of view, it is extremely difficult to get information about subsistence activities, partly because of the large number of small scattered farms, and partly because goods and services that are not traded for money are very hard to find out about. Subsistence output thus contrasts with the marketed output of a product such as Virginia tobacco, all of which is sold through a single marketing organization. The Tobacco Board is able to supply excellent information on output and prices.

In trying to value subsistence output the statisticians use the fiction that the farmer produces something (output), buys it from himself (expenditure) and receives income as a result (income). In principle, if the amount and value of output are known then expenditure and income are also known. But even in the case of, say, maize production where prices are known, a problem remains. Because the farmer consumes his own product there are no transport and distribution costs – transport and distribution services are not needed. In recording *output*, therefore, it is correct to value maize at the 'farm gate' price, that is, the price paid to a commercial farmer if his maize were to be collected from his farm. The price is of course lower than the price of maize at a centralized market, and both are lower than the price of maize as sold by traders.[6] In addition the manufacturing process of converting maize to maize meal is commercialized in towns, and the cost and profits of millers are incorporated in the price paid for maize meal by urban consumers. If, therefore, one wishes to compare the *welfare* of urban consumers and subsistence farmers, by valuing their consumption of basic foodstuffs, then clearly the correct price to use is the urban price of maize meal. In other words, one would have to impute to subsistence output some sort of value added by non-existent transport and distribution services, and the 'manufacturing' activities of the farmer's wife in converting maize into meal.

The almost invariable practice of national income statisticians in Africa is to value output of foodcrops only, and to value them at prices which make *output* figures comparable, that is, to use farm gate prices. While this is a perfectly sound procedure if primary interest is in agricultural output, it is wholly inadequate in comparing the *welfare* of rural and urban people. Yet this is what is implied by taking subsistence output, dividing it by the population dependent on subsistence farming and then comparing this derived figure of subsistence income per head with the urban wage income per head of the urban population. Clearly like is not being compared with like, and the result is absurd.

In trying to make sensible use of published estimates of subsistence output, it is absolutely essential, therefore, to be clear as to what it is that has been measured. Thus if most estimates of subsistence output are in fact estimates of the output of the main food crops, and if the estimates are good ones, then they can be quite useful in providing information on, say, changes in the amount of food grown and eaten by subsistence farmers. But such estimates are not only useless but thoroughly misleading if used to compare the incomes of subsistence farmers with the incomes of urban dwellers. The town dweller has to pay cash for his housing, fuel, lighting, transport to and from work, beer, entertainment, water and for all sorts of public services via local taxes. The subsistence farming family provides most of these services for itself.

It would in theory be possible to record the fact that the subsistence farmer enjoys home-brewed beer, shelter, fuel and so on, but it is not even theoretically possible to put a value on these goods and services. It is true that even in the most isolated village most goods and services are exchanged occasionally for cash, but the price implied by such a transaction cannot necessarily be taken as typical, precisely because cash transactions themselves are not typical. Services performed for others in a village form part of a whole network of rights and obligations, the time scale of which can be as long as a man's lifetime. The money that changes hands on any particular occasion may thus represent all sorts of considerations additional to the actual service performed at that time. Where cash transactions are the norm, as in towns where most men perform specialized jobs for cash, and buy everything they need for cash, prices reflect more truly what goods and services are worth to the buyer, and the impersonal nature of *most* transactions excludes other considerations. Of course, even in town traders give discounts to friends and family, friends lend money interest-free whereas banks and hire purchase companies charge interest; but in the urban market economy, impersonal transactions are the rule rather than the exception.[7]

Again, even in the monetized, market-dominated sectors of an African economy there are some services which some people perform for themselves while others pay to have them done. For example one man may paint his own house, another may pay a professional decorator. The service performed by the do-it-yourself householder almost certainly is left out of the GNP estimates, while the output of the professional decorator should be, and probably is, included. But by and large the bulk of output in the market sectors is included in the official estimates of GNP. Value added by mining companies, by supermarket chains, by steelworks and by hotels is recordable and is recorded. And value added by the big organizations is very large compared with the anomalies and omissions. None of this is true in the subsistence sector.

In practice, the subsistence output estimate for Zambia is totally useless. It is based on very out-of-date estimates, for only a few districts, of the *dietary* habits and needs of the rural population. It is then assumed that the farmers grow (and catch in the case of fish) these requirements. This 'estimate' is then updated by almost equally shaky estimates of the growth in population. What this process therefore does is to *assume* answers to many of the questions that ought to be asked. It does not tell us whether in fact farmers have succeeded in supplying themselves and their families with the food they need, nor does it tell us anything about variations from year to year or changes in the trend of production over time. The figures are thus useless for assessing or preparing government policy, or indeed for anything else.

At first sight it might appear that the error is unimportant in Zambia's case, since in 1970 subsistence farming output was shown as K64 mn which was only about 6% of GNP. This means that even a 100% error in estimating subsistence output would only have produced a 6% error in estimating GNP. But the estimate of subsistence output affects the largest and probably the poorest group in the population,[8] and is used for many purposes. In other African countries, subsistence output is much more important both in terms of population and in relation to GNP.

In addition to variations in the importance of subsistence farming, different countries use different 'production boundaries'. Items that are within the production boundary are those that are included in GNP, and the production boundary varies much more in estimates of subsistence output than in estimates for other sectors of the economy. For example hut-building, fuel-gathering, the 'manufacturing' services of wives, are treated as being inside the production boundary in some countries, outside it in others. Furthermore different countries use different ways of measuring the items that *are* included.[9]

Given the extremely difficult problems, both conceptual and practical, in estimating subsistence output, there is real doubt as to whether it is worthwhile at all. Van Arkadie and Frank, for example, seem to conclude that all measures are worthless. Certainly the variations between countries make it quite as invalid to use the published statistics to make comparisons of rural standards of living in different countries as it is to use estimates of subsistence output for making welfare comparisons between rural and urban people.

Even if quite good estimates of food crop production by small farmers were available, and these estimates were used purely to estimate change over time within the same rural communities, there would remain considerable conceptual problems in using the figures. Some of these problems are common to both monetary and non-monetary sectors of the economy, but they tend to be more fundamental in the villages.

Firstly, national income accounting puts no value on leisure. If people become more productive and are able to produce the same quantity of goods in less time, they are better off provided that they put a positive value on leisure; but this is not recorded in national income. The growth of welfare in industrialized economies tends to be under-recorded because of this factor, since working hours have been gradually reduced over time. In the village economy, on the other hand, the growth of output, perhaps of new crops for export, may be at the expense of leisure, so that the growth of welfare is exaggerated by the statistics. This is especially important when leisure is used for maintaining vital kinship and other relationships, vital because of the risks involved in small-scale, low-technology farming, and the need for help with tasks like hut-building and harvesting.

Secondly, national income accounting tends to take no account of the gradual movement of transactions into the market economy. Again, this occurs in the urban industrialized world, as people use rising incomes to pay for services previously performed within the household and thus not recorded in the statistics. But the change is a more basic one in rural Africa, since village life is moving from a situation in which only a small proportion of 'economic' activity is included, towards one in which most goods and services will be exchanged for cash. It is thus probable that the growth of income in the villages will be exaggerated by official statistics as commercialization of village life proceeds.

Thirdly, there is a much greater interconnection between rural and urban life than has been suggested so far. Just as the conventions of national income accounting are ill-suited to a situation in which 40% of the male labour force work in another country (as in Lesotho) or in which a big proportion of the highly skilled are temporary residents (as in Zambia), they are also ill-suited to making sense of the *internal* patterns of migration. Photographs of people queuing to vote in the 1968 general election showed an overwhelming proportion of women, children and old people – most of the men of working age were absent in the towns, working or seeking work. These men send money to their families and bring money and goods with them when they return, temporarily or permanently, to their villages. In addition, people from the villages visit relatives in town, or send children to visit, in order to enjoy access to urban amenities. The extent to which rural people depend on urban income varies sharply with the ability and opportunity to earn income from farming. For example Deane estimated in 1945 that only 15% of men were absent from villages in the Southern Province, which had easy access to markets for agricultural produce, but that up to 70% were absent from the Eastern Province.[10] After Independence there was some adjustment in this pattern as families joined the men in towns.[11] Nevertheless, a study of small farmers in Mumbwa and Katete in 1968/9 showed that among farmers whose farming was intended mainly for their own consumption, the largest source of cash income was from non-agricultural employment.[12]

The same study of small farmers tells us much more about small farmers than the official figures have ever done, even though the study covered only two small areas which were inevitably not typical of Zambia as a whole. In the context of the interconnection between rural and urban life, the study shows that the sample farmers received only quite small sums of money in the form of gifts; but the very nature of the sample excluded the returning migrant and the cash and goods brought with him.

Nevertheless it is interesting to compare the UNZALPI income figures with those implied by the official figure for subsistence output. The latter was K64 mn in 1970, or about K20 per person if one assumes that some three million of the population lived in the rural areas and were dependent to some extent on subsistence production (the official figure does *not* pretend to cover all the output of small farmers since it excludes the value of any output marketed through official channels).

The UNZALPI figures are shown below. The distinction between 'farmers' and 'villagers' is based on *attitudes*, farmers being those who were seeking (successfully or unsuccessfully) to derive an increasing cash income from farming, and villagers being those who regarded farming as being mainly a means of providing for their subsistence needs. Villagers do sell some of their output since they aim to produce a surplus in a normal year as an insurance against bad years.[13]

TABLE 2.6

UNZALPI figures for consumption of own product per head

	Number of families	*Number of people per family*	*K/head*
Mumbwa: villagers	68	5·1	9·80
farmers	67	8·0	20·00
Katete: villagers	77	4·7	13·47
farmers	27	6·8	17·60
Total sample	239	6·0	15·60

Source: UNZALPI, Report No. 3, Tables 1/9 to 1/12, pp. 147–50, as corrected by Report No. 5, p. 111.

These figures suggest that the official estimates are in fact too high, especially as Mumbwa and Katete are considered to be relatively prosperous areas. On the other hand, the two areas are also relatively well placed for the earning of cash income. Nevertheless, villagers in

TABLE 2.7

UNZALPI figures for annual income per head

	Subsistence output K/head	*Other income K/head*	*Total K/head*
Mumbwa: villagers	9·80	18·20	28·00
farmers	20·00	43·60	63·60
Katete: villagers	13·47	11·18	24·65
farmers	17·60	5·20	22·80
Total sample	15·60	24·90	40·50

NOTE: 'Other income' for 'farmers' in Mumbwa is much larger than for the rest of the sample because a few farmers earned quite a large income from using their tractors to plough and carry goods for others.

Source: As Table 2.6.

Mumbwa spent only K1·15 per head on food, and villagers in Katete only K0·70 per head, so that subsistence output represented by far their most important source of food.

Total income as calculated for the sample included the proceeds of crop and livestock sales, employment (mainly but not entirely non-agricultural), fishing (very small), cash gifts and sales of beer. Total income per head for the four groups of Table 2.6 is shown in Table 2.7.

The figures for total income per head in Table 2.7 do *not* of course include any imputed income except food consumption and even consumption of home-grown food is valued at the farm gate price. It thus includes nothing for the manufacturing services of housewives, nor for transport and distribution which would normally have to be paid for by the urban consumer. In other words, even when a very detailed survey is carried out (and the UNZALPI survey was very detailed indeed, involving daily visits to each farm in the sample, over a period of two years) so that the facts are known as well as it is possible to know them, it is still not possible to compare rural and urban welfare. Apart from the pricing problem and the impossibility of putting any value on the general pleasantness of living in country or town, the UNZALPI figures contain no imputation for the value of housing, fuel, recreation (except beer), water, etc. It would thus be absolutely incorrect to say that the average family in the UNZALPI sample was living at the same standard as an urban family with an income of K40 or so per head. Clearly an urban family would need more than this, but how much more it is impossible to say.

6 FACTOR COST AND MARKET PRICES

In the modern sectors of the Zambian economy almost everyone works at something fairly specialized, receives cash income as a result, and then buys the goods and services wanted, out of that cash income. It is therefore reasonable to estimate the output of goods and services on the assumption that prices roughly reflect the value that people place on them. Increases in the amounts of goods and services produced will be reflected in statistics of purchases and sales, scarcity will be reflected in prices, and so on. There are however some exceptions, even in the modern sectors of the Zambian economy.

In the first place some goods and services are taxed, and others subsidized. For example cigarettes and beer are taxed, maize meal is subsidized. There are thus two ways of valuing such goods; at the market price, the price actually paid by the buyer, including the tax or minus the subsidy; or at the 'factor cost' of production, that is the amount which goes to the various factors of production in wages, rent and profit, but not including taxes or subsidies. There are thus two ways of measuring GDP: 'GDP at market prices' and 'GDP at factor cost'. The relation between the two is:

GDP at factor cost = GDP at market prices
minus indirect taxes
plus subsidies.

Thus if the government levies a tax on bottled beer, the market price paid by the consumer includes the tax; the price received by the producer excludes the tax, so that the cash available for distribution to the factors of production, the factor cost of production which is necessary in order for production to take place, is the market price minus the tax. Similarly, if the government subsidizes the cost of fertilizer to farmers, then the market price paid by farmers is less, by the amount of the subsidy, than the amount of money received by the producer and available for paying the 'factor costs' of production, including profit (if any).

The main items in the Zambian accounts where there is a major difference between factor cost and market price are:[14]

commercial agriculture – tobacco and maize are subsidized;
manufacture of beverages and tobacco – alcohol and cigarettes are heavily taxed;
transport – the railways are subsidized;
mining – royalty and export tax were indirect taxes.

The case of mining needs further explanation. Until 1970 there were three taxes on copper mining: royalty, export tax and income tax. The first two were levied on *output* and were thus treated in the accounts like other indirect taxes; the income tax was a tax on profits, and so was ignored in distinguishing between factor cost and market prices. In practice, since the price of copper is determined by world market conditions and is normally outside the control of the Zambian mining companies, all three taxes were simply paid out of mining profit, which is the difference between the world price of copper and the cost of mining, refining, transporting and selling it. In 1970 the tax system was changed as part of the takeover arrangements and all copper taxation is now levied directly on profits. In order to make pre-1970 and post-1970 figures for GDP at factor cost comparable it is thus necessary (as well as conceptually more consistent) to add royalty and export tax to the published figures for GDP at factor cost up to and including 1970 (the position in 1970 and 1971 was complicated by the transition to the new copper tax system which came into force in April 1970).

The official figures in the *Monthly Digest of Statistics* have in fact done this, by dropping the old series of GDP (and its components) at factor cost. In Sections 2 and 3 of this chapter GDP has been shown at factor cost but *including* the royalty and export tax on mining profits. In Section 4, GDP was shown at current market prices, or as it is expressed in the new tables, at 'current purchasers' values'.

7 IMPUTED INCOME IN THE MODERN SECTOR

Another problem in calculating GDP is that even in the monetized modern sector of the economy, not all services are bought and sold. The most important examples are housing and housewives' services. People who own their own houses do not pay rent, although they derive the same service from housing as people who live in rented housing. The statisticians therefore *impute* income to owner-occupiers, that is they assume that a man living in his own house receives an income equivalent to the rent he would have to pay if he did not own the house, and that this income is then spent on buying housing services from himself. The recorded output of housing services is thus increased by an imputed amount.[15]

Housewives' services are on the other hand ignored by the statisticians, mainly on the grounds that it is too difficult to value them and too difficult to discover the quantity produced. In practice, even the domestic service which is paid for in cash is almost certainly underestimated by the statisticians. For years after Independence the employment figures showed an unchanging number of domestic servants employed (35,000) and then in 1971 this statistic was dropped altogether, so that employment figures are now shown exclusive of domestic servants. This is an example of a type of employment in which statistics are extremely difficult to obtain. Another example would be self-employed car-washers and vegetable sellers. Conceptually there is no difficulty since their production is equal to the value of their services as paid for by their customers, less any purchased inputs, but the difficulty lies in obtaining the facts about their activities.

8 GOVERNMENT SERVICES

The final 'sector' of the economy to be included is government. It has been argued from time to time that many government services, such as defence and the maintenance of law and order, are really intermediate products which are necessary in order for economic activity to take place. There is some virtue in this point of view, but it is extremely difficult in practice to distinguish between government services which ought to be classified as intermediate products and government services which are final products to be enjoyed by the public like any other product. For example education is partly a necessary input into economic activity, since much modern sector production depends on educated manpower, and partly a service to be enjoyed by the participants in the same way as some of the services provided by private businessmen, for example cinema shows or football matches. In principle, some private sector services and commodities, such as transport to work and working clothes, could also be treated as intermediate products.

In practice all government services are treated as part of national product. They are valued at *cost* even though this means that the methods of valuation in government and non-government sectors are different. Government services provided free or at cost contain no element of profit in their valuation as do private sector goods and services. This is inevitable because there is normally no way of estimating what the value of government services would be if they were produced and sold by private businessmen for profit.

Provided the range of services supplied by government stays the same then GDP estimates will remain roughly comparable from one year to the next; but if sectors of the economy move into or out of the government sector then comparison over time will become invalid as the method of valuation changes. For the same reason, comparison of GDP between countries with differing proportions of production in the government sector will suffer from the same problem of differing methods of valuation.

Including all government services in GDP means assuming that all such services are valued by the community, particularly if GDP estimates are used as a measure of the wealth and welfare of peoples. For example if defence expenditure increases, people may or may not feel better off, depending on how seriously they view the problem of the nation's security. Yet excluding government spending from GDP would not necessarily improve matters, since even defence services have some value to everyone, and other services like health and education are of obvious and immediate value to most people.

It should be clear, though, from this discussion of government services that the *composition* of GDP, as well as its actual size, is very important; and that changes in the composition of GDP may be as important as changes in its size. For example, if a country goes to war local factories will start to produce war materials, imports will be of tanks and fighter aircraft instead of motor cars and passenger airliners. The people will be heavily taxed to pay for war spending while at the same time fewer consumer goods are available because production and imports have been switched to guns and tanks. Because GDP includes government services valued at cost, it is possible that GDP will appear as the same in wartime as in peacetime. GDP may even appear higher in wartime as unemployed people are employed as soldiers. But to deduce from this that the people are in some sense better off is clearly misleading, since the composition of GDP as between government spending on defence and the provision of other goods and services has changed so drastically.

9 DOMESTIC PRODUCT, NATIONAL PRODUCT AND THE INCOME OF FOREIGNERS

The total of value added for all sectors of the economy, plus the total of government services valued at cost, is equal to Gross *Domestic* Product. Domestic is the word used to describe production within a country's borders. But in a country like Zambia a great deal of the value added by domestic industry is transferred abroad. There are two main reasons for this. Firstly, a large part of Zambian industry is owned by foreigners who must therefore be paid their share of dividends.[16] Secondly, a large proportion of skilled, high-level manpower in Zambia is still expatriate, and these people, although resident in Zambia, send a significant proportion of their incomes out of the country. The calculation of Gross *National* Product takes account of profits sent abroad (less any profits received) but takes no account of expatriate remissions. This is because GNP is defined as the income available to residents of the country, a definition derived from use in developed countries at a time when 'resident' was normally not sufficiently different from 'national' to make very much difference.

Because almost all of them expect to be in Zambia temporarily, the large number of highly paid expatriates send large amounts of savings abroad, and take the savings they have accumulated in Zambia with them when they leave at the end of their contracts. Many also educate their children abroad, which accounts for a further outflow of domestic income. These items were over K100 mn in 1970 and 1971, that is, some 10% of GNP. The temporary nature of expatriate residents, and their financial importance in a country like Zambia, makes the normal definition of national income yield this rather odd result: that income remitted abroad, by people resident in Zambia for very short periods, is nevertheless treated as part of national income. Although these sums of money are at the command of residents of Zambia, they are really very similar in principle to profits sent out of the country, that is, payments for the use of foreign resources: physical resources and know-how in the case of profits, human resources in the case of expatriate savings and other remittances. Clearly this problem is not permanent, since expatriates will eventually nearly all be replaced by Zambians; but it will remain substantial into the 1980s at least.

Another problem which occurred between 1970 and 1973 concerned the compensation payments to shareholders in the copper mines at the time of the government's 51% takeover in 1970 – a minimum of K28 mn a year. Technically these payments were capital transfers, being redemptions of a loan made by the shareholders to the government to finance the original 51% share purchase. In practice what happened was that a minimum of two-thirds of the government's 51% share of copper dividends was being used to pay out the shareholders, who as a result received a greater cash flow than they would have received had the takeover not taken place. The point here is that capital transfers do not affect the national income figures, whereas profits paid abroad are subtracted from GDP in arriving at GNP. The non-technically minded person would rightly observe that if the figures showed a *drop* in net income paid abroad, while foreign shareholders were getting a *rise* in receipts of cash from copper mining profits, then the figures were slightly crazy *even if* at the end of ten years or so the government would have paid for its 51% share in the mines. The important thing for the student of the Zambian economy is to understand what was happening, namely that dividends paid to Mindeco were recorded as part of GNP as Mindeco is a Zambian-owned company, but that Mindeco had to use most (if not all) of these dividends to redeem its overseas debt, so that the money promptly left the country. In 1973 the government redeemed Mindeco's debt by using the foreign exchange reserves and by borrowing from European and American banks. Redemption of the new loan also counts as a capital transaction, so the new arrangements were much the same in principle although different in detail. In both cases, redemption of debt had to come from mining profits in one way or another.

On both these issues, expatriates sending money out of the country and the purchase of a share in the mines out of the mines' own profits, the published GNP figures are liable to be misleading because of the unusual structure of the Zambian economy. In fact the new system of national accounts adopted in 1970 (known as the 'New SNA') took account of the problem of expatriate remittances by creating a new concept 'National Disposable Income'. This is arrived at as follows:

	1970 in K mn
GDP at market prices	1185
less profits paid abroad	33
= Gross National Product	1152
less 'Other current transfers to the rest of the world'	105
less 'Consumption of fixed capital' (Depreciation)	122
= 'National Disposable Income'	925

It would be rather clearer if the new concept was known as 'Net National Disposable Income' since it is in fact net of depreciation of fixed capital. Nevertheless it is undoubtedly a better concept than the old one of GNP which only took account of foreign ownership of capital.

If national income statistics were only used by professional economists with a close knowledge of the Zambian economy, who could be expected to know the peculiarities of the system, then these points would be of little importance. But the statistics are used much more widely – by politicians to make political points, by international agencies to decide which countries get various forms of aid. And it is the older concept of GNP which continues to be used. For example, the International Development Agency is the 'soft loan' member of the World Bank group; that is, the IDA lends at very low interest rates and with very long periods of repayment to countries with *GNP* per head of less than US$375 (in 1974). Countries with GNP per head of more than US$375 must borrow at the much higher rates and shorter repayment periods of the World Bank. In these sorts of circumstances the definition of national income is of more than technical statistical interest. In 1970 the cut-off point for IDA lending was a per capita GNP of US$300. So officially Zambia was too rich a country to be allowed to borrow cheaply from the IDA in 1970. If National Disposable Income were to be used instead, 'per capita NDI' in 1970 would have been US$308, only just above the cut-off point. If the per capita income of *Zambians* could be calculated it would obviously have been considerably lower than US$308. So Zambia was considered too rich to borrow cheaply from the World Bank group partly because of having a lot of highly paid non-Zambians resident in the country. Zambia is of course much better off than the great majority of black African countries so it is perhaps right that cheap lending is reserved for the latter. The point here is that estimates of national income per head are not just empty statistical calculations; they are used for official purposes, of which IDA lending is only one example. Equally, this is only one reason why international comparisons of GNP can be misleading; others are dealt with in Part II of this chapter.

It is interesting to compare the statistical treatment of the well-paid expatriates in Zambia with that of the low-paid migrant labourers who go to work in South Africa, from countries such as Lesotho, Mozambique and Malawi (a small number used to go from Zambia but this was stopped after Independence). These men leave their homes and families to work mainly on South African mines and farms. The typical contract for such migrants is for a year to eighteen months, not so very different from the typical two-year expatriate contract in Zambia (which can work out at 21 months if leave is taken out of the two years). Yet the African migrant labourers are treated as residents of their home country since both their consumption (abroad) and their remittances are added to GNP. The difference perhaps is that migrant African labourers normally leave their families at home; but as Zambia's expatriates frequently have children at boarding school outside Zambia and a substantial proportion of the African migrants are single men seeking to save enough money to buy some cattle and to pay bride-money, the differences in family circumstances have some (if not many) similarities. The more general point here is again that the GNP definitions originating in industrialized countries have been awkwardly adapted to African conditions, sometimes to the practical disadvantage of African countries.

NOTE

See pp. 38, 39 for footnotes to Chapter 2, Parts I and II.

2 *Measuring National Income II*

1 CHANGING PRICES

In the first part of this chapter, the figures for national income, whether calculated by product, income or expenditure method, were all in 'current prices' – this means that the statistics use the prices actually paid at the time. The trouble with this concept is that if prices change significantly over time then national income figures will reflect changes in prices as well as 'real' changes. 'Real income' in this context means the goods that a man can actually buy, as opposed to his 'money income'.

Since the Second World War prices in all countries have tended to rise continuously. Nearly everyone is aware therefore that his real income, his economic welfare as represented by the goods and services he is able to buy, has gone up less fast than his money income. A man whose income is twice as large as it was is *not* able to buy twice as much of everything.

The national income statistics attempt to allow for changing prices by calculating GNP at 'fixed prices'. This means estimating GNP in, say, 1970 at the prices prevailing in 1965. In principle, this should show how much real or physical output has increased, and therefore the amount by which the nation as a whole has more goods and services at its disposal.

Although prices of different goods and services have a tendency to change in the same direction at the same time, obviously they do not all move together, nor do they change by the same amounts. It is necessary therefore to calculate *average* price increases. The best-known of these averages is the 'consumer price index' which attempts to average the change in the prices of the consumption foods and services bought by the average citizen. There are many other price indices – for wholesale prices, building materials, commodity prices, etc. – but they all attempt to solve the same problem, namely how to express the *average* price rise for a group of items.

How do you work out such an average? There is no perfect way. There are however various methods which give reasonable answers – provided that the components which make up the average or index are fairly homogeneous. This is a necessary condition for all averages. If a class of adult students are all within six inches of each other in height, then an average height for the class is a meaningful figure. But if a two-year-old child is two feet tall and his father six feet, then their average height is a meaningless and misleading figure, which tells you nothing about the group to which they belong. Similarly, it is only because prices have a general tendency to change together by similar amounts that price indices are worth calculating.

How do you work out a price index? *Firstly:* – it is not helpful to say that (for example) the price of bread has risen by 3n and that of meat by 10n, so the average price rise is 6½n. Such a statement is meaningless, because nothing is stated about the original prices or about quantities. *Secondly:* – if the price of a box of matches has risen from 1n to 3n (a 200% rise) and that of a pound of beef from 40n to 50n (a 25% rise), is the average price rise 112½%? No. Why? Because meat is much more important than matches, so we must somehow give more *weight* in the argument to the relatively small rise in the price of meat, and less *weight* to the relatively very large rise in the price of matches. These are the two main points.

How do you discover what weight to give to each product? *The only way* is to conduct a budget survey, which means examining the spending habits of a representative sample of people, and discover what the typical consumption of each commodity is – that is, if you are investigating the 'cost of living'. All price indices face exactly the same problem – what weight to give (that is, what relative importance to give) to each commodity, each stock or share, or whatever.

Take a very simple example. Suppose in an average week a man spends K5 on food, K2 on clothing, K2 on drinks and K1 on transport – total expenditure K10. To make the whole thing very simple suppose also that food is expressed in 'units' such that he buys 5 units at K1 each, and also that he buys 2 'units' each of clothing and drink at K1 each, and one 'unit' of transport, at K1 a unit. In an average week the following year, he buys 8 units of food, 3 each of clothing and drinks, and 1 of transport; at prices of K1·50, K1·80, K2·20 and K2·00 respectively. This can be summarized:

	Year 1		*Year 2*	
	Price	*Quantity*	*Price*	*Quantity*
Food	K1	5	K1·50	8
Clothing	K1	2	K1·80	3
Drink	K1	2	K2·20	3
Transport	K1	1	K2·00	1
Total expenditure	K10·00		K26·00	

There are now *two* basic ways of answering the question: how much has his cost of living gone up? *Firstly*, by answering the question – how much would it cost him in year 2 to buy exactly what he bought in year 1? In year 1 he spent K10·00. To buy the same in year 2, would cost him 5 × K1·50 for food, 2 × K1·80 for clothing, 2 × K2·20 for drink, and K2·00 for transport. This adds up to K17·50. Thus it would cost him K17·50 in year 2 to buy what he bought in year 1. In one sense his 'cost of living' has therefore gone up to 175% (K17·50/K10·00 × 100) of what it was before.

The prices of three out of the four items he buys have gone up by more than 75%, but because of the great importance of food, whose price rose least, the average price rise was only 75%. This particular index is called a *'base year'* index, because of using the quantities bought in the base, or first, year.

Secondly, the other basic type of index is obtained by answering the question – how much would it have cost him in year 1 to buy exactly what he bought in year 2?

In year 2 he spent K26·00 (see table). To have bought the same in year 1 would have cost him 8 × K1 for food, 3 × K1 for clothing, 3 × K1 for drink, K1 for transport – K15·00 in all. So his cost of living has gone up to 173·3% (K26·00/K15·00 × 100) of what it was before. Notice that this method gives a slightly lower figure for the average price rise, because of using the weights of year 2; in year 2 he has increased his purchases of food by more (60%) than he has increased his purchases of other commodities and the price of food has risen least. In fact he probably increased his food purchase by more *because* the price rose least. This second index is called a 'current year' index because the weights of the current year were used. As you can see, the answer given by each is not very different, and there is no way of deciding which is better.

Which is used in practice? The base year index is used almost always, because you can go on using the same weights year after year. If you use a current year index you have to recalculate the weights each year, which would mean an expensive budget survey every year.[17] Very few statisticians are in a position to do this. Of course if you go on using a base year index for very long, the weights become out of date. So periodically a new, more up-to-date base year is chosen.

You can see this in successive issues of the *Monthly Digest*. For the eleven years 1954/64 the base year used was 1954. Then it was updated, and a new series was started using 1965 as a base year. In 1969 this process was repeated. Another interesting facet of the Zambian statistics is that *two* types of consumer price indices are calculated – one for 'higher incomes' and one for 'lower incomes' (Tables 48 and 49, *Monthly Digest*). A combined index is also calculated, but clearly the Central Statistical Office regards the difference in consumption habits of the two groups as being so different as to make it worthwhile to show the two indices differently.

One final point: if you have a price index, and wish to use it to discover how some figure or other has moved 'at fixed prices', or 'in real terms', DIVIDE by the price index, and multiply by 100. Thus if a man's income rises from K1,000 to K1,200, and the consumer price index rises from 100 to 110, then the man's real income has risen to

$$K\frac{1{,}200}{110}\times 100 = K1{,}090 \text{ (approx.)}.$$

Of course, this assumes that his spending pattern as an individual is the same as the 'average' person's, which is used in calculating the weights for the index. If a large part of a rise in the index is caused by price rises in drink and tobacco (as was the case in Zambia in February 1968, just after the budget; see Table 48, *Monthly Digest*, November 1968) and the man does not smoke or drink, then he is better off than is indicated by the crude calculation above.

Even if all the components of national income have been suitably 'deflated' to give a series free of the effects of inflation, there remains one problem peculiar to countries like Zambia. If the price of copper goes up, the current value of copper production rises even if physical output in tonnes of copper remains the same. In 1966, for example, copper output actually fell because of fuel shortages. Most importantly, there was a shortage of coal for smelting as a result of the problems caused by Rhodesia's UDI. But because of an increase in the price of copper, from an average of K923 per tonne in 1965 to K1,090 per tonne in 1966, the *value* of copper output rose from K343 mn to K465 mn. Because the whole of copper output was exported at that time[18] the country was better off in the real sense of being able to buy more goods from abroad. At first the official figures showed a fall in national income at fixed prices in 1966, but later the figure was adjusted to show a rise. Once again neither figure is absolutely correct. The country was better off in real terms, that is the buying power of the nation had increased so that it was correct to show a *rise* in 'real' national income. On the other hand, physical output of copper had fallen. Because of the dominance of copper in Zambia this was enough to offset the increase in physical output of all the other sectors, so that it was also correct to show a *fall* in 'real' national income.

The same problem can arise in other countries dependent on a single export commodity whose price fluctuates widely; Ghana with its dependence on cocoa is a good example. In industrialized countries, which have a very diversified export trade made up mainly of manufactured goods with fairly stable prices, it simply does not arise. Although prices of exported manufactures *do* change, they do not change suddenly, and changes are in any case usually partly or wholly offset by similar changes in import prices. Of course even in Zambia the value to the country of a rise in the copper price can be partly offset by increasing import prices – indeed this has invariably been the case in recent years. Because of this factor the official figure for GNP at 1965 prices is shown as having been 'adjusted for changes in terms of trade'. This means that account has been taken of changes in both import and export prices. The factors which make the Zambian case so different from that of an industrialized country are the extreme movements in the copper price (very much greater than movements in import prices) and the enormous importance of copper, not only in exports but also in GNP.

2 MAKING INTERNATIONAL COMPARISONS OF NATIONAL INCOME

Estimates of national income are well known to be very inaccurate. Many forms of income are only guessed at, many are left out. Prices do not reflect economic welfare. In particular, the incomes of small farmers and their families are very seriously underestimated and are not comparable with urban incomes. Yet the majority of the population is often in this rural category. Even in Zambia with its great wealth from copper and relatively large modern urban sector, some 65% of the population live in the rural areas and are partly or wholly dependent on subsistence output. In Tanzania and Malawi the figure is over 90%.

In spite of their well-known drawbacks, national income figures, usually divided by population estimates (which may be almost as shaky as income estimates), are widely used. Nearly every book on the economic development of underdeveloped countries quotes the United Nations figures for per capita income of poor and rich countries, and invites the reader to compare them. The typical table looks like this:

TABLE 2.8

Per capita GNP of selected countries in 1970. At current market prices, in US dollars

USA	4,294	Columbia	366
Britain	1,986	Zambia	342
Japan	1,658	Tanzania	93
Chile	678	Ethiopia	62
Portugal	600		

Source: *UN Statistical Yearbook*, 1972, Table 187.

The notes at the end of the table in the *UN Statistical Yearbook* actually say 'The estimates ... are designed to facilitate international comparisons of economic activity.' The UN is of course only trying to offer a useful service by gathering into one volume all the national income figures provided by the various governments. The fact is, however, that the figures as published, and so often quoted, are quite meaningless. What they appear to say is that the average level of income in Ethiopia is the same as could be bought in the USA for $62. That is wholly absurd. An annual income of $62 in the USA would mean quite simply – starvation. A person with $62 to spend in a year would be quite unable to buy enough food to stay alive, quite apart from clothing, housing, fuel for cooking and keeping warm in the winter, etc.

The comparison between rich and poor countries is basically absurd for the same reason that comparison between urban and rural income is almost impossible – namely that the town-dweller has to buy many things that the country-dweller enjoys for nothing or provides for himself. Such things are either left out of national income accounting, or grossly undervalued in terms of a welfare comparison. In addition, the price level in low-income areas is usually lower than in high-income areas. These two points have been discussed already.

There are further reasons why international comparison can be very misleading. Figures are converted to dollars at official exchange rates, but the latter seldom reflect at all accurately the purchasing power of currencies. For example, throughout the 1960s Kenya and Zambia maintained the same exchange rate with the dollar, but inflation was much worse in Zambia than in Kenya. The difference in rates of inflation was *not* reflected in the exchange rates of the Kenya shilling and the Zambian Kwacha.

People in different countries have different consumption habits and priorities. As a result, even countries at a roughly similar stage of development cannot be accurately compared. The French put a higher priority on good food and wine than on housing; the Americans prefer hygiene to good food; large numbers of Indians do not eat beef or drink alcohol for religious reasons, so their perceived needs are different from other peoples'. These factors make welfare comparisons impossible.

Different climates make a big difference. In cold countries whole industries are devoted to providing warm houses, warm clothing, sunny foreign holidays, heated swimming pools. All of this activity counts as production and is thus included in GNP. In hot countries warmth comes free but nobody adds an extra amount to GNP to allow for this.

The contribution of public services to welfare is enormous but difficult to value. For example it can be quite cheap to lay on fresh drinking water in a shanty town. The increase in government spending is thus quite small and will show up as a small increase in GNP and GNP per head. But the increase in welfare, in improved health, in a reduction of the back-breaking labour of fetching water, in the sheer pleasure of drinking and washing in clean water, is immeasurable. Similarly, it can be quite cheap to remove some diseases, thus greatly improving people's prospect of a healthy life.

Averages for income per head conceal the distribution of income. If the rich get richer but the poor remain as poor as ever, *average* income goes up but it is difficult to believe that the nation is better off. Before independence in countries like Kenya and Zambia the white population was as well if not better off than the average for industrialized countries like Britain, but the *per capita* national income figures showed a much lower figure and concealed the fact that Africans were mostly very poor, and were denied access to education, to land, indeed to most of the things enjoyed by the whites. The same is still true of Rhodesia and South Africa.

Finally, income figures take no account of insecurity. If people frequently lose their jobs, or if they even *think* they are likely to lose their jobs, then they are worse off than people in steady employment at the same average income. That is why relatively secure jobs in the civil service and in large stable institutions like banks are greatly prized when unemployment is very bad. Similarly farmers, especially small farmers in tropical countries, are constantly threatened by uncertain rains, diseases that attack cattle and crops, fire, locusts and marauding elephants. That is why they tend to save more (proportionate to their income) than urban workers. A settlement scheme for growing coffee in the Northern Province of Zambia was finding it difficult to attract people, I was told in 1971. The men who were being employed to clear and prepare the land wanted to continue in employment and wanted the government to run the scheme as a state farm. The reason was that they preferred the certainty of a rather lower income in employment to the risks of a new crop, running into debt, and the uncertain prospect of a slightly higher income. Uncertainty, not only about income but about the prospect of being able to get medical treatment if members of the family need it, and of being able to get an education for one's children, is not measured by estimates of GNP.

3 COMPARING THE STRUCTURE OF OUTPUT BETWEEN COUNTRIES

Tables 2.9 and 2.10 show the contribution of the main economic sectors to GDP for several African countries in 1970. In Table 2.9 the sectoral contributions are shown in a common currency (US dollars) in order to give an idea of absolute size; in Table 2.10 the breakdown is given in percentages in order to avoid the problems of converting to dollars when exchange rates may be bad indicators of currency values.

TABLE 2.9

Sectoral contributions to GDP for several African countries, 1970: in US dollars (millions)

	Zambia	*Kenya*	*Ghana*	*Nigeria*	*Uganda*	*S. Rhodesia*	*Tanzania*
Agriculture	106	485	1026	2400	643	223	473
Mining	609	68	38	345	20	94	15
Manufacturing	179	183	297	393	108	307	112
Trade	168	157	244	637	126	173	156
Government	189	217	200	403	102	80	} 529
Other	408	508	412	1131	324	612	
GDP	1659	1618	2217	5309	1323	1489	1285
Remitted abroad	−192	−68	−58	. .	−20	−31	+5
GNDI	1467	1550	2159	. .	1303	1458	1290

NOTES

(1) 'Other' includes electricity, gas and water; transport and communications; financial and other services (including tourism).

(2) 'Remitted abroad' includes profits *and* other current transfers (net).

(3) GNDI is National Disposable Income plus depreciation (i.e. Gross).

Source: UN

TABLE 2.10
Sectoral contributions to GDP for several African countries, 1970: percentages

	Zambia	Kenya	Ghana	Nigeria	Uganda	S. Rhodesia	Tanzania
Agriculture	6	30	46	45	49	15	37
Mining	37	4	2	7	2	6	1
Manufacturing	11	11	13	7	8	21	9
Trade	10	10	11	12	9	12	12
Government	11	13	9	8	8	5	} 41
Other	25	32	19	21	24	41	
Total GDP	100	100	100	100	100	100	100
Remitted abroad	−12	−4	−3	. .	−2	−2	—
GNDI	88	96	97	. .	98	98	100

Source and notes as for Table 2.9.

Although the tables do give a broad picture of the breakdown of these countries' economies, the student should note the following points:

(i) The larger is the contribution of agriculture, the more unreliable is the total (and the relative contributions of the other sectors) because agriculture is so difficult to measure.

(ii) Because the bulk of the population are rural in all these countries (even Zambia) the figures give a very inaccurate picture of their output, income and welfare.

(iii) On the other hand, the figures are relatively reliable for the modern sectors of the economies.

(iv) Definitions of sectors are a bit arbitrary and vary between countries – for example the processing of copper ore (as opposed to digging it out of the ground) could be treated as manufacturing rather than mining.

(v) Domestic income remitted abroad gives only a partial picture of dependence since it does not show the structure of debt and thus of current and future *capital* liabilities.

(vi) The figures are shown at market prices and so exaggerate the contribution of heavily taxed sectors (see the next section for Zambia's figures at factor cost).

(vii) The proportion of GDP contributed by sectors producing for export tends to vary with export prices. For example, the proportion of GDP contributed by agriculture in Ghana is higher when the cocoa price is high, while the proportions contributed by all other sectors are necessarily smaller.

4 COMPARING THE STRUCTURE OF OUTPUT OVER TIME: ZAMBIA

Table 2.11 shows how the structure of Zambian GDP has changed since Independence.

TABLE 2.11

Zambian GDP by economic sector, 1965 and 1970 (at factor cost and current prices)

	Percentages 1965	1970
Agriculture: commercial	2·7	2·4
subsistence	6·2	5·7
Mining and quarrying	44·7	38·9
Manufacturing	6·5	8·1
Electricity, gas and water	0·9	1·3
Construction	6·4	7·3
Wholesale and retail trade	11·6	10·1
Hotels and restaurants	1·7	1·0
Transport, etc.	5·3	5·0
Financial institutions	1·7	3·7
Real estate	1·5	3·6
Business services	1·5	1·5
Public administration and defence	4·9	5·6
Education	2·4	3·6
Health	1·4	1·2
Other services	0·6	1·2
GDP	100·0	100·0

Source: National Accounts 1964–5 and 1970.

The most important point to be made about Table 2.11 is that it is extremely difficult to alter the structure of an economy like Zambia's when it is so dominated by one sector. The post-independence boom allowed the government to increase spending very fast; manufacturing expanded rapidly as a result of the ending of federation, UDI and rapidly rising income; and other services responded as well. But the high and rising copper prices that fuelled the boom meant that the value of copper production also rose quite fast, although not as fast as GDP, as shown in Table 2.12. The net result was only a small reduction in the share of mining in GDP.

TABLE 2.12

Sectoral growth rates in Zambia, 1965–70 (at factor cost and current prices)

	Average annual growth rates Percentage
Agriculture	11
Mining	10
Manufacturing	18
Trade	10
Government	17
Other	18
GDP	13

5 CONCLUSION

Perhaps it is just as well that income levels (as measured conventionally) do not measure welfare. The prospect of *all* the countries of the world attaining similar levels of income to those of the industrialized, rich countries is extremely remote. It may be quite simply impossible because there are not enough resources, especially of raw materials.

It is not entirely the fault of the statisticians that national income figures are wrongly used. The figures were asked for in the first place by economists and by governments who had been influenced by economists. There is now a growing realization that other indicators of development are of equal if not greater importance. Seers has suggested three main indicators: the absolute necessities of life (food, clothing, shelter), a way of earning one's own living so as not to be dependent on others (a job, a farm or a business), and a reasonable level of equality of income. A country cannot claim to be better off if absolute poverty, unemployment and inequality have not been reduced.[19]

Others have added long lists of 'social indicators' measuring life expectancy, availability of education and health services, prevalence of various diseases, and so on. This is definitely a desirable trend. Ideally, national income statistics should be used only by professional economists and statisticians who fully understand their limitations and their uses. They *are* useful, particularly in the modern sectors of the economy and when used in relation to output rather than welfare; but the trouble is that it seems impossible to impose such restrictions.

NOTES

1 See Section 9, p. 25, for a discussion of foreign-owned income.

2 Always look carefully at any statistical table to see what the units are – in this case thousands of Kwacha.

3 It is assumed here that rent is paid to an individual. If it is paid to a property company, for example, then it becomes an intermediate payment for the shoe factory, and part of gross 'sales' of the property company.

4 Changes in the amount of 'work-in-progress', that is in the amount of goods actually in the middle of being processed, are treated in the same way as additions to stocks of finished goods, since they too are part of production.

5 Recent changes in national income accounting recommended by the United Nations include the estimation of depreciation on government assets such as schools and hospitals – for a discussion of this see Chapter 2, part II.

6 The general tendency to underestimate the income of poor countries and poor areas, because these areas have lower price levels, which in turn is caused by the structure of transport costs, is dealt with at length in Dan Usher, *The Price Level and the Meaning of National Income Statistics*, Oxford, Clarendon Press, 1968, especially Chapter 1.

7 For an account of village life and the difficulty of applying economic concepts and national accounting principles to it, see Phyllis Deane, *Colonial Social Accounting*, Cambridge University Press, 1953, Chapter IX.

8 'Affects' because many farmers who are dependent mainly on subsistence output also have other sources of income. 'Probably' the poorest because some shanty town dwellers may be as badly or worse off than small farmers.

[9] See B. Van Arkadie and C. Frank, *Economic Accounting and Development Planning*, Nairobi, OUP, 1966, Chapter XII, for several examples of these variations from East and Central Africa.

[10] P. Deane, *Colonial Social Accounting*, op. cit., pp. 21, 22.

[11] Between 1963 and 1969 the urban male population increased at 7·6% a year, the urban female population at 10% a year. *'Second National Development Plan'*, Lusaka, 1971, p. 50.

[12] The figures for the proportion of cash income earned from non-agricultural employment were 48% in Mumbwa and 35% in Katete. Universities of Nottingham and Zambia Agricultural Labour Productivity Investigation (UNZALPI), Report No. 3, pp. 147 and 149, Nottingham and Lusaka, 1970.

[13] See W. M. Allan, *The African Husbandman*, London, Oliver and Boyd, 1967, for further description of the 'normal surplus' and its effect on the amount of maize sold by small farmers from year to year.

[14] See National Accounts 1970, Table 7.

[15] The fact that many people in Zambia live in heavily subsidized housing is in fact ignored by the statisticians, who should really increase the recorded output by the amount of the subsidy.

[16] Dividends are that part of profit paid out to shareholders, who are the owners of a business. There are 'exchange controls' which lay down rules about how much of foreign-owned profits may be sent out of the country: see Chapter 8.

[17] In fact using a monthly index, one would strictly need a new survey every month and one would have to delay the publication of the index number until the survey had been tabulated.

[18] Most of copper output is still exported – but since 1970 about 6,000 tonnes a year have been used by the copper fabrication plant (ZAMEFA), out of total output of the order of 700,000 tonnes.

[19] Dudley Seers, 'What are we trying to measure?', *Journal of Development Studies*, April 1973.

3 *Excess Demand and Spare Capacity*

1 THE LINK BETWEEN NATIONAL INCOME CONCEPTS AND AGGREGATE DEMAND, SUPPLY AND INCOME

There is a clear link between the concepts of aggregate demand, supply and income of Chapter 1, on the one hand, and the national accounting concepts of expenditure, output and income of Chapter 2, on the other.

Demand is not exactly the same as expenditure, but the two are very similar. Both can be broken down into the same categories for analysis: the main categories are government demand and spending, and demand and spending for investment, consumption and exports. Demand is not always expressed as actual spending because the goods and services are not always available, or because buyers cannot get credit even though they may be creditworthy. Thus demand may be greater than expenditure. In general, it is not possible for demand to be less than expenditure. If goods and services are available demand can be realized in the form of actual spending. The one exception to this is that producers may be unable to sell all of their output, so that stocks may accumulate involuntarily. Since increases in stocks are assumed to be 'bought' by firms from themselves, then in this case 'spending' can be greater than demand.

The supply of goods and services is the same as output (or product). There are two exceptions. Firstly, goods can be supplied from accumulated *stocks* which were produced in some previous period. In such a case supply would be greater than current production. In this case, however, supply would be the same as output as defined for national income purposes, since that definition includes changes in stocks. Secondly, supply also includes *imports* – it is possible for a country to import more than it exports and to pay for the difference out of accumulated savings of foreign exchange, or by borrowing from foreign countries. Imports cannot normally be paid for in local currency, so that if imports are greater than exports payments have to be made out of the earnings of past production (that is, an earlier excess of exports over imports) or out of future production, when a future excess of exports over imports will have to be used to repay foreign loans.[1]

The two concepts of income are very close. Income accrues in the form of profits, wages and salaries and self-employment income (including income from farming), some of which is re-spent within the country and some of which is sent out of the country in the form of dividends to foreign owners of local business, interest on loans and expatriates' savings. The important factors concerning income are thus *who* gets it, which should reveal something of how it is likely to be disposed of, and whether the income is available to be spent within the country or not.[2]

2 EXCESS DEMAND

If demand is greater than supply, there are various ways in which the economy can react. Demand could exceed supply for many reasons – for example as a result of a big wage increase granted by the government or the copper mines, or as a result of a big foreign loan which is spent on building new schools or railways or roads. Alternatively, excess demand may occur because of sudden reductions in supply, for example because of a poor harvest or problems with international transport routes, such as occurred after UDI in 1965 and the Rhodesian border closure in early 1973.

The possible reactions to excess demand are categorized below. Basically the supply of goods for sale can be increased in four main ways – by increasing output, reducing accumulated stocks, increasing imports, reducing exports. In addition demand can be frustrated or prices can rise. These are not alternatives since all six possibilities can occur simultaneously or in any number of combinations. The discussion of these possibilities that follows is by no means a comprehensive one: most of them are discussed at much greater length in later chapters. The intention at this point is to give a rapid overview which should help in understanding the rest of the book.

(1) A reduction in accumulated stocks of raw materials, work-in-progress and finished products. Sometimes businesses carry stocks precisely in order to be able to meet sudden increases in demand. In Zambia, sellers of imported goods need to keep large stocks because the country is so far from its major foreign suppliers that it can take a long time between ordering increased supplies and the arrival of the goods. The government through its marketing boards should also try to carry stocks of basic foods, especially maize, which can be used if there is a poor harvest. Clearly there is a limit to meeting excess demand by running down stocks. If demand continues at the new higher level then some other reaction is bound to occur. In practice, moreover, the normal reaction to a period of rising aggregate demand is for there to be an overall *increase* in stocks throughout the economy. In general, the bigger the national income the bigger the level of stocks should be. Certainly that is what has happened in Zambia since Independence – there has been an increase in stocks in most years, in spite of great difficulties with import routes.

(2) An increase in production. For an increase in production to occur, there must be unemployed resources which can be used in combination. Thus manufactured output can be increased if there is labour available with the right skills and in the right place, if there are machines available with unused capacity and if other inputs (fuel, raw materials, services, transport) can also be increased. Most commonly this situation exists if factories have dismissed men in some recent period of time, because of a lack of demand for their products. In such circumstances labour with the right skills is probably available locally, since the workers should be able to return to their old jobs. They might of course have found other jobs, or returned to their villages, in which case output would not be able to increase so quickly or easily. In the case of agricultural output, production of most goods cannot be increased in the short term, that is in less time than it takes to grow a crop. The commonest time lag is thus a year, but many agricultural goods take even longer, for example an increase in the breeding and rearing of beef cattle, or the seven years it takes to get a cocoa crop from the time of planting.

(3) An increase in imports. Even if there is no spare capacity *within* the economy, there is usually spare capacity somewhere in the world, so that increased demand can usually be met by importing. Nevertheless, there are various other reasons why imports may not increase in response to an increase in aggregate demand: the country may not be able to *pay* for additional imports, imports may be controlled by bureaucratic means, international transport routes may not have spare capacity. Zambia introduced import licensing in 1971 *because of* a lack of foreign exchange at a time of low copper prices. There were other reasons for introducing controls, most importantly to change the structure of imports, but one effect was to slow down the growth in total imports.[3]

(4) Diversion of exports to the home market. Because 95% of Zambia's exports are copper, and because the copper fabrication plant only absorbs a tiny proportion of production, excess demand in Zambia cannot really be absorbed by diverting exports to the home market. In many other African countries the same applies: Ghanaians consume little cocoa, Ugandans little coffee compared with the amounts exported. In principle, however, excess demand *could* be met in this way. For example rising demand for maize would mean less available for export, and the same applies to timber and tobacco, both of which are exported *and* bought locally. When the power station on the north bank at Kariba is completed it is possible that the country's capacity for producing electricity will be big enough to allow some to be exported, but rising home demand will gradually reduce this amount. If Zambia develops its *manufacturing* sector to the point where exports of manufactured goods become significant, then there will be a possibility of meeting excess demand by diverting manufactured exports to

the home market. Clearly this can only happen if manufacturers have no spare capacity to meet excess home demand by increasing output, and if manufacturers are prepared to deny their overseas customers in favour of customers at home.

(5) Demand may be frustrated. If goods and services are not available then demand, whether from consumers, government, businesses or the overseas buyers of Zambian exports, may simply not be expressed as actual expenditure. Zambia's recent history provides many examples of this because of the very rapid increase in aggregate demand after Independence. Thus the government actually underspent the budget in 1966 and 1967, because of the enormous difficulty of coping with huge increases in government budgets at a time when many posts were unfilled and many civil servants (Zambian and expatriate) were new to their jobs. Some consumer demand has also been frustrated, the most obvious example being petrol which was rationed on two occasions. Frustrated demand may either be postponed, in which case expenditure will be higher at some later date (than it would have been otherwise), or it may never take place. For example, motorists who did not use their cars so much as they wanted to during petrol rationing could not make up for it afterwards – weekend trips not taken have gone for ever. Similarly, a government post not filled means a salary not paid, and unless the government hires two people to clear the backlog of work, that money does not get spent later. Permanently frustrated spending is clearly more effective in coping with excess demand, but even delays can serve a very useful purpose since the *capacity* of the economy may have increased by the time the money comes to be spent.

(6) Rising prices. If supply, from home or abroad, cannot be increased and if demand cannot be contained by rationing or the simple non-availability of goods and services, then prices will be driven up by excess demand. This has happened in Zambia, as in most countries of the world, in recent years. There have undoubtedly been other reasons why prices have risen, but excess demand has contributed to inflation in spite of price control measures.

3 EXCESS SUPPLY

An imbalance between supply and demand can also, of course, mean that demand is *less than* supply. This can cause reductions in output and imports, an involuntary build-up of stocks or more goods available for export (provided that there is a market abroad for goods not wanted at home). The cut in Zambian government spending in 1969, for example, did result in a fall in new construction work and a fall in imports. Stocks, on the other hand, *fell* which suggests that the desire to reduce stocks in the face of falling demand was greater than any involuntary build-up of production which could not be sold.

Clearly there is no mirror image of frustrated demand – if demand is less than supply all demand can probably be met (some types of demand may still be frustrated, but in aggregate this will not be so) and there is normally no equivalent way in which excess *supply* can be absorbed. However if a period of excess supply follows quickly after a period when a lot of demand was frustrated, then it is possible that for a while producers will be able to maintain production, by meeting a backlog of orders accumulated during the earlier boom period.

In principle, prices may fall in a period when demand is less than supply – the analysis of markets suggests that this should be so. But prices in the modern world are notoriously 'sticky downwards'. By this is meant that while prices are quick to rise in response to excess demand, they do not usually fall in the reverse situation. There are many reasons for this: for example government guarantees some important prices such as the prices paid to farmers for agricultural goods; and manufacturers and traders are often very reluctant to reduce prices, because they fear the damaging effects of competitive price cutting and are doubtful about whether demand for their products will increase as a result of lower prices. Most importantly, wage earners resist very strongly any attempt to cut wages, especially in those sectors with strong trade unions. The result of successful resistance to wage cuts is that the *cost* of labour to employers does not fall in a situation of excess supply, and this makes it harder for employers to reduce the prices of their products. Certainly in Zambia in 1969, when demand fell, prices rose less fast than before, but did not fall. A reduction in the rate of inflation may be a very significant achievement, but it is different from an actual fall in prices, especially in its feedback effects.

4 FEEDBACK EFFECTS

Increases in output and rising prices clearly increase the incomes of producers. In both cases the value of sales increases, incomes therefore increase and unless the whole of the increase in incomes is saved, or taxed and not spent by the government, then spending will increase further. Increases in income and rises in prices are not in any sense a *solution* therefore to a situation of excess demand, since increases in income will feed back into aggregate demand. Since it is normal for some part of increases in income not to be spent (or to be spent on imports with minimal feedback effects) each successive feedback will be smaller than the previous one suggesting that some sort of balance or equilibrium between supply and demand might eventually be reached – if no new event occurred to prevent that possibility in the meantime. The conditions under which equilibrium might be reached, and how much output and prices might rise in achieving it, will be discussed at much greater length in subsequent chapters. For the moment, the essential point is that disequilibrium can lead to further disequilibrium as a result of feedback – responses to excess demand which increase incomes must lead to further increases in demand.

If additional goods are put up for sale out of accumulated stocks, then in principle no new income is created. The *production* of stocks is theoretically assumed to generate income; selling off the stocks, therefore, yields no new income, and thus has no feedback effects. This process does mean however that firms exchange physical assets (accumulated stocks) for cash. It is not possible to 'spend' stocks, although a firm can borrow using stocks as security. It *is* possible to spend cash. Firms might therefore increase their spending if they had been unable to borrow for some reason. Firms' reaction to a reduction in stocks also depends on why they built up stocks in the first place. If the stocks were involuntarily accumulated for lack of demand, then no further action need be expected. But firms might react by trying to rebuild stocks to their former level, or even to a new higher level in keeping with a higher level of demand. In these circumstances, a secondary reaction would be increases in output with the attendant feedback effects.

The diversion of goods from exports to satisfy domestic demand creates no new income. Producers get the same income by selling in overseas or home markets – unless of course prices are different. Various service industries may lose or gain from the process – retailers may gain from selling the goods locally, transporters may lose by not carrying the goods out of the country. Technically these ups and downs in services are changes in the output of service industries; in any case they are probably small in relation to the increase in the domestic supply of goods, which does *not* have any feedback effects.

An increase in imports creates income for foreigners who are not likely to spend that income in Zambia. As explained in Chapter 1, only in a very large country is there likely to be any feedback effect. As the number of industrialized countries grows it is unlikely that any one country will again dominate world trade as Britain and the USA once did, so that any individual country will be able to ignore the feedback effects of increasing its imports. Of course some local income increases if imports increase; traders selling imported goods do very well. In Zambia a large range of goods is still imported because of the low level of industrialization, so that most traders sell some imported goods and some sell nothing else. Again, traders' income is technically local output and so should be analysed as such, but it should be remembered that some local income is directly dependent on the level of imports.

The frustration of demand clearly has no impact on income. If money is not spent, then no income is received. If demand is postponed, then increased spending at some time in the future will have an effect on income at that time, but the immediate effect of the frustration of demand is quite simply that the circular flow of income is stopped to the extent that spending does not take place. Perhaps this explains the attraction of bureaucratic attempts to frustrate demand. A government trying to control a situation of excess demand faces the problem that some of the possibilities create further income and thus further demand, whilst increases in supply from imports and export diversion both damage the balance of trade and so create problems of their own. Rationing, which is a bureaucratic way of frustrating demand, may then seem the only solution. But bureaucracy has its own cost since extra civil servants have to be paid, or existing ones diverted from other duties; and rationing is politically unpopular and may lead to the development of uncontrolled illegal (or 'black') markets. In addition, the frustration of demand does not provide a channel for the unspent income. It *may* be saved, but in Zambia that means an increase in the sending of savings abroad if it is expatriate demand that has been frustrated, and that too damages the balance of payments.

5 EQUILIBRIUM AND DISEQUILIBRIUM

Situations of excess demand and excess supply are forms of disequilibrium, by definition. An economy is described as being 'in equilibrium' if aggregate demand equals aggregate supply. That is, equilibrium exists if the demand for goods and services of consumers, government, businesses and export customers is equal to domestic output and imports. This concept of equilibrium is a 'static' or short-term one since it excludes long-term changes in the production capacity of the economy. In contrast, a 'dynamic' equilibrium in a growing economy is one in which long-term growth in supply is matched over time by long-term growth in demand.

Most of this book is concerned with short-term equilibrium and disequilibrium. This is not because the long-term growth and development of an economy are not important. On the contrary, long-term solutions to the problems of poverty and backwardness are of absolutely fundamental importance and occupy a great deal of the attention of the Zambian government as of other governments in Africa and elsewhere.

Short-term problems remain however, and have to be understood in order to be tackled. As a working definition of the difference between short term and long term, short term will be taken as a period within which the *capacity* of the economy to produce goods and services can be assumed to be unchanged. This means assuming that although investment may be taking place, the increased output made possible by investment is not yet available, and that the capacity of the work force, although growing in the long term through growth in population and through better education and training, is unchanged. Some of these assumptions will be relaxed at times, since it is not possible to dissociate short term from long-term problems. The reaction of an economy to a short-term disequilibrium will almost invariably have an important influence on its long-term development.

A great deal of macroeconomic analysis consists of examining the effects of disequilibrium in an economy. For example, in Zambia the effects on the economy of changes in the production of copper, and of changes in the price of copper, are of great importance. A convenient way of analysing these effects is to assume that the economy is initially in equilibrium, with aggregate demand and supply equal to each other, and then to examine how much the various macroeconomic aggregates will change as a result of, say, a change in the copper price, and to try and determine what their new levels will be if and when a new equilibrium is reached.

Because of the feedback effects, of changes in output for example, it is clear that equilibrium will not be immediately restored by the reaction of the economy to a situation of disequilibrium. However, in a situation of excess demand, further increases in demand via increases in income are usually smaller with each round of the circular flow of income. Taking an increase in aggregate demand caused by, say, an increase in government spending, the income of consumers and businesses will increase as a result. But not all of these increases in income will be spent. Some will be taxed, some will be saved, and some of the spending will be on imports, which does not create new domestic income. In short, leakages from the circular flow of income gradually reduce the size of successive rounds of spending. Eventually, therefore, it is possible that a new equilibrium could be reached, at a higher overall level of economic activity and of national income, provided that no new injections into the circular flow of income occur in the meantime. Emphasis on comparing the hypothetical equilibrium values of national income before and after a state of disequilibrium is why macroeconomics is often called 'national income analysis'.

6 EQUILIBRIUM EXPRESSED IN TERMS OF SAVING AND INVESTMENT

Saving is defined as that part of income that is not spent on current goods and services. In other words, saving is income minus consumption. Investment is defined as spending which is not for current consumption but for future consumption or to increase the capacity to produce in the future. In other words investment is total spending minus consumption.

Since total spending has been defined in such a way that it is equal to total income, both being equal to GNP, it follows that saving equals investment. Both are equal to that part of national income which is not consumed (that is, not used up during the current period and so available in some way for the future).

It may help to make this clear if the relationship is expressed in symbols. If

Y=income (GNP)=output available for consumption or investment
C=consumption by individuals
I=investment (fixed domestic investment plus increase in stocks)
G=government current spending on goods and services
X=exports
M=imports

then because total supply equals total spending

$$Y+M=C+I+G+X$$

or as it is more frequently written

$$Y=C+I+G+X-M$$

Now savings consist of that part of income which is not consumed, so

$$S \text{ (savings)} = Y-C-G$$

Since Y (domestic output) is the same as income, and consumption consists of consumption by individuals plus collective consumption by government, it follows that

$$S=Y-C-G=I+X-M$$

But the difference between exports and imports ($X-M$) is a form of investment. If the country exports more than it imports then foreign exchange reserves will rise, or foreign loans can be repaid. Either way, net foreign assets increase, which is a form of investment. Like all forms of investment, it will allow greater future consumption than would otherwise have been possible – because of the existence of additional foreign reserves, or because loans no longer have to be repaid.

In other words saving equals investment, if 'investment' includes investment abroad.

Although saving and investment are by definition equal after the event (or 'post hoc' which means 'after this event' in Latin) the intentions of savers and investors before the event (*ex ante* in Latin) may not be equal. The reason is that some saving is *not* done by the same people who make investment decisions. Individuals save out of their incomes, and put money in a box under the bed, or deposit money in a bank or building society. Investment is *mainly* undertaken by government and by businesses, in pursuit of their various interests, and both government and businesses are normally net *borrowers* of money. To some extent the saving and investment decision is the same: businesses retain profits rather than distributing them to shareholders *in order to* invest; and government runs a current surplus of revenue over current spending *in order to* finance its capital spending. Individuals also save in order to invest in housing, but the normal practice in private house-buying, as in capital spending by businesses and government, is for investment to be partly (or even mainly) financed by borrowing.

Now if saving is a result of decisions by one group and investment is the result of decisions by another group, there is no reason to suppose that savings plans and investment plans will be equal, even though the two groups overlap a bit. If savers plan to save more than investors plan to spend, total demand, which consists of consumption demand plus investment demand, will be less than income and thus less than output. This amounts to a situation of excess supply.

Similarly in the reverse situation, if investors plan to spend more than savers plan to save, investment demand will be more than the resources released by saving (or non-consumption), which amounts to a situation of excess demand. It is thus possible to express equilibrium and disequilibrium in terms of savings and investment rather than in terms of aggregate demand and supply.

The supposed advantage of focusing on savings and investment is that this also focuses attention on financial markets and financial institutions. The main way in which money not spent by consumers is made available to investors is through 'financial intermediaries'. Thus if a saver puts money in the Post Office Savings Bank, that is a loan to the government. Savings deposited in a commercial bank may be lent to business borrowers, or to the government by purchase of government stocks and bills.

But not all investment is financed out of borrowing, as has been explained; and investors are not the only borrowers. A significant proportion of consumption is also financed by borrowing, especially the purchase of 'consumer durables' (long-lasting items such as cars and refrigerators). This form of credit, known as consumer credit, is of greater importance in rich countries where production and sale of consumer durables is a greater proportion of economic activity than in Africa. But it is of growing importance in Africa. Furthermore, some African governments (for example, Malawi) have borrowed to finance *current* expenditure; while Zambia, at the other extreme, has several times had an annual surplus of tax revenue over both current and capital spending, which means that in those years investment by government (a very large proportion of total investment) was financed without any borrowing at all.

It seems, therefore, that there is no great advantage in paying as much attention to the savings-investment relationship as is done in other textbooks. The important things for the student to know are firstly, that

actual (or post hoc) saving = actual (or post hoc) investment.

This statement is simply true by definition. Secondly, the student should know that

planned (or ex ante) saving is *not* necessarily equal to planned (or ex ante) investment because plans are made by different (but overlapping) groups of people. As far as the equilibrium of the economy as a whole is concerned, it is much more useful to concentrate on the relation between aggregate demand (which could be described as planned spending) and aggregate supply, since all the factors affecting equilibrium are then included.

7 SPARE CAPACITY AND 'UNEMPLOYMENT'

If an increase in demand is to be met by increased domestic output there must obviously be some sort of spare production capacity in the economy. More specifically, unused resources must be available in the right combinations and the right places so that production can increase in response to the increased demand. Thus it is not sufficient to have unemployed labour in the country if that labour is in the wrong place, has the wrong skills or has no capital goods with which to work.

In industrialized countries the scarcest resource is nearly always labour. Spare capacity is thus usually referred to as unemployment, meaning unemployment of people. A situation of full utilization of capacity (that is, a situation where no further increase in output is possible) is normally called 'full employment', since as output increases labour becomes scarce while there is still an adequate amount of capital available.

In Zambia the scarcest resources are skilled labour and physical capital.[4] Thus the expansion of the economy after Independence in 1964 was greatly hindered by shortages of skilled labour and the absence of capital goods. Probably the most obvious immediate capital shortage was in transport, especially after UDI; while the shortage of skilled labour was prolonged by the shortage of schools and other educational institutions. At the same time there was some urban unemployment of relatively unskilled workers.

The emphasis on the level of unemployment as the key indicator of capacity to increase output in an industrialized economy dates from the 1930s when the 'great depression' caused millions of workers to lose their jobs. In an industrialized economy, workers depend on jobs for their living. They no longer have any link with the rural sector, which is much too small anyway to absorb a significant number of unemployed urban workers. In Zambia, by contrast, the copper miners thrown out of work by the great depression simply returned to their villages. Many had not even brought their families to town, and there was enough land for all.

The sort of unemployment which occurred in industrial economies in the 1930s, where factories are closed for lack of demand for their products, is sometimes called 'demand deficiency' unemployment. It is also called 'Keynesian' unemployment because the English economist Keynes is credited with finding the solution – namely to stimulate demand. If somehow demand can be increased labour can return to work at very short notice and output can quickly increase. That may seem very obvious, but at the beginning of the great depression governments reacted to falling demand and growing unemployment by *reducing* their spending, which made things worse.

The existence of unemployment in Zambia is an important social and political problem, but very little of it has been caused by lack of demand. The very rapid growth of government spending after Independence has more often led to a situation of excess demand. Nevertheless, a cutback in government spending did cause some unemployment in 1969 and 1970, especially in the construction industry, and this must have had some feedback effects on other sectors. It is always very important therefore for aggregate demand to be maintained at a level which employs as many people as possible, so that there is no *unnecessary* unemployment. The scarce resources of skilled labour and capital should be used as fully as possible.

'As fully as possible' suggests that other considerations may be important. This is so. Most importantly, high levels of demand lead to a high demand for imports. So long as Zambia enjoys a high price for exports of copper, imports can be increased and paid for, but a falling copper price may mean having to reduce demand even at the risk of throwing men out of work. Another important consideration is inflation, since a high level of demand may cause prices to rise faster than desired.

If unemployment in Zambia is only marginally caused by lack of demand, what does cause it? Before describing the main cause, some relatively unimportant forms of unemployment should be dealt with first. In all countries there is a small proportion of the work force that is basically *unemployable*. Some people are unemployable because of physical or mental limitations or because they are simply 'work-shy'. In addition, some people are unemployed because they are in the process of changing their jobs. Provided their next job is fairly certain such people are not really a problem. Unemployment statistics usually try and identify this group in a rough and ready way by distinguishing between those who have been unemployed for a short time, for example less than six weeks, and those who have been unemployed for longer. This type of unemployment is called *frictional*.

More serious as a social and political problem is so-called *structural* unemployment, which consists of people thrown out of work because their industry is in decline and their skills are becoming obsolete. This is a serious problem in the older industrialized countries. Britain, for example, has serious structural unemployment in mining, shipbuilding and textile industries which are declining because substitutes have been found (oil for coal, cheaper or more efficient overseas labour in shipbuilding and textiles) or because other nations have overtaken Britain and can compete by making a cheaper product (Japan in shipbuilding, Hong Kong in textiles). Structural unemployment is often associated with *regional* unemployment, so that workers have not only to learn new skills but to move to new areas, or the government is faced with trying to persuade new industries to go to the declining areas.

Zambia has too 'new' an industrial economy to face much of this type of structural unemployment, except for the decline of tourism in Livingstone, which is due to political rather than economic factors. In a sense, however, it would perhaps be possible to describe Zambia's main form of unemployment as structural. People whose rural skills are of no use in the modern sector of the economy are seeking work in towns, where there is a shortage of people with industrial skills and advanced education but a surplus of job-seekers who are unskilled in the modern sense and have little or no education. The problem is in fact made worse by an oversupply of primary school leavers seeking urban jobs and not willing to farm in the rural areas where spare land exists. At the moment secondary school leavers and university graduates can get jobs,[5] but the experience of other developing countries and the manpower forecasts in Zambia suggest that unemployment will soon shift up the educational scale.

Thus the number of primary school leavers was about 64,000 in 1970, of whom only 1 in 5 could go on to secondary school. Yet the number of jobs expected to be created during the five years of the Second National Development Plan is only 100,000, or an average of 20,000 a year. The First National Development Plan did not reach its target of 100,000 new jobs even though the rate of increase of government spending was much higher at that time than it is likely to be during the SNDP.[6]

The Zambian employment problem is thus 'structural' in very different ways from the meaning of that word in industrial countries. Zambia is investing heavily in education and training in order to replace the foreigners who still dominate the higher skill levels; at the same time many of the ablest rural inhabitants are leaving their villages and farms to seek employment in the towns. Not only do the most enterprising tend to be the ones who leave, but the education system has the effect of selecting the ablest children and funnelling them up through the educational system. The farther up they go, the less likely are they to return to their villages, and to agriculture as a way of making a living. The more efficient are the selection methods at each stage of education, the more efficiently does education remove the ablest, in an intellectual sense, from the rural areas.

The problems of urban–rural migration and unemployed school leavers cannot be tackled here.[7] Clearly some sort of two-pronged attack, involving the creation of better opportunities to make a living in rural areas and the creation of more jobs for the unskilled, is necessary. Equally clearly the problem has little to do with short-term equilibrium and disequilibrium in aggregate demand and supply. The latter remains important, but can only have a relatively small effect on unemployment.

One further type of unemployment should be mentioned – *disguised* unemployment. This refers to workers who are not actually unemployed but whose usefulness in their work is so low that production would fall by very little if they ceased work. In the extreme case, disguised unemployment is defined as a situation in which workers have zero marginal productivity. The situation is supposed to arise in agriculture where there is a severe shortage of land so that there are more workers than are needed to maintain production; or in the urban sector where employers hire more workers than they need, because of very low wages and widespread unemployment. The concept has little relevance to Zambia's rural areas because land is not scarce; it is possible that some urban employers do in fact hire more workers than they need, perhaps as a result of political pressure, but it is unlikely that there is a significant amount of disguised unemployment – among other things, wages are not particularly low.[8] In Kenya, on the other hand, the government actually tried to compel all employers to increase their labour force by 10% regardless of their labour needs. To the extent that this move was successful there must have been some disguised unemployment as a result.

8 OUTPUT AND EMPLOYMENT

Short-term fluctuations in output are normally reflected in employment. If the short term is defined as a period during which the stock of capital does not change, which must mean that skills and productivity cannot change either, then output changes can only occur by using more or less labour. Normally this will be reflected in the number of people employed. However, those in jobs may work longer or shorter hours, so that instead of an increase in employment there is an increase in overtime; and instead of a reduction in employment there is a reduction in overtime and an increase in short-time working – for example the four-day week.

Employment may not respond to changes in output because of the practice of 'labour hoarding'. Employers may prefer to retain (or 'hoard') their workers rather than dismiss them when output falls, because they expect the fall in output to be temporary. In this situation it is often more efficient to keep the labour force together than to dismiss workers who may not be available when demand and output recover.

The government in Zambia may also put political pressure on employers to maintain employment. For example, the copper mines maintained and even increased their labour force in 1966 in spite of a fall in output. The mining management knew that the fall in output was probably temporary since it was caused by shortages of coal and coke from the Wankie mine in Rhodesia; so there was a sound economic reason for hoarding labour. At the same time, it would have been very difficult politically for the mines to have reduced their labour force at that time. In contrast, the construction industry reduced its labour force in 1969, mainly because of a reduction in the government's capital budget. In this case there was no way of knowing how long the reduced level of spending would last, so that labour hoarding would have been much more risky, especially as labour cost is a much higher proportion of total cost in construction than in mining.[9]

NOTES

[1] Two other possible sources of foreign currency are: money sent home from abroad by migrant workers, and grants of aid.

[2] The conventional distinction is between domestic income and national income. But as explained in Chapter 2, this distinction would only deduct from domestic income money accruing to overseas residents – mainly shareholders in Zambian businesses. Money sent out of the country by short-term expatriate residents in Zambia is sent out *in order to* be spent abroad, and should not really count as domestic income.

[3] The value of imports grew by less than 5% in 1972, compared with annual growth rates of 16% in 1971 and 9% in 1970. The average annual growth in the value of imports 1964–72 was about 13%.

[4] Physical capital means machinery, lorries, trains, buildings, roads, etc.

[5] There is already some evidence, however, that secondary school leavers are beginning to have difficulty getting jobs.

[6] For these figures see *Second National Development Plan*, Lusaka, 1971, Section D.

[7] There is a lot of published material on this subject. The student should at least be familiar with the relevant sections of the two development plans, 'Zambian Manpower', Development Division, 1969, and the earlier 'Manpower Report' Cabinet Office, 1966, and T. C. Coombe and C. Angi, *The Primary School Leaver Crisis and Youth Programmes in Zambia*, University of Zambia, School of Education, 1969.

[8] But see the last section of this chapter on labour hoarding, which could be described as a form of short-term disguised unemployment.

[9] According to the 1967 Input-Output Table the number of Zambian workers employed per K1,000 of final demand was 0·2 in mining and 0·75 in construction; see J. Fry and C. Harvey, 'Copper and Zambia', Table 4, in J. Cownie and S. Pearson (eds.), *Commodity Exports and African Economic Development*, Boston, Lexington Books, 1974.

4 *The Consumption Function*

1 DEFINITION OF CONSUMPTION

The economic meaning of consumption is the using up of economic resources so that they are not available in the future. From the point of view of the individual, consumption is that part of income that is spent on 'consumer goods' – the remainder of income being defined as savings. It is actually possible for the individual to have consumption greater than income, by spending past savings or borrowing, in which case the individual has 'dissaved' or had 'negative savings'.

From the point of view of the national economy, consumption includes current spending by government; and saving by the nation as a whole includes not only saving by individuals out of their incomes, but also saving by government. Government saving occurs if current government revenue from taxation and other sources is greater than current government spending. Government saving, like private saving, can be negative, if the government runs a current deficit and has to borrow to pay for its current spending.

Business income, or profits, is technically part of the private income of the individuals who own the business. Nevertheless a business is described as 'saving' if it retains part of its profits rather than distributing them as personal incomes to owners. Some of the distributed income may also be saved, but this is usually described as being part of private saving.

Commercial farms are a form of business. Commercial farmers can consume or save their cash incomes in the same way as other businessmen. Subsistence production of, say, maize can either be consumed or 'saved' in the form of accumulating stocks. Subsistence production of investment goods, such as the clearing of land or the building up of cattle herds, is a form of income which is by definition saved and invested simultaneously.

These definitions give rise of course to a number of problems. For example, a great deal of spending by individuals is on goods which are not immediately 'consumed'. The most obvious of such goods are the large, expensive, long-lasting items like cars, refrigerators and furniture, known as consumer durables. Precisely because these items have a fairly long life they can very often be obtained on credit by means of loans or hire purchase arrangements. Nevertheless they are defined as consumption, as are more obviously consumable items like tins of food which are bought and stored in the home without being consumed at once. The only item of private spending which is *not* treated as consumption is the purchase of a house.

This definition of consumer spending by individuals means that the purchase of an item like a car for private use is treated as consumption, but when it is bought by a business it is investment. The importance of consumer durables is, however, relatively minor in poor countries; and demand for consumer durables has less immediate effect on the economy of poor countries since the poorer the country the more likely are consumer durables to be imported. Even those items which are manufactured locally are mainly assembled from imported parts so that the local value added is small.

2 IMPORTANCE OF CONSUMPTION

Of the four main components of demand – private consumption, investment, government current spending and exports – private consumption is normally the biggest. In Zambia, however, the copper industry is so large in relation to the rest of the economy that export demand is normally greater than demand from private consumers. For the same reason, investment is a larger than normal proportion of demand: the large profits made by the copper industry when the copper price is high make possible a high rate of capital formation, especially by government which levies a high rate of tax on copper company profits. The orders of magnitude for 1970 are shown in Table 4.1.

TABLE 4.1
The components of final demand: Zambia 1970

	K mn	%
Private consumption expenditure	458	27
Government consumption expenditure	198	12
Gross fixed capital formation	328	20
Increase (or decrease) in stocks	– 13	– 1
Export of goods and services	685	42
TOTAL SUPPLY (GDP plus imports)	1656	100

Source: *Monthly Digest of Statistics*, November 1973, Table 56.

Another way of looking at it is to examine the way in which national disposable income is spent. National disposable income is a new concept, recently introduced into Zambia's official statistics. It consists of Net National Product (GNP minus depreciation) at market prices, with an item consisting mainly of expatriates' remittances also deducted. This is shown in Table 4.2.

Table 4.2 shows that in 1970 Zambia consumed about 70% of national disposable income, and saved and invested about 30%. These proportions vary quite a lot in the short term because of variations in the copper price. When it is low as in 1971 and 1972 the country is forced to reduce its holdings of foreign exchange in order to maintain

TABLE 4.2

Expenditure out of National Disposable Income, 1970

	K mn	%
Private consumption expenditure	458	49
Government consumption expenditure	198	21
Net domestic investment	192	21
Net foreign investment (net lending to the rest of the world)	62	7
Statistical discrepancy	15	2
National disposable income	925	100

Source: *Monthly Digest of Statistics*, November 1973, Tables 56 and 58.

essential imports. Even if there is no other change this tends to reduce total investment by making foreign investment into a negative item, and so to increase the share of consumption expenditure. The reverse happens when the copper price is very high. In 1969, for example, total consumption (private and government) was only 55% of national disposable income, because exports were valued at K863 mn compared with only K685 mn in 1970.

3 THE DETERMINANTS OF CHANGES IN PRIVATE CONSUMPTION

It is obvious that over any length of time, consumption by individuals must be determined principally by their income. To a much lesser extent, some people are able to spend on consumption out of past savings or by borrowing. The main problem to be examined here, though, is the effect on consumption of *changes* in income, and other short-term changes in the economy. Since private consumption is a very large component of total demand it is also a very large part of the feedback from changes in demand. Thus the important thing to investigate is the short-term *change* in consumption that occurs as a result of a *change* in income. This is called the 'marginal propensity to consume' or the 'mpc'. Basically it describes the feedback effect via consumption of a change in income:[1]

$$\text{mpc} = \frac{\Delta C}{\Delta Y}$$

if C = private consumption,
Y = income.

On the other hand, the 'average propensity to consume' or the 'apc' is simply the proportion of total income that is consumed:

$$\text{apc} = \frac{C}{Y}$$

These are simply definitions. There is a *theory* which says that consumption is related in a particular way to income, thus

$$C = a + bY$$

where a and b are positive *constants*. What this theory is suggesting is that consumption increases or decreases with income in a particular way, namely that consumption is determined by income according to a linear formula. Some consumption, represented by a, is independent of changes in income; the remainder varies with income in such a way that b is in fact the marginal propensity to consume (see below for an algebraic demonstration of this). This theory is attributed to the English

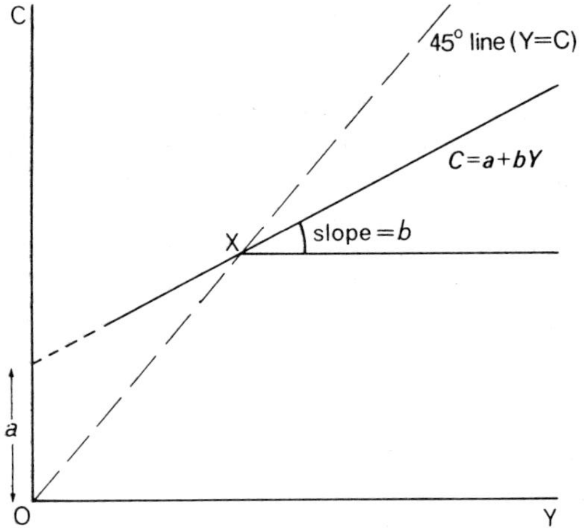

Figure 4.1 Consumption function $C = a + bY$

economist Keynes, and is called the Keynesian consumption theory (or consumption function). On a graph it looks like Figure 4.1. The theory of $C = a + bY$ implies several things about consumption, including:

(1) consumption is greater as income is greater, and less as income is less;

(2) if income changes from Y to Y^1, then the new level of consumption will be

$$C^1 = a + bY^1$$

compared to

$$C = a + bY$$

Subtracting one equation from the other gives

$$C^1 - C = b(Y^1 - Y)$$

or

$$\Delta C = b\Delta Y$$

or

$$\Delta C/\Delta Y = \text{mpc} = b$$

The theory thus implies that the marginal propensity to consume is a constant, b.

(3) the average propensity to consume, $\frac{C}{Y}$, is

$$\frac{C}{Y} = \frac{a}{Y} + b$$

so that the apc gets *smaller* as income increases. This is the same as saying that the average propensity to save gets *bigger* as income increases. In other words, the richer people get the more they save.

(4) if income is very low, consumption will equal income, so that no saving takes place at all. This is shown in the figure by the point X where the line $C = a + bY$ cuts the dotted line $Y = C$ (the line at 45° from the origin, O). If income is even lower than at the point X, then consumption is greater than income, saving is negative and so is investment. This can happen to a subsistence farmer, for example, if he has a poor crop and survives by eating stocks of food accumulated in a previous period. In such a situation the farmer is dissaving and disinvesting. It can happen to a nation if net investment is negative, that is, if depreciation of the nation's capital is greater than gross investment; in these circumstances saving is also negative.

The Keynesian consumption theory seems quite plausible. But so did the consumption theory in use before Keynes wrote his *General Theory* in 1936.[2] This earlier theory, now known as 'classical theory', suggested that saving was mainly determined by the rate of interest offered to savers. If the rate of interest on bank savings accounts and other investments was high, then people would save more and of course a low rate of interest would reduce the incentive to save and so cause an increase in consumption. This theory therefore put the emphasis on saving, suggesting that people first decide how much to save, the remainder of the income being available for consumption. Keynesian theory puts the primary emphasis on consumption.

The only way to decide which theory is correct is to examine the facts. Before doing so, however, it is worth pointing out that the classical theory as described above does not take full account of the possible effect of changes in the rate of interest paid on savings. If the rate of interest rises, people's savings will be worth more in the future so that the need to save is reduced, and people may save less. In practice, research has failed to find any connection between interest rates on the one hand, and the division of income between savings and consumption on the other hand. In Zambia, the interest rates available on individual savings have changed very little since Independence so that it is not possible to investigate the classical theory. There is no apparent reason, however, for thinking that Zambia is different from other countries in this matter.

Some evidence is available on the relationship between income and consumption in Zambia. The Urban Budget Survey conducted from 1966 to 1968 gave the results shown in Figure 4.2.

The points representing the two lowest income brackets should probably be ignored, since expenditure is shown to be much higher than total receipts including loans and that is not possible. There must have been some errors of measurement, presumably in underestimating receipts, since 269 households with an average membership of five persons could not have survived on total receipts, including receipts of goods as well as of cash, of just over K10 per month. Assuming the remaining data are reliable, they show a quite clear relationship between income and consumption, of the type suggested by Keynes. The points approximate quite closely to a line of the type $C=a+bY$.

The figures in the Urban Budget Survey are, however, derived from a cross-section analysis – that is, the figures show the spending of people with different incomes at a particular point in time. They do not necessarily show how people would react to an increase in income. If, for example, there is a general increase in income, the people with the lowest incomes will have larger incomes but will still be worst off – as a result they may behave differently from those who had this income previously but were then better off than some. In other words, relative income as well as absolute income may have some influence on spending.

There has not been any Zambian research into *changes* in consumption as a result of changes in income. There are annual figures for wage and salary income but large numbers of employees are probably excluded from the official figures. Furthermore, changes in the figures for 'Operating Surplus' (profits) are dominated by copper company profits which fluctuate a great deal with the price of copper. Changes in the price of copper have very little effect on consumption however. All one can say is that Zambian consumption behaviour does not appear to be inconsistent with the results of research in other parts of the world – but this is only an impression gained from the figures, not a scientifically based statement. And of course it relates principally to the urban, modern sector of the economy.

Research elsewhere into *changes* in consumption and income has revealed a difference between the short-term and long-term relationship between consumption and income. In the short term the Keynesian function is a fairly good explanation of consumption behaviour, but there are some important time-lags which the function does not explain. Basically it seems that people's consumption habits are fairly stable, so that they do not react immediately to changes in their income. This process is not symmetrical: people try and *maintain* their consumption

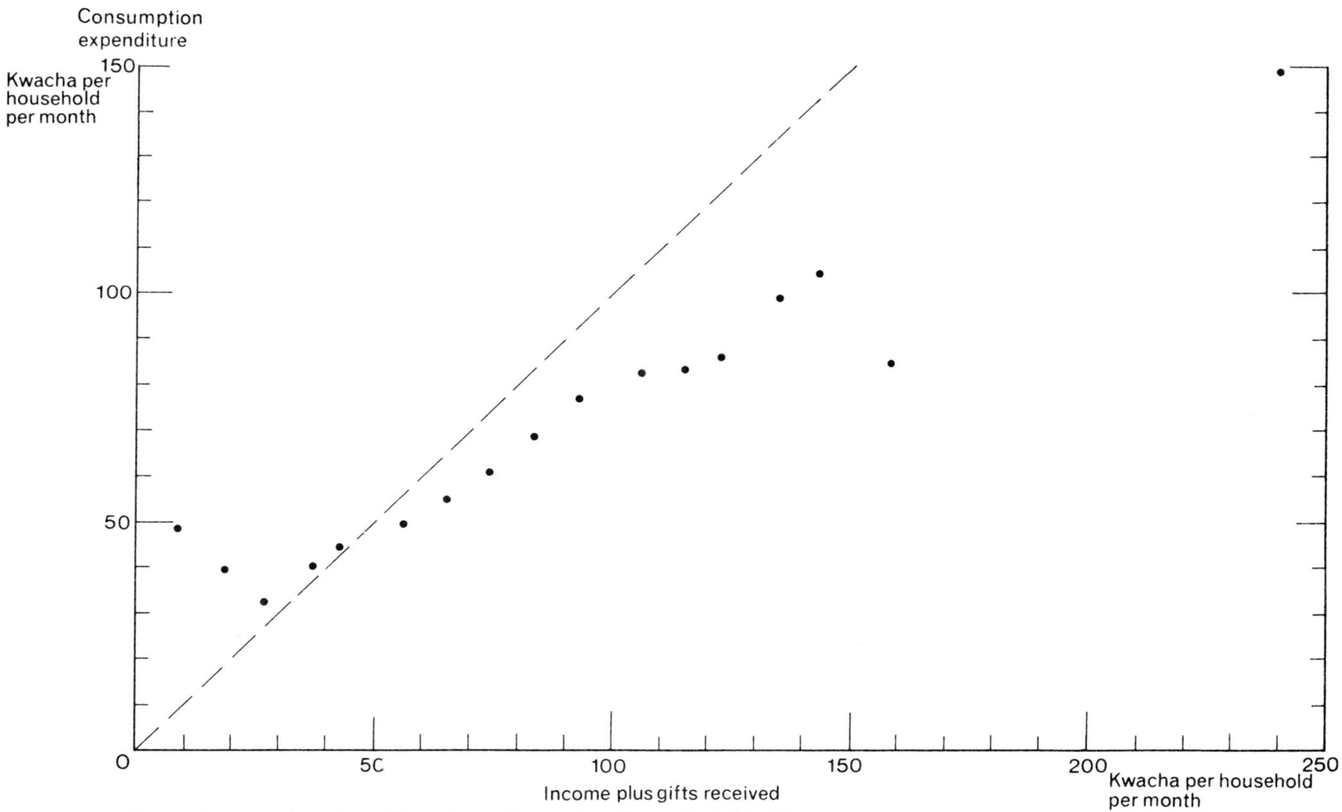

Source: *Some important tables o' Urban Budget Survey: 1966–68*, Lusaka, C.S.O., 1973

Figure 4.2 Cross-sectional figures for consumption and income of urban households (and thus their standard of living) when their income falls, by using up savings or by borrowing; they are less slow to react to increases in income, although even then there may be some time-lag so that savings increase for a while as people adjust to new income levels.

Various theories have been put forward to explain these variations on the simple Keynesian consumption function. The 'permanent income' hypothesis suggests that people consume according to what they estimate their income is likely to be in the long term, or permanently. Short-term variations of income away from these expectations are therefore ignored as far as possible. An alternative theory is that consumption depends on the 'previous peak' income; that is, people adjust their spending to the highest that their income has ever been. If income increases above its previous peak level, consumption increases accordingly; if income falls below its previous peak level, consumption does not fall, or does not fall to the level it had reached when income was previously at that point.

Both the permanent income hypothesis and the previous peak theory have received quite strong confirmation from American data. Clearly they are theories with main relevance for growing, industrialized economies where changes in incomes are marginal, that is, relatively small in relation to total income. One would not necessarily expect them to apply to the predominantly agricultural economies of Africa. In fact American research has discovered that farmers have significantly different savings habits from the rest of the population – they save more at all levels of income. This factor makes only a small difference in industrialized economies because farmers are a small proportion of the population (less than 10% in America). But in Africa it is very important. Furthermore, the most likely reasons why farmers save more than urban workers at similar income levels are, firstly that they face greater uncertainty and so need savings against natural disasters and price variations ('precautionary' savings); and secondly, that they are both businessmen and ordinary consumers at one and the same time which means their incomes have some of the characteristics of business incomes – saving is usually much higher out of profits than out of wages and salaries. Clearly the first of these factors, uncertainty, is much greater for African than for American farmers. Against this, African farmers generally have much lower incomes so that their *ability* to save is less.

The UNZALPI data shows that small farmers *do* save in Zambia, even at very low income levels. The results of the Urban Budget Survey show lower savings, see Table 4.3, p. 63. Both these sources were cross-sectional surveys and so do not reveal the marginal propensity to consume out of changes in income.

Research into the *long-term* relationship between consumption and income reveals a rather different picture. This should be clear from Figure 4.1. If an economy has been growing over time, then income at some time in the past must have been so low that it was actually less than the point on the graph where income equals consumption. But this would mean that total consumption was greater than total income at that time. Clearly that was not so, since the economy could

TABLE 4.3
Monthly savings of rural and urban low income households

	Income per head *K*	*Savings per head* *K*	*Savings as % of income*
UNZALPI farmers and villagers	3·37	1·02	30
Urban Budget Survey	12·08	0·97	8

NOTE: These are monthly figures, so multiply by 12 to compare with Table 2.7.
Sources: UNZALPI as in Table 2.2; *Some Important Tables of Urban Budget Survey: 1966–68*, Lusaka, C.S.O., 1973.

not have grown over time with negative savings. So the short-term consumption function $C=a+bY$ *cannot* also represent the long-term function.

The explanation is partly given by the previous peak income theory already discussed. It is also partly explained by the concept of relative poverty. People are influenced in their consumption spending not only by the absolute level of their income, but by the incomes of the other people in their society. As average incomes rise, therefore, what was once an adequate income, out of which people could save, becomes an inadequate income out of which people are unable to save because of the higher consumption standards set by a richer society. This is sometimes called the demonstration effect.

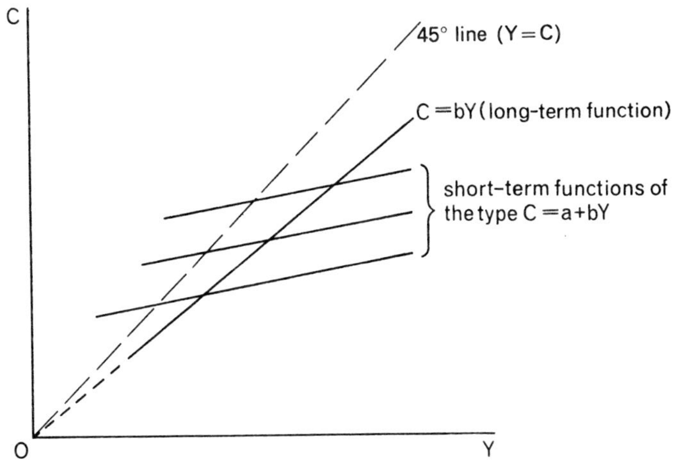

Figure 4.3 Short-term and long-term consumption functions

In the less developed countries there is a particular type of demonstration effect arising out of contact with people from richer countries. This *international* demonstration effect, particularly strong in Zambia with its large expatriate labour force, pushes up consumption. This is not only because of imitation, but because Zambianization of expatriate jobs gives Zambians both expatriate salary levels[3] and expatriate housing – which in turn makes all sorts of expenditure necessary, especially on private cars. The infrastructure created for the highly paid expatriates does not disappear with the expatriates when the latter are replaced by Zambians.

For whatever reason, it appears from research in industrialized economies that over the long term, decades rather than years, consumption is *proportional* to income; the long-term consumption function is thus of the form $C=bY$. If the short-term consumption function is of the form $C=a+bY$, then it must shift upwards on the graph as economic growth pushes up people's incomes. This is illustrated in Figure 4.3.

4 OTHER FACTORS AFFECTING CONSUMPTION

The possession of assets makes additional consumption possible. 'Liquid' assets, that is cash or assets that can be turned quickly and easily into cash, probably have a greater influence on spending; but even illiquid assets like housing can be used to increase spending because they make borrowing easier, and because the possession of assets reduces the need to save. However, this factor is almost certainly very small in Zambia. No research has been done on it, but even in rich countries only a very small proportion of the population has significant personal assets. In Zambia the proportion is certainly smaller and what is more, a big proportion of the asset-owning part of the population has its assets abroad, where they are rather less likely to be an influence on consumption.

The availability (but not the cost) of consumer credit has a considerable influence on the buying of consumer durables. This factor is again of much greater importance in rich countries. In Britain, for example, the government has from time to time laid down conditions controlling consumer credit by enforcing minimum down payments (or deposits) and maximum repayment periods. This has a considerable effect on consumption of consumer durables and thus on the income generated in the relevant industries.

The distribution of income has some influence on the level of consumption. If poor people consume a higher proportion of income than rich people, then a redistribution of income from the rich to the poor should lead to an increase in consumption. It is rare however that a major change in income distribution occurs over a short period, so that this factor is unlikely to have much effect on the analysis of short-term changes in the economy. Similarly, the migration of rural people to town is likely to result in consumption being higher than it would otherwise have been, if urban workers consume more at each level of income than farmers. The situation is complicated in Zambia by the large, well-paid expatriate labour force whose savings are sent out of the country. A redistribution of income from the rich to the poor in Zambia could result in an increase in consumption, and thus a reduction in savings by residents; but at the same time savings retained within Zambia could actually increase if the savings of the lower-paid, all of which are retained in the country, were greater than the reduction in *local* saving by the higher-paid Zambians.

A final influence on consumption which has received a great deal of attention in economic writing is the 'real-balance effect', also known as the 'Pigon effect' after the English economist who first discussed it. If prices rise, the real value of money balances is reduced: other things being equal this will reduce consumption since people's liquid assets have fallen. Conversely, if prices fall, the real value of money balances increases, increasing consumption. The argument applies to assets other than money balances whose value is fixed in money terms. For the same reasons that assets, liquid or otherwise, have a very small influence on consumption, the real balance effect is also small. Those with substantial money balances are in any case precisely those who are least likely to allow their standard of living to fall as a result of rising prices.

5 THE IMPACT OF THE CONSUMPTION FUNCTION $C=a+bY$

Despite the reservations and complications already discussed, a consumption function of the type $C=a+bY$ is quite a good first approximation to consumption behaviour in the short term. The function expresses two very important ideas: firstly that income is the main influence on consumption, secondly that there is a marginal propensity to consume which expresses the amount of a *change* in income that gets spent and thus creates further changes in income. The marginal propensity to consume is thus a measure of the amount of *feedback* from a change in demand.[4]

Suppose that there is an increase in investment, for example the building of a factory or the construction of a road. The spending of money for investment will create income for those who work on the project and for those who supply inputs to the project in the form of cement, bricks, machinery, etc. Those who receive additional income will spend it according to their marginal propensity to consume and so create yet more income. The total rise in income will therefore be greater than the original increase in investment spending. Clearly the total rise in income will depend on how much income is created by each successive round of spending – in other words the total rise in income will depend on the marginal propensity to consume out of an addition to income.

By assuming that consumption is given by the formula $C=a+bY$ it is possible to calculate very simply the total rise in income that could occur from a change in demand.

Assume that there is no government and no foreign trade, so that demand is made up of consumption and investment demand only. This assumption is made here purely in order to make it easier to understand the working of a simple model; clearly it is unrealistic, but as will be seen in subsequent chapters, introducing government spending, taxation and foreign trade into the model makes it rather more complicated but does not alter the basic principle of the model as explained here.

Assume also that the economy is temporarily in equilibrium so that aggregate demand and supply are equal, and both are equal to income. This can be expressed thus:

$$Y=C+I=\text{demand} \tag{i}$$

The only other assumption needed is that

$$C=a+bY \tag{ii}$$

If the value of C in equation (ii) is substituted in equation (i) then

$$Y=a+bY+I$$

or

$$Y-bY=a+I$$

or

$$Y(1-b)=a+I$$

or

$$Y=\frac{a+I}{1-b} \tag{iii}$$

What equation (iii) expresses is that at each level of investment spending there is a value of income (Y) at which the economy will be in equilibrium. In other words at each level of investment spending there is a level of income which will be just the right amount for *savings* out of that income to be equal to investment demand.

Now suppose that for some 'exogenous' reason, that is some reason not explained by this simple model of the economy, investment demand increases from I to I^1. This will create new income, some of which will be spent. If investment demand were to continue at the new level, I^1, then a new equilibrium level of income, Y^1, would eventually be reached; at this new income level, savings out of income would also have risen to the new investment level. The new equilibrium level of income would be given by the formula in equation (iii) so that:

$$Y^1=\frac{a+I^1}{1-b} \tag{iv}$$

Subtracting equation (iii) from equation (iv) gives the *difference* between the two equilibrium levels of income, thus:

$$Y^1-Y=\left(\frac{a+I^1}{1-b}\right)-\left(\frac{a+I}{1-b}\right)$$

or
$$Y^1 - Y = \frac{a + I^1 - a - I}{1 - b}$$

or
$$Y^1 - Y = \frac{I^1 - I}{1 - b}$$

or
$$Y^1 - Y = (I^1 - I)\left(\frac{1}{1 - b}\right) \quad \text{(v)}$$

Equation (v) expresses the fact that the change in income caused by a change in investment demand is a *multiple* of the change in investment demand. The multiple is $1/(1-b)$, and is thus determined entirely by the marginal propensity to consume. An alternative way of expressing equation (v) is

$$\Delta Y = k\,\Delta I \quad \text{(va)}$$

where ΔY is the change in income caused by a change in investment ΔI, and k is the 'multiplier'. Another way of defining the multiplier is to say that where a change in demand causes a change in income, then the multiplier is the ratio of the change in income to the change in demand – algebraically $k = \Delta Y/\Delta I$.

In reality, the value of the multiplier is not simply determined by the marginal propensity to consume. It is also affected by other leakages from the circular flow of income, most notably by tax rates and by the amount of spending on imports. These complications will be dealt with in later chapters, but, as has been said already, the *method* of finding a formula for the multiplier remains essentially the same.

6 ANOTHER WAY OF DERIVING THE MULTIPLIER FORMULA

There is another way of deriving the formula for the multiplier which uses slightly more difficult algebra, but which often helps students to understand the process better.

Suppose as before that investment increases by an amount ΔI. This will create new income. Some of this income will be spent. The actual amount spent is $b\,\Delta I$, since that is the meaning of b, the mpc. For example if the marginal propensity to consume out of an increase in income is $\frac{2}{3}$, then $\frac{2}{3}$ of ΔI will be spent on consumption.

The spending of $b\,\Delta I$ will create new income of that amount. Some of this new income will in turn be spent, namely $b(b\,\Delta I)$ will be spent. This creates new income of $b^2\,\Delta I$. Of the new income $b^2\,\Delta I$, $b(b^2\,\Delta I)$ will be spent, creating new income of $b^3\,\Delta I$. This process continues indefinitely. As a result the total increase in income, ΔY, is

$$\begin{aligned} Y &= I + bI + b^2I + b^3I + \ldots \\ &= I(1 + b + b^2 + b^3 + \ldots) \quad \text{(vi)} \end{aligned}$$

Of course each successive addition to income is smaller than the previous one, since *some* of each increase in income is saved and so does not create new income. It so happens that there is a formula for the sum of an infinite series of the type $(1+b+b^2+b^3+\ldots)$ where b is less than 1. The formula is $1/(1-b)$. The proof is as follows.

Multiply out the expression

$$\begin{aligned}&(1-b)(1+b+b^2+\ldots+b^n)\\ &=1+b+b^2+b^3+\ldots+b^n\\ &\quad -b-b^2-b^3-\ldots-b^n-b^{n+1}\\ &=1-b^{n+1}\end{aligned}$$

Rewriting,

$$(1+b+b^2+\ldots+b^n)=\frac{1-b^{n+1}}{1-b}$$

Now suppose n becomes infinitely large, then b^{n+1} tends to zero, because b is less than 1, and the formula becomes

$$1+b+b^2+b^3+\ldots=\frac{1}{1-b}$$

Equation (vi) for the change in income caused by a change in investment demand then becomes

$$\Delta Y=\Delta I\frac{1}{1-b}$$

or

$$\Delta Y=k\,\Delta I \qquad \text{(vii)}$$

This equation (vii) is exactly the same as equation (va) – as indeed it should be since both methods, if correct, must give the same answer.

7 ASSUMPTIONS UNDERLYING THE MULTIPLIER FORMULA

It is extremely important for the student to understand the assumptions behind the multiplier formula, and to know under what conditions it is likely to give a good approximation to reality.

Close study of the algebra helps greatly in establishing the assumptions. The first set of assumptions arise from using a consumption function of the form $C=a+bY$. Thus in the short term it is assumed that:

(1) consumption is a function of income *and of nothing else*, that is, interest rates, assets (liquid or illiquid), prices, etc., have no effect on consumption;

(2) consumption is a *linear* function of income.

The second set of assumptions arises from the simple algebra used to derive the formula for the multiplier. Thus when equation (iii) is subtracted from equation (iv) it is necessary to assume that:

(3) *a* and *b* are constants (this is essentially the same as assuming that the consumption function is linear);

(4) investment remains at its new level I^1 until the new equilibrium level of income is reached – in other words it is assumed that investment demand is not affected by changes in the level of income.

The last set of assumptions is not apparent from the formula, and will probably not become fully clear until later chapters have been read. Nevertheless, the student should note at this stage that nothing has been said about the effect of changes in investment and income on money and credit, nor of the effect of the changes on prices, nor, since the economy has been assumed to have no government or foreign trade, of the effect on the budget and the balance of payments. It is necessary to assume, therefore, that:

(5) no monetary restraint prevents income from rising as indicated by the formula.

It is probably also *wise* to assume that:

(6) the economy has spare capacity to meet the increases in demand by increasing output.

In a situation where increases in demand cannot be met by increases in output, either demand will be frustrated, in which case income will *not* rise to its new equilibrium level; or increases in demand will cause prices to rise, in which case all sorts of additional factors must be considered. It is best to defer the study of inflation until it can be done thoroughly in Chapter 10.

In stressing the difference between two equilibrium levels of income the model may be rather unrealistic. Economies are seldom in equilibrium. One disequilibrating factor is usually imposed upon the effects of another, and further disturbances usually occur before an equilibrium position is reached.

The multiplier formula is useful, nevertheless, in indicating an order of magnitude for a rise in income caused by an increase in demand, under conditions of spare capacity. It stresses the key importance of the marginal propensity to consume and shows that because of the fact that new income is partly spent, as expressed by the mpc, income can change by more than the original change in demand.

The analysis is equally useful for indicating the size of a fall in income that may result from a *fall* in demand when the economy has *not* been experiencing rapid inflation – under inflationary conditions other factors must be considered.

NOTES

[1] For those who have done no calculus, 'ΔC' is simply a short way of writing 'a small change in C'; and ΔY means a small change in Y. Δ is a Greek capital D, and is written 'delta'.

[2] J. M. Keynes, *The General Theory of Employment, Interest and Money*, London, Macmillan, 1936.

[3] Often the actual salary is less by the amount of expatriate inducement allowances, but the order of magnitude is the same. Basic salary scales are and should be the same for obvious reasons of justice.

[4] *Any* consumption function of the form $C=f(Y)$, that is, where consumption is a function of (determined by) income, implies by definition a marginal propensity to consume. In calculus terms mpc$=dC/dY=f^1(Y)$.

5 *Government Expenditure*

1 DEFINITION

In the national accounts, government consumption expenditure is defined to include spending by local authorities as well as by the central government, on the provision of services. In Zambia, local sources of revenue are relatively small so that local authorities rely fairly heavily on grants from the central government. Spending by the central government is thus a good indicator for total consumption spending by government even though the two are not the same. This is important since central government spending figures tend to be easily and quickly available, and, at the time of the annual budget, estimates of central government spending are published for the year ahead. Statistics based on the national income definition are published some two or three years after the event.

The national accounting definition of government consumption spending excludes 'transfer payments'. These include the payment of pensions, and subsidies to parastatal organizations such as the National Agricultural Marketing Board. The reason for this distinction is that such transfer payments are not direct purchases of services and so should not be counted as part of the national income. They are not the same as payments to teachers for example, which directly create a service forming part of national output. Transfer payments do not actually purchase a service and so do not create any output. From the point of view of this chapter, however, the question is whether transfer payments create demand. Payments to people create demand indirectly, as they are spent by their recipients, but this demand is less than the transfer payment by the amount of any saving. Subsidies, for example subsidies on the price of maize, are paid to farmers who spend this income less any savings. Pensions were only 1·1% of the 1974 current budget and subsidies under 8%. They were even smaller proportions of total spending, current and capital. For most of the rest of this chapter the distinction between consumption expenditure and transfer payments will be ignored. The figures quoted for government spending will be as quoted in official statistics with the exceptions noted in the next two footnotes.

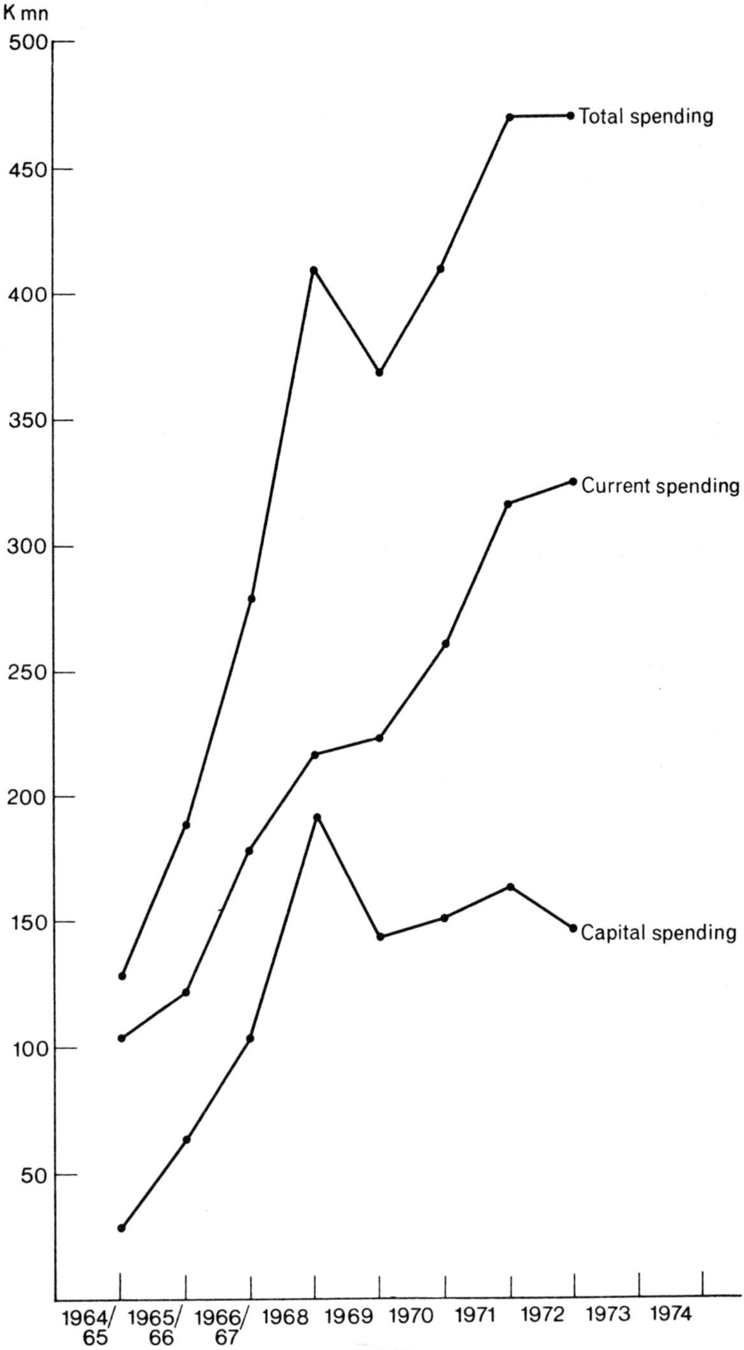

Source: as for Table 5.1

Figure 5.1 Central government spending 1964–72, Zambia

2 GROWTH SINCE 1964

The growth of current government spending in Zambia since 1964 has been spectacular. In the budget year 1964/5 central government current spending was K101 mn; by 1972 it had grown to K325 mn and the 1974 budget forecast was for K411 mn.[1] In ten years therefore, current spending multiplied four times, an average annual rate of increase of about 16%. Furthermore, government capital spending, on things like roads, schools and hospitals, has grown even faster. In 1964/5 it was only K28 mn; by 1972 it had grown to K146 mn. The estimate for 1974 capital spending was more than K170 mn.[2] Capital spending thus increased over ten years by more than six times, an annual growth rate of about 19%.

However, Figure 5.1 shows that the progress of government spending was not very regular. Current spending increased in every year but capital spending fell after reaching a peak in 1968, and still had not recovered to the 1968 level some six years later. Furthermore, budget estimates of government spending have frequently been very different from what the government eventually spent. Budget estimates indicate what the government plans to spend. If the estimates are underspent it suggests that government cannot always obtain the resources it wants, even though the money is there to be spent, having been approved by the Ministry of Finance and the Cabinet and voted by parliament. It is, of course, possible that over- or underspending of budget estimates simply indicates that government changed its intentions during the year. But it is also possible that government does not wholly control its own spending, in which case the student should ask just what *does* determine the level of government spending, since this is enormously important in the determination of national income.

3 GOVERNMENT CONTROL OF SPENDING

In both 1969 and 1972 the government tried to reduce current and capital expenditure for macroeconomic reasons. In 1969 the government was worried about the balance of payments and about inflation. The

TABLE 5.1
The attempt to reduce government spending in 1969 *K mn*

	Actual 1968	*Estimate 1969*		*Actual 1969*	
Current spending	216	190	(−26)	223	(+7)
Capital spending	190	127	(−63)	144	(−46)
Total	406	317	(−89)	367	(−39)

NOTE: Figures in brackets show changes compared with actual spending in 1968.

Sources: Financial Reports and Estimates of Revenue and Expenditure, with adjustments as explained in footnotes (1) and (2), p. 87.

previous year the budget had run into deficit for the first time since Independence and inflation had accelerated. The government therefore tried to cut both current and capital spending, by a total of K89 mn. But in the event current spending rose by K7 mn instead of falling by K26 mn as estimated. Capital spending did actually fall, by K46 mn, although the government tried to reduce it by K63 mn. These figures are summarized in Table 5.1.

Much the same thing happened in 1972. Faced with very rapidly falling reserves, a low copper price and no apparent prospect of improvement, the government tried to cut current spending by K49 mn and capital spending by K15 mn. The result is shown in Table 5.2.

TABLE 5.2
The attempt to reduce government spending in 1972 — *K mn*

	Actual 1971	*Estimate 1972*	*Actual 1972*
Current spending	315	266 (−49)	325 (+10)
Capital spending	157	145 (−12)	146 (−11)
Total	472	411 (−61)	471 (−1)

Sources: As for Table 5.1.

Thus in 1972 the government was again unable to cut current spending at all, let alone by as much as K49 mn; but it was able to reduce capital spending by the fairly small amount of K12 mn, in line with the estimates.

An examination of the Financial Reports for 1969 and 1972 reveals clearly enough why the government found it so difficult to reduce its current spending. A large part, about 25%, of current spending is on salaries for civil servants and roughly the same amount is spent on 'recurrent departmental charges'. These are simply the expenses associated with employing people and providing them with the means to get on with their jobs – offices, desks, transport, telephones, typewriters and the like. Government does not normally dismiss civil servants, nor can it break the contracts of expatriates without paying compensation. Salaries therefore must normally be paid. Even among workers paid daily government policy may be to maintain employment. The 1972 Financial Report contains many footnotes referring to the 'extra costs due to policy of not declaring any redundancies'.

Civil servants' expenses are rather more vulnerable to cuts. Repairs and maintenance of vehicles and buildings can be delayed or simply neglected, civil servants can be forced to economize in the use of office space, paper and transport. Thus in the period 1969 to 1974, during which great efforts were made to restrain the growth of public expenditure, salaries grew by 71% while recurrent departmental charges grew by only 34%. Such economies can lead to great inefficiency and therefore be counterproductive. It usually pays in the long run to maintain property continuously and it is pointless to employ someone to do a job if he is not provided with the means to do that job properly. On the other hand the period of rapid expansion from 1964 to 1969, when money was very freely available, may have created a good deal of 'fat' in the public services so that the scope for economizing without creating inefficiency may have been quite large. Certainly this argument was frequently put forward at the time.

The second important point is that the huge increase in capital spending from 1964 to 1968, from K28 mn to K190 mn, created a need for *current* spending to make use of the new capital. Thus schools and hospitals, once built, must be manned and equipped if they are not to be wasted. Only in the most appalling crisis would government be willing to allow buildings and equipment to lie empty and idle once they had been built and paid for.

The third point is that many of the government's commitments are very open-ended in various ways, that is, commitments once entered into may involve the government in much greater expenditure than it had originally intended, or even imagined. Such commitments are of many sorts. For example a guaranteed producer price for maize or tobacco costs the government more if the rains are favourable and the crop is good; in 1971 the cost of maize producer subsidies was down (by K1 mn) because of a very poor harvest, but the government had to pay over K10 mn in subsidizing the cost to consumers of the very expensive maize imports. The government also has commitments to parastatal bodies: in 1969 part of overspending was in meeting the deficit of Zambia Airways and providing additional finance for the Credit Organisation of Zambia (because its customers had failed to provide finance by paying back their loans). Sometimes parastatal bodies manage to finance their losses by borrowing, but if the deficits do not become surpluses eventually, the government is faced with paying off accumulated losses, as it did for the National Agricultural Marketing Board in 1972 and for COZ in 1971.

A fourth point is that some expenditure is dictated by external pressures. The most obvious is defence which since 1969 has been buried in the item 'Constitutional and Statutory Expenditure' so that the amount spent is not revealed to the public. After 1969, when defence spending was only K10 mn, constitutional and statutory spending increased very rapidly, from K23 mn to K161 mn in 1974, or from about 20% to over 35% of the recurrent budget. Because the figures for defence are no longer public, these very large increases are not debated by parliament and indeed are effectively outside all of the usual systems of expenditure control. Other examples of spending dictated by external events are the costs of rerouting external trade after UDI in 1965, and after the Rhodesian border closure in 1973. Again and again the spending figures contain large items for contingency planning and emergency expenditure.

A fifth point is that the rapid growth in the budget and in the duties of civil servants, combined with the shortages and lack of experience of skilled people since Independence, has meant that control over expenditure has been less than complete. Many items of expenditure have been greater than voted by parliament and nothing has been done about it in spite of such spending being illegal. Measures to tighten up control, including instructions to the Bank of Zambia not to allow ministries to spend more than their allocations, were announced in the 1974 budget speech.

In the most general sense the government of the day commits itself, politically and sometimes legally as well, to do certain things: to maintain law and order, to defend the country from external threat, to cram as many students into existing schools and as many sick people into existing hospitals as the buildings can hold, to maintain embassies abroad, to provide cars for cabinet ministers and to do innumerable other things. If they cost more than estimated then in normal times the government will foot the bill, either by introducing supplementary estimates, or simply by 'illegally' overspending the money voted by parliament.[3]

From Tables 5.1 and 5.2 it would seem that it is much easier to reduce capital spending than current spending. The main reason is that capital spending is less continuous. In any particular year a number of projects will be ending so that annual spending can be reduced if new projects are not started. Another way of reducing capital spending is by spreading projects over a longer period so that spending in any particular year is reduced. Neither of these methods is as easy as it sounds. Many large projects cost very little in their early stages, while engineering studies are conducted, tenders invited and contractors appointed. Starting them later may therefore save very little actual spending in the short term. Spreading a project over a longer period may lead to inefficiency; and if the project is integrated with others, a late finish may cause huge problems. For example, a new road to serve a new mine *must* be ready for when the mine needs it.

As far as total spending is concerned therefore, the inability of the government to control current spending has made it impossible to reduce total spending on the two occasions it has been attempted, even though capital spending has been more responsive to government controls.

The fact that government spending tends to have a life of its own and frequently turns out to be more than planned by the government is fairly well known. Less obvious is the fact that very rapid *increases* in government spending may also prove impossible to implement. The main reason is that physical resources are not always available. Just as it may be difficult to dismiss civil servants, so it may be difficult to hire new ones quickly, especially where there is a severe shortage of skilled manpower. Thus Zambia's expenditure has sometimes been less than planned because of the delays in recruiting skilled people from abroad. In addition, existing civil servants may be unable to cope administratively with the problems thrown up by very rapid increases in spending, so that delays occur and spending is less than planned. A third reason for delays in Zambia is the lack of capacity on import routes: with local industry unable to supply more than a narrow range of goods, many projects, especially capital projects, depend heavily on imports and may thus be delayed when import routes are unable to cope with the demands made on them. The problems caused for imports by UDI and the 1973 border closure are well known, but the capacity of the port at Dar es Salaam is a continuing problem. In several years general imports have been badly held up by the need to give priority to bulk imports of such commodities as maize and fertilizer. The Zambian economy, land-locked, very distant from the sea, with hostile countries on several sides, seems at times to lurch continuously from one transport crisis to another.

Given the very rapid increases in spending after 1964, it is not therefore surprising that in some years the budget has been underspent, mainly in the immediate post-Independence period. Also, because of the greater dependence of capital spending on imports (and on the construction industry) capital spending was more frequently underspent than current. This is shown in Table 5.3.

TABLE 5.3

Actual and estimated expenditure compared, 1964–8 (actual spending as a percentage of budget estimates)

		Percentages	
	Current spending	*Capital spending*	*Total spending*
1964/5	117	102	114
1965/6	113	96	107
1966/7	104	67	85
1967 July to Dec.	87	98	91
1968	111	117	114

Since 1966/7 the current budget has always been overspent, in spite of increasing every year, while the capital budget has hovered between K120 mn and K160 mn, usually overspent and once underspent, never by very much either way.

4 GOVERNMENT SPENDING AND TAX REVENUE

Clearly the amount of revenue received by government from taxation could have some influence on the level of government spending. Taxation is not the only source of finance for government – some revenue accrues from government's trading activities, government can borrow both domestically and from abroad, some finance is received in the form of aid and government has the power to create money by 'borrowing' from its central bank (see Chapter 8). But tax revenue is the most important source of finance.

Indeed, the amount of tax revenue available is often treated *politically* as the best indicator of the correct level of government spending. In its extreme form, this point of view holds that the budget should always be balanced, with expenditure equal to current revenue. This very old-fashioned view has now been replaced because of a better understanding of the needs of the economy. Basically, the level of government spending should be decided by two main factors: the capacity of the economy, that is, the potential level of internal supply; and the external position, that is, a combination of the physical ability to supply imports and the financial ability to pay for them.

In the post-Independence period the finance to pay for imports was abundantly available, either from a large current account surplus on the balance of payments[4] or from accumulated reserves. The size of the government's spending programme should really, therefore, have been decided by the internal capacity of the economy and the capacity of import routes (internal and external) to meet the demands being made on them.

In practice, the large increases in spending (planned and actual) were a result of two main factors. The first was the huge neglect of the colonial and Federal periods, which meant that the newly independent government had an enormous desire to try and catch up on national needs.

The second factor was the huge increase in tax revenue. During the Federation period large amounts of tax revenue raised in Northern Rhodesia were spent in Southern Rhodesia. Furthermore, royalty on copper production was paid to a foreign company, the British South Africa Company. Tax revenue available to the new Zambian government was thus at first much greater than its ability to spend it. What is more, tax revenue grew very fast at first, because of high copper prices and because of the growth of the economy. This rapid growth was itself stimulated by the government's own spending programme and by the commercial opportunities offered by Independence and (after November 1965) by UDI. The government thus had a very strong urge to spend, to catch up on the backlog of such items as education, and the situation with plenty of money available, was apparently ideal for spending.

However, the idea that tax revenue allows the government to spend is based on the assumption that taxation reduces domestic spending. In many cases this assumption is broadly correct: if the tax on cigarettes is increased, for example, consumers will pay more for cigarettes and have less to spend on other things. Or they will buy fewer cigarettes. Either way, aggregate demand is reduced so that an increase in demand via government spending should be possible without creating excess demand.[5] If, though, an increase in tax revenue is paid out of income that would otherwise have been saved, or that would otherwise have left the country, then aggregate demand has *not* been reduced and supply capacity has *not* been made available to government.

In Zambia, as in many African economies very dependent on the export of one or a very few commodities, this distinction is absolutely fundamental. It is possible in Zambia for tax revenue to increase very rapidly indeed *entirely* as a result of an increase in the price of copper. About 73% of an increase in the price of copper accrues to the government, and the figure was little different, at 74·4%, before 1969.[6] As a result, rising copper prices can increase government tax revenue very rapidly indeed. Yet a rising copper price does not increase the *internal* capacity of the economy at all. What it *does* do is ease the balance of payments financial constraint, by making more foreign exchange available to buy imports. If government spending has been held down because of a foreign exchange shortage, a rising copper price might make possible an increase in government spending.

In Zambia, therefore, it is quite wrong to look just at the forecasts of tax revenue to see how large an increase in government spending is justified. Equally, a fall in forecast tax revenue need not mean that government spending should be reduced. If the fall in tax revenue is caused by a fall in the copper price, this does not reduce the amount of goods and services that could be supplied by the domestic economy. So the government can maintain (or continue to increase at the same rate) its spending *provided that* enough foreign exchange is available in spite of the falling copper price.

There is a very important distinction, of course, between how the government ought to try and control its spending and how it actually tries. Furthermore, since the government is not always able to control its own spending, actual spending may not in any case reflect the government's intentions.

TABLE 5.4

Budget forecasts: changes in expenditure and revenue (forecasts compared with actual for the previous year) K mn

	Forecasts of total revenue	*Forecasts of total expenditure*
1965/66	+12	+46
1966/67	+30	+128
1968	−29	+78
1969	−9	−89
1970	−67	−2
1971	−87	+58
1972	−48	−64
1973	+83	−8

NOTE: Figures for 1966/67 based on the 18-month period July 1966 to December 1967, reduced by ⅓ to give a comparable annual rate.

Source: As for Table 5.1.

Various sorts of evidence are available. Budget speeches make no distinction between tax revenue from mining and other sources of revenue. This suggests that the government ignores this distinction or else thinks it too complicated to explain to parliament and the general public. If the first is true then perhaps changes in expenditure are based on changes in total tax revenue, but there is no evidence from Table 5.4 that this is so.

If the government bases its expenditure plans on its forecast of non-copper revenue, then there should be some relationship apparent from the figures. Again this is not apparent from Table 5.5.

TABLE 5.5

Budget forecasts: changes in expenditure and non-copper revenue (forecasts compared with actual for the previous year)

K mm

	Forecasts of non-copper revenue	*Forecasts of total expenditure*
1965/66	−3	+46
1966/67	+17	+128
1968	−3	+78
1969	+15	−89
1970	−7	−2
1971	+2	+58
1972	+15	−64
1973	+68	−8

NOTE: As for Table 5.4.

Source: As for Table 5.1.

There is another possibility, namely that government spending adjusts in some less obvious way to tax receipts. For example it may be that when tax revenue is increasing faster than forecast then supplementary estimates are more easily permitted. In other words ministers of finance find it harder to refuse requests for more money when tax revenue is known to be high. The reverse might be true when revenue is falling. Both suggestions might be true with a time-lag.

These suggestions are rather more difficult to test. Some indication might be expected from comparing changes in actual spending with actual tax receipts, but none appears from Table 5.6.

The student should try plotting the figures in Tables 5.4, 5.5 and 5.6 on a series of graphs – a completely random pattern appears. There seems to be no systematic connection between changes in tax revenue and changes in government spending, whether planned beforehand, or after the event.

This result is not all that surprising. After all, low copper revenue but high foreign exchange reserves add up to no financial constraint on imports;[7] and non-copper revenue is an imperfect indicator of internal capacity. Transport capacity on import routes is another vital factor. Finally, the level of government spending is an important political

TABLE 5.6

Changes in revenue and expenditure: actual figures *K mn*

	Non-copper revenue	*Total revenue*	*Total expenditure*
1965/66	+10	+60	+58
1966/67	+39	+61	+92
1968	+15	+27	+127
1969	+36	+95	−39
1970	+15	+31	+42
1971	+14	−123	+43
1972	+47	−11	−4

NOTE: As for Table 5.4.
Source: As for Table 5.1.

variable. From the point of view of building up a model of the economy it does mean, therefore, that there is no obvious equation for *G*, government spending. Certainly it is not a simple function of tax revenue.

In very broad outline therefore, government spending plans *ought* to be based on internal capacity (and internal taxation since it affects internal demand) on the one hand, and on the balance of payments situation on the other. An additional consideration from time to time is the physical capacity of import routes, which includes not only domestic transport capacity but also foreign transport capacity affecting Zambia.

5 ABILITY TO BORROW

Another source of finance for government spending is borrowing. Domestic borrowing from companies and individuals in Zambia, reduces the lenders' capacity to spend. If it does reduce private sector spending, then it reduces aggregate demand and it is therefore reasonable for government to increase its spending accordingly. Borrowing from the banking system does not on the whole reduce spending power in quite the same way. This topic is best postponed until after the chapters on money and banking. The important point to grasp here, however, is that if government wants to increase its demands on the economy it can reduce private demand for resources *either* by taxation, *or* by borrowing from domestic spenders.

Borrowing from abroad, however, does not reduce domestic demand. If a project is financed by foreign loans, or by foreign grants for that matter, it eases the government's financial position but does not release any domestic resources. That is why projects with foreign finance still have to be approved by the Ministry of Finance. Otherwise a whole series of externally financed projects might result in excess demand. Presumably the balance of payments constraint is eased, because of the foreign loans,[8] but domestic resources may not be adequate.

An interesting exception is the first part of the building of the Tanzam railway from Dar es Salaam. This railway is financed entirely out of a loan from the Chinese government, which is also supplying all the imported equipment. In these aspects the railway is not so very different from other externally financed projects. But the building of the railway began in Dar es Salaam, so that until it reached the Zambian border (in 1973) actual spending on its construction was outside Zambia and thus made much smaller demands on Zambian domestic resources than most projects. About the only comparable expenditure, capital formation outside the country, is the purchase or building of foreign embassies and, possibly, Zambian aid to the Tanzanian government for port improvements at Dar es Salaam. The railway is very much bigger than such projects. It demands some local resources, administrative time for example, but the Chinese have even supplied the skilled and much of the semi-skilled labour, so the domestic economy really was very little affected.[9]

6 THE IMPACT OF CHANGES IN GOVERNMENT SPENDING

A change in government spending is a change in aggregate demand and therefore has feedback or multiplier effects. These effects are precisely similar to those of a change in investment demand, as described in the last chapter. However, when government is introduced into a model of the economy, it is obviously necessary to investigate how taxation affects the model. If government spends more money, then under most systems of taxation some of it will come back to the government in the form of income tax and taxes on the goods that people buy out of their increased incomes. About the only tax that is *not* affected by changing incomes is the poll tax – for example as had been levied on Africans in Zambia before Independence. Basically then, tax receipts are a function of income. As a first approximation, domestic tax receipts (other than from copper) can be assumed to be a linear function of income as shown in Figure 5.2, so that a tax function would be of the form

$$T = \bar{t} + tY \qquad (1)$$

where T = total tax revenue
Y = income
and $\bar{t}$ and t are constants.

Figure 5.2 shows the relation between non-copper tax revenue and national income *minus* the 'operating surplus' in mining.[10] This is the simplest way of removing from the income figures the influence of changing copper prices. Another way would have been to value copper production at a constant price in calculating income: the effect would be the same, namely that non-copper revenue is very closely determined

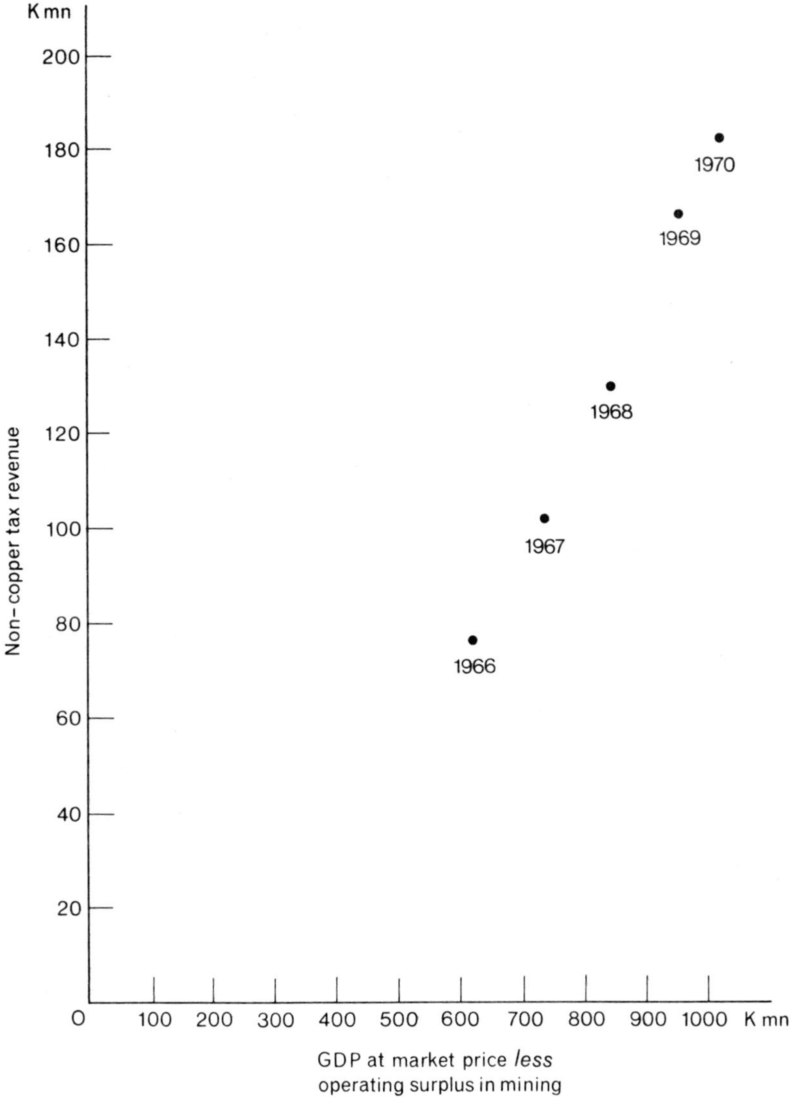

Figure 5.2 Non-copper taxation compared with GDP at market prices *less* operating surplus in mining

Source: *Financial Reports and National Income Accounts*

by income. Essentially what this implies is that the copper price is being assumed constant in the model so that the effects of changing government spending on income can be studied, including the effects on non-copper taxation. The effects on the economy of changes in the copper price will be dealt with in the next chapter.

What the tax function expresses is that tax revenue depends on income only. Furthermore, if income changes from Y to Y^1 then tax revenue will be

$$T^1 = \bar{t} + tY^1 \tag{2}$$

Subtracting equation (1) from equation (2) gives

$$T^1 - T = t(Y^1 - Y)$$

or

$$t = \frac{(T^1 - T)}{(Y^1 - Y)}$$

Therefore t is the ratio of a change in tax revenue to a change in income; in other words

t = the marginal propensity for tax receipts to change in response to a change in income.

In common language, t could be called the marginal tax rate – *not* in the personal sense of the marginal tax rate paid by an individual on an increase in his income, but in the national, macroeconomic, sense of the marginal tax rate for the economy as a whole always assuming constant export (copper) prices.

In some economies the amount of tax that is independent of income ($\bar{t}$ in the equation) may be fairly small – mainly taxes on capital such as death duties (on the wealth of people who have died) and poll taxes where they exist. In Zambia, the whole of taxation on copper is independent of changes in national income *in the short term*. Clearly copper taxation depends not only on the price of copper but also on the amount of copper produced and on mining costs, which can change substantially over time. But in the present context, the short-term effects of a change in government spending, copper taxation is indeed exogenous to the simple model of the economy. In Zambia's case therefore, the term $\bar{t}$ is very large, but independent of the other variables in the model. It is not, in the long term, constant – but in analysing the effects of a change in government spending on the economy it is reasonable to assume revenue from copper as constant in the absence of knowledge to the contrary. In any case, even if copper revenues *do* change there is usually very little further impact on the domestic economy in the short term, as will be explained in the next chapter.

The simple model of the economy, with government spending and taxation included, is now

$$Y = C + G + I \tag{i}$$

$$\begin{aligned} C &= a + b(Y - tY) \\ &= a + bY(1 - t) \end{aligned} \quad \text{(ii)}$$

The consumption function has been modified on the assumption that consumption is a function of disposable income, that is income after the payment of domestic taxes (for simplicity at this stage the difference between direct and indirect taxes is ignored). Consumption has been assumed to be unaffected by the level of copper taxation, $\bar{t}$.

No equation has been added for G. In a situation where government spending has been very severely restrained to protect the balance of payments, it may be possible to take the brakes off very fast – a lot of spending plans will already be in existence and ready to go. But even in these particular circumstances the response will be to a change in the balance of payments prospects, that is to a rise in the copper price and therefore in copper tax revenue, which is exogenous to the model. So it seems best to assume G as constant in the short term, or as determined by exogenous factors. Both amount to the same thing in terms of the model, namely that G is not a function of any of the other variables in the model.

Substituting for equation (ii) in equation (i) gives

$$Y = a + bY(1 - t) + G + I$$

or

$$Y(1 - b + bt) = a + G + I$$

or

$$Y = \frac{a + G + I}{1 - b + bt} \quad \text{(iii)}$$

A change in government spending, from G to G^1, would eventually lead to a new level of income Y^1

$$Y^1 = \frac{a + G^1 + I}{1 - b + bt} \quad \text{(iv)}$$

Subtract equation (iii) from equation (iv) to get the *change* in income resulting from a change in G, and

$$Y^1 - Y = \frac{G^1 - G}{1 - b + bt}$$

or

$$Y^1 - Y = (G^1 - G)\frac{1}{1 - b + bt}$$

In other words the modified multiplier formula is

$$k = \frac{1}{1 - b + bt}$$

There is an additional positive term (bt) on the bottom line, indicating that this multiplier is smaller than the formula derived in the last chapter ($k = 1/1 - b$). The economic explanation is that taxation is an additional leakage from the circular flow of income. If demand increases, income will increase but some of this income accrues to the government in the form of taxation. If the government does not respend this income, but adds to its reserves or repays borrowing (and those repaid do not spend the money), then income will not increase by as much as it would have done in the absence of taxation. Each successive round of spending is smaller because some income and some spending accrues to government and is not respent at once.

The larger is t, the marginal tax rate, the smaller is the multiplier. In other words, fluctuations in income are dampened or reduced by the existence of taxes responsive to income and spending, and are the further reduced the higher is the marginal tax rate. The economy is thus stabilized by the existence of a large government sector requiring high rates of tax. This stabilizing factor is not as powerful as it might be in Zambia because so few people pay income tax. Basic exemptions from income tax are so high as to exclude the bulk of industrial workers. Changes in their disposable incomes are *not* reduced by tax. On the other hand taxation is heavy on beer and cigarettes which are bought by all income groups; and a wide range of imported goods, especially clothes, are bought by all but the poorest, so that changes in income (and therefore in spending) *are* reflected in tax receipts.

7 ASSUMPTIONS BEHIND THE MULTIPLIER ANALYSIS

In analysing the effects of a change in government spending a number of assumptions have been made. Some are the same as described at the end of the last chapter: consumption is a linear function of income, investment remains unaffected as income changes. To these must be added two more: government spending is unaffected by changes in receipts from taxation, taxation is a linear function of income[11] and of nothing else. Finally, nothing has been said about the budget surplus or deficit. If government spending changes and as a result tax receipts also change, then the balance between the two will also change. For the time being it is necessary to assume that the changing budget position is financed in such a way that there are no further feedback effects on income and spending. Thus an increase in the deficit is assumed *not* to be financed by increased borrowing from the public, or if this does take place such borrowing is assumed not to reduce private sector spending (consumption or investment). Similarly, it is necessary to assume that an increased surplus is not used to repay earlier government borrowing from the private sector, or that such repayment is not then respent.

As before, the analysis is best suited to a situation in which changes in demand are reflected mainly in changes in output, since some of the assumptions are particularly unrealistic under inflationary conditions. When prices are fairly stable it does give some idea of how the economy reacts to changes in demand, with necessary emphasis on the marginal propensity to consume, and the marginal tax rate (in the macro-economic sense).

In this chapter emphasis has been placed on control of government spending by the government itself, other determinants (if any) of government spending and what it *ought* to be from the point of view of the management of aggregate demand. The differences between current and capital spending have therefore been ignored except in so far as *control* of total capital spending may be easier than control of total current spending. Capital spending is, however, a part of investment and capital spending decisions by government have some common features with private investment decisions. Discussion of this aspect of government spending is postponed to the chapter on investment.

NOTES

[1] Budget years ran from July to the following June until 1966/7 when an extra six months' budget for July to December 1967 was introduced. Since then, starting with 1968, budget years have been the same as calendar years. The figures quoted for current spending exclude repayments of public debt, which are included in official figures of current government spending (under the heading 'Constitutional and Statutory'). They are really a financing item. All figures quoted in this chapter have been similarly adjusted.

[2] Capital spending figures, which include central government loans to other government bodies such as local authorities and parastatal companies, are here quoted *net* of capital repayments of such loans. Government borrowings from the public and from abroad have not been deducted, however, being financing items.

[3] Supplementary estimates averaged 16% of original estimates for the four years 1969 to 1972. Not all voted money was always spent however – actual spending was on average 1·3% lower than the combined total of original and supplementary estimates – only in 1972 was actual spending *in total* greater than all estimates combined.

[4] Balance of payments will be explained in the next chapter.

[5] Reduction in demand for cigarettes releases productive resources (for cigarette making) which are not much use to government. *Some* useful resources are released because the cigarette industry has less demand for transport, electricity, etc.

[6] For a more detailed analysis of taxation *see* Chapter 12.

[7] In 1971 the government forecast that internal, non-copper taxation would hardly rise at all. At the same time the copper price was low and expected to remain low (copper revenue was forecast to fall). Presumably, the government felt able to plan an increase in spending of K58 millions, because the foreign exchange reserves were still quite high.

[8] Provided that not too many foreign loans are contracted. They all have to be repaid out of future earnings of foreign exchange, or yet more borrowing.

[9] This may be the reason why it has sometimes been omitted from spending statistics; but it should surely have been included in the 1974 estimates, since in 1974 it had become a domestic project.

[10] 'Operating surplus' is the national income accounting definition of profit, taken from the National Accounts: 1970 and earlier versions.

[11] If T is a function of Y, and if G is not a function of T, then G is not a function of Y either.

6 *Exports and Imports*

1 DEFINITIONS

Exports are goods and services that earn foreign exchange. Imports are goods and services that have to be paid for with foreign exchange. The main Zambian export is copper; in return Zambia imports a very wide range of goods because local industry is relatively undeveloped.

Buyers of Zambian copper pay for it in their own currency or in one of the international currencies (British pounds and American dollars are the main ones). These foreign currencies must then be sold to the Bank of Zambia, which holds them for the government. Similarly, Zambian importers must pay their suppliers in foreign currency since to the foreign supplier the Kwacha is of no use. Importers therefore buy foreign currency from the Bank of Zambia, paying for it in Kwacha. If there is an excess of *earnings* of foreign money from exports over *payments* of foreign money for imports then the Bank of Zambia's stock of foreign currency will rise.[1] This stock of foreign currency is called the country's foreign exchange reserves.

Copper is not the only Zambian export although it is by far the largest. Other 'visible' exports (that is, of goods) include lead and zinc, mined at Kabwe since long before the large-scale mining of copper, cobalt (a by-product of copper), tobacco, timber, groundnuts and (in good years) maize. 'Invisible' exports are services provided by Zambia which are paid for, like exports, in foreign currency. In Zambia, as in most underdeveloped economies, one sort of invisible export is tourism. Foreign visitors must buy Kwacha to pay for their hotel bills and other expenses while in Zambia, and they pay for Kwacha with foreign currency. It is paradoxical, if not absurd, to describe a foreign tourist stepping off the plane at Lusaka airport as an 'invisible' export but the earning of foreign exchange is just as valuable financially whether it is from tourists or copper wire-bars. Other services which earn foreign currency are transport (Zaire uses Zambia Railways for imports and exports via Rhodesia) and interest earned on foreign exchange reserves (the 'service' here is the loan of money to foreign countries).

'Invisible' imports are services which must be paid for in foreign currency such as bank charges, foreign shipping and foreign travel. These items together are always much larger than the foreign currency earned from invisible exports. So Zambia has to pay for a deficit on invisibles by earning a surplus on visible trade. This is shown in Table 6.1.

TABLE 6.1

Exports and imports in 1970

Visible trade	*K mn*		*K mn*
Exports f.o.b.		Imports f.o.b.	
Copper	640	Food etc.	32
Zinc	11	Electricity and oil	35
Lead	5	Chemicals	26
Cobalt	6	Machinery	132
Other	7	Other manufactures	105
Re-exports	5	Other	11
	674		341
Visible trade surplus: 333			
Invisible trade	*K mn*		*K mn*
Exports		Imports	
Transport and travel	5	Transport and travel	93
Investment income	29	Investment income	62
Other services	7	Other services	30
Private transfers	2	Contract transfers	35
		Emigrants' transfers	25
		Other private transfers	48
		Government transfers	3
	43		296
Invisible trade deficit: 253			
Current account surplus: 80			

NOTE: 'f.o.b.' stands for 'free on board' which means *before* the payment of insurance and freight charges. Imports and exports on which insurance and freight charges have been paid are described as 'c.i.f.' – 'cost, insurance and freight'. Totals may not agree due to rounding.

Source: *Monthly Digest of Statistics.*

There are several points of interest in Table 6.1. First of all, the overwhelming importance of copper, which accounts for 95% of visible exports and 89% of *all* foreign exchange earnings. These proportions vary with the price of copper but are always very high.[2] Invisible earnings are very small. Zambia has a very small tourist trade compared with, say, Kenya where tourism is the largest single earner of foreign exchange. The main invisible earnings are from interest on the foreign exchange reserves which are invested in London. Because the foreign exchange reserves fell in 1971 and 1972 investment income was only K14 mn in 1972.

The very heavy cost of invisible imports is due mainly to Zambia's need to employ a large number of expatriates. Despite the big effort to Zambianize since Independence, the very long time-lags in education and the rapid growth of the economy have meant that the demand for skilled labour has continued to exceed local supply. The number of 'non-Africans' employed in 1972 was 26,000 compared with about

30,000 in 1964. What is more, the tendency has been for the long-term people to leave taking their savings with them (emigrants' transfers), to be replaced by short-term contract employees from further away (thus increasing travel costs, met by Zambia, to and from Europe as opposed to Rhodesia and South Africa) and with a desire to save and send their savings home (contract transfers) and to educate their children outside Zambia (a large part of other private transfers). Only a relatively small part of invisible imports is accounted for by insurance and freight payments on visible imports and the sending abroad of profits earned by foreign-owned companies.

An important item is missing from Table 6.1, namely 'Net errors and omissions'. Because the amount of foreign exchange held by the government and the Bank of Zambia at the end of the year is known, the sum of international receipts and payments, including movements on capital account (borrowing and repayment of borrowing, inflow and outflow of private investment capital) should add up to the change in foreign exchange reserves. It never does, of course, since even the most efficient statistical service cannot measure everything accurately. In recent years in Zambia, however, the error has always been negative, suggesting that it is not just a minor statistical problem, but a failure to measure an important outflow of foreign exchange. In 1970 it was only K15 mn, but in the four years 1969–72 it averaged K38 mn. This roughly represents an unrecorded, probably illegal outflow of money as a result of people trying to get more of their money out of Zambia than is allowed by the exchange control regulations. Various much publicized court cases show that such people sometimes get caught.

It was probably inevitable that Zambia would have to have tough exchange control regulations because of the large number of individuals and businesses that did not see a future for themselves after Independence. If they all took their money out at once Zambia would have no foreign exchange at all. The pressures have increased since the economic reforms and the policy of the government to move faster towards economic independence. The situation is very difficult. Those trying to get money out of Zambia regard themselves as being justified in trying to ensure their own futures with their own money; the Zambian government cannot afford to let this happen and anyway regards some of the money as the result of various forms of exploitation. The moral issue is thus not at all clear. Meanwhile an added complication is the incentive towards corruption: as a general rule, the greater the financial gain from an administrative decision, the greater is the likelihood of attempts to corrupt.

2 EXPORTS AND THEIR IMPORTANCE

Copper mining was not the first modern industry in Zambia, since lead and zinc were mined at Kabwe before copper, and the railway line was completed through what became the Copperbelt before mining began there. But the development of the modern sector of the Zambian economy is almost entirely bound up with the growth of the copper mining industry and the growth of its links with the rest of the economy. Furthermore, the lack of development of the traditional economy is also linked with the growth of the copper industry.

To begin with, the copper mines were a fairly extreme case of an 'export enclave'. The product was exported, most of the inputs were imported (including all the skilled labour), tax in the form of a royalty was paid to a foreign company, many of the other taxes were not spent within Zambia and the mines were owned by foreigners so that much of the post-tax profit also left the country. There is a sharp contrast with, for example, the development of cotton exports in Uganda or cocoa exports in Ghana, where the crops were grown by local people on their own land so that a much higher proportion of value added remained in the country.

The main feedback into the Zambian economy at first was through the payment of (very low) wages to unskilled local workers. A colour bar imposed by the white trade unions impeded the learning of skills by local people; and white settlers arrived and farmed a lot of the land near the railway to supply the food requirements of the new urban population. These farmers were partially successful in discriminating against African farmers in the marketing of maize and beef.

The ease with which food could be imported probably hindered agricultural development; the absence of large numbers of men in the towns removed the people most likely to use opportunities to develop the villages; the import of cheap manufactures probably destroyed a lot of village manufacturing; the arrival of the rifle eliminated wild game from most areas outside game parks and so eliminated meat from many people's diet.

Zambia thus paid a high price at first for its copper industry. The industry did however gradually increase its positive impact on the economy. By 1957 it was buying K41 mn a year from other local industries and paying K13 mn in African wages, K31 mn to expatriate workers and K64 mn in taxes (not all of which were spent locally). The big breakthrough occurred after Independence, not only because of the capture of the royalty and ending of Federal transfers of tax to Southern Rhodesia, but because the government actively pursued a policy of developing local industry. The most obvious industrialization policies were import substitution to supply consumer demand and the mines. Thus purchases from local sources increased rapidly, as did African wages as a result of wage increases and Zambianization. This is shown in Table 6.2.

Further linkages since 1969 include local manufacture of explosives, local mining of coal and a copper fabrication plant which uses a small proportion (about 1%) of refined copper output.

TABLE 6.2
Domestic payments by the metal mining sector — *K mn*

	1956/7	*1967*	*1969*
Payments to Zambian industrial sectors			
Metal mining	n.a.	14	28
Electricity, gas and water	12	15	17
Construction	16	16	25
Distribution	n.a.	15	33
Financial and business services	n.a.	9	26
Metal products, machinery	2	17	10
Others	11	12	39
	41	98	178
African wages	13	52	56
Other wages	31	40	37
Taxes	64	171	334
Total local payments	149	361	605
Gross output	273	495	820
Local payments as a % of gross output	55%	73%	74%

NOTES: Figures for 1956/7 incomplete and so probably under-estimated (n.a. means not available); tax figures for 1967 and 1969 calculated on basis of indirect taxes as quoted in National Accounts plus 45% (income tax rate) of operating surplus – some of this income tax would have been paid in the following years. The figure for local payments as a percentage of gross output is therefore partly imputed, but it gives a correct order of magnitude.

Sources: For 1956/7, Table 2.4 in R. E. Baldin, *Economic Development and Export Growth: a study of Northern Rhodesia 1920–60*, Berkeley, 1966; for 1967 and 1969 'National Accounts and Input–Output Tables', Lusaka, C.S.O.

3 THE DETERMINANTS OF CHANGES IN EXPORTS

Changes in export proceeds occur for two quite separate reasons: output changes and price changes. Virtually all Zambia's exports, not just copper exports, are sold at prices determined on world markets. The price received is thus outside Zambia's control. Various attempts to control commodity prices have been made; and copper was sold at a 'producer price' determined by the main copper-exporting *companies* for the three years or so ending in April 1966. The main copper-exporting countries are members of CIPEC but this international organization has not yet succeeded in controlling copper prices in the way that the better-known OPEC has done so successfully.[3]

Production of copper is virtually all for export. Differences from year to year between output and exports occur because of transport difficulties in getting the copper out of the country or difficulties in the various stages of production. For example, UDI resulted in a shortage of coal for smelting in 1966, so copper concentrates were stockpiled and smelted and refined in later years.[4]

In the short term production, and therefore exports, have an upper limit set by the mining and processing capacity of the mines. Fluctuations below that limit are normally because of something going wrong, as in 1966. The government does not at the moment try to restrict production deliberately, although this would be one way of trying to keep up the price. It would only work if done in co-operation with other exporters. It is possible that rising internal costs, for example increases in wages or electricity prices or transport costs, could render some mines or some parts of some mines unprofitable to operate, thus reducing production. Since local costs are to some extent determined by the aggregate demand and supply situation in the country, it could be argued that copper output might be affected by domestic conditions – that is, by other variables in the macroeconomic model. But this has not occurred in recent years and is unlikely to occur in present conditions. It would only happen with a low copper price and the companies would probably maintain production in such circumstances, hoping for a price rise or pressing for a subsidy. The government, for its part, would be very unwilling to allow a mine to close unless it had no hope of being profitable in the future.

Zambian output has *some* influence on the world price of copper, since it is roughly 10% of world output and 25% of world exports. The indications are, however, that a fall in Zambian output causes a smaller rise in the world price as determined on the London Metal Exchange (LME). The arithmetic of the situation is very simple, namely that a 1% fall in output must generate a rise in price of more than 1% if Zambia is to be better off as a result.

The LME price of copper reflects not only the supply and demand position in the world, but also speculative beliefs about future supply and demand. Events in the main producing countries thus affect the price. For example, the prospect of a strike by American copper miners, the coup in Chile, the closure of Zambia's Rhodesian border all tend to push up the price because of the *expectation* of future supply shortages. Thus Zambia may have done quite well out of the border closure because the price rose, but deliveries of copper did not, in the event, fall so that Zambia benefited from a high price and from high levels of exports. It is not possible to be certain about this because there are always many factors affecting the price and it is never possible to know what the price would have been if certain events had not occurred.

The position of other mineral exports is similar to that of copper in being largely independent of domestic factors. In theory, exports of maize might be influenced by the level of domestic income since maize is consumed in Zambia. Thus higher domestic income would result in higher local maize consumption and a smaller surplus for export. In practice, the amount of maize available for export depends mainly on the size of the harvest which is in turn determined by the acreage planted, the weather and the efficiency of the marketing services in supplying inputs like fertilizer and in buying the output. Acreage is mainly determined by the government price for maize and how it compares with other crops. Consumption of maize is probably very little affected by short-term changes in income because it is a staple food. Consumption of non-essentials tends to fluctuate much more. A year with a high producer price and good weather, for example 1970/1, resulted in exports of 8600 tonnes of maize in 1971, compared with only 1455 the next year. But the difference in export receipts was K0·1 mn which is negligible in relation to copper, and very small even in relation to tobacco.

Exports are thus yet another exogenous variable in the model. Short of making CIPEC effective in controlling the copper price, there is little that Zambia can do to control the price; and output and export volume in a high-risk industry with long transport routes through foreign countries will never be wholly within domestic control.

It is possible that the level of domestic demand may one day have a significant influence on exports. The necessary condition for this is that both domestic consumption and exports are large. For example if half the production of the car assembly plant at Livingstone were exported and half bought locally, then a rise in domestic demand would reduce the cars available for export if the factory had no spare capacity and if the management was willing to neglect export markets in favour of the home market. If the factory had spare capacity supplies to the home market could increase without affecting supplies to the export market. Indeed, increased production might lower average costs and so make it easier to sell cars in competitive export markets. The latter argument has been used by the British car manufacturers.

The argument about the effect of domestic demand on exports has not really been resolved in countries which export manufactured goods. It is of no relevance to Zambia at present. Negligible amounts of the important exports are consumed in Zambia; and where domestic consumption *is* important, as with maize, exports are negligible. It is sensible therefore to ignore the effect of domestic demand on exports in the Zambian case, but to realize that it can be significant in other countries and could be significant in Zambia in the future.

4 THE DETERMINANTS OF IMPORTS

In the absence of government controls and physical constraints, the level of imports is mainly determined by the level of home demand. The more income people have, the more imports they will buy. In Zambia, as in many underdeveloped countries, it is seldom as simple as that. In the years after Independence import routes were unable to cope with demand, so that some demand was frustrated by shortages and, in the case of petrol, by rationing. After UDI a system of import licensing was introduced (in December 1965) in order to control imports from Rhodesia and to allocate existing transport capacity to priority imports. In the early 1970s import licensing was greatly strengthened for a quite different reason, namely to protect the balance of payments – at that time transport capacity was less of a constraint than the ability to pay. Tough import licensing had reduced imports for two reasons, firstly because that was the intention of the government and secondly because of the delays caused by the setting up of a new bureaucratic system. The delays eased over time as the new system began to work more efficiently.

In normal times, some invisible imports are very closely related to visible imports. Thus payments for insurance, banking charges and freight are unlikely to vary differently from payments for visible imports. But the major switch in imports, from Rhodesia to other suppliers and from using the route through Rhodesia to using other routes, caused a sharp increase in the cost of freight, insurance, etc. These items were 12% of the cost of visible imports in 1964 and rose to a peak of 19% in 1968 and 1969. The biggest increase was in 1966, the year after UDI. The remarkable shift in sources of imports is shown in Table 6.3.

TABLE 6.3

(*1*) *Changing import sources, 1964–72* — *K mn*

Source of imports	*1964*	*1968*	*1972*
Rhodesia	62	23	12
South Africa	32	76	59
United Kingdom	27	76	96
Japan	3	18	38
West Germany	4	14	22
Other	28	118	177
	156	325	404

(*2*) *Changing import sources, 1964–72: percentages*

Source of imports	*1964*	*1968*	*1972*
Rhodesia	40	7	3
South Africa	21	23	15
United Kingdom	17	23	24
Japan	2	6	9
West Germany	3	4	5
Other	18	36	44
	100	100	100

Source: *Monthly Digest of Statistics*

To reduce imports from Rhodesia by so much and so quickly, at a time when total imports were rising so rapidly, was a remarkable achievement. It is even more remarkable than appears from the figures since about three quarters of imports from Rhodesia in 1968 consisted of electricity from Kariba. Zambia owns this power source jointly with Rhodesia and electricity from it only counts as an import because the power station is on the south bank. The opening of Kafue in 1972 allowed further reduction in this 'import' of electricity.

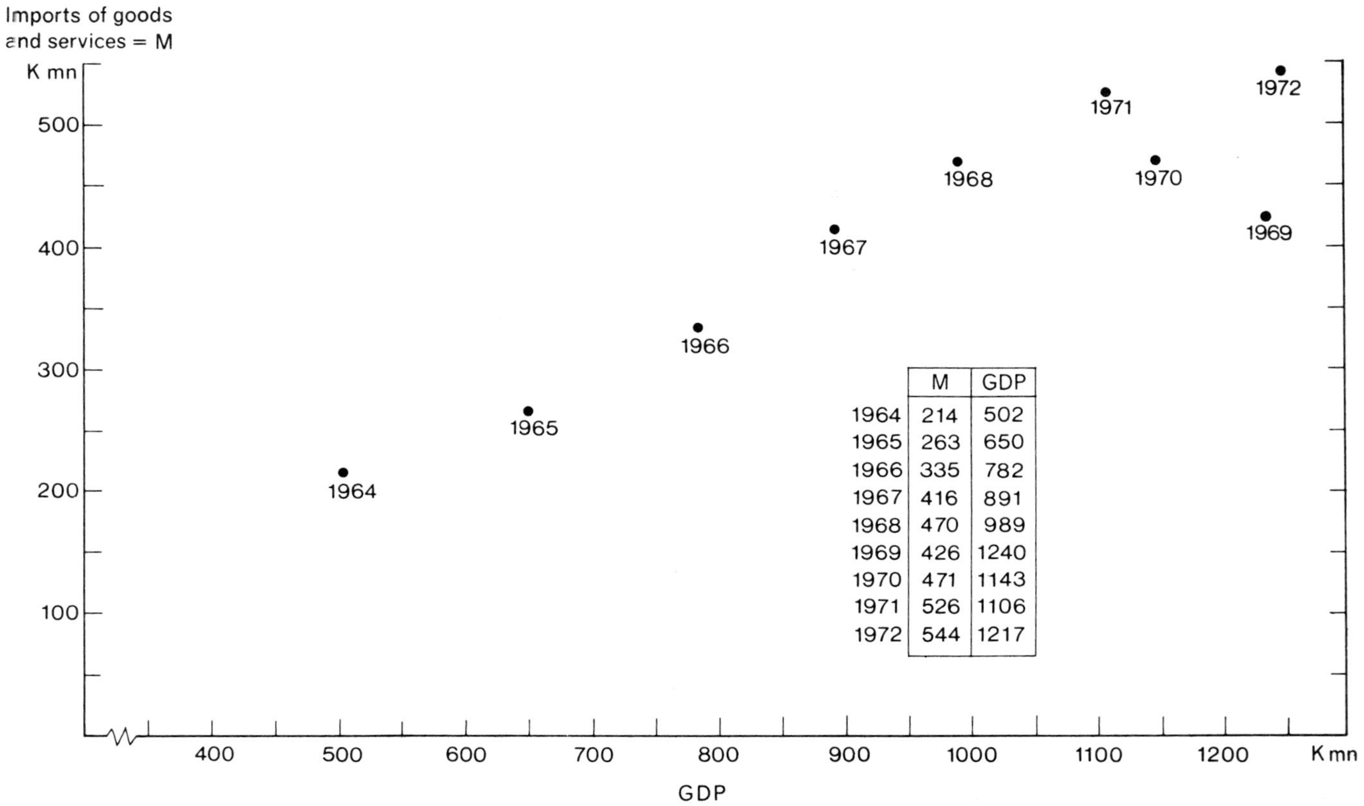

	M	GDP
1964	214	502
1965	263	650
1966	335	782
1967	416	891
1968	470	989
1969	426	1240
1970	471	1143
1971	526	1106
1972	544	1217

Figure 6.1 Imports and GDP

Since 1968 imports from South Africa have also been reduced, a process sharply accelerated by the border closure in early 1973 – imports from South Africa in 1973 were down by 35%. In general Zambia has diversified import sources very considerably, greatly reducing the importance of individual countries and thus the political risks of disruption. This did add to some invisible import costs however, as already shown.

Other invisibles, for example travel abroad (mainly by expatriates) and the cost of foreign embassies, are not related at all to the level of visible imports, although they are linked to the level of income.

Despite all the upheavals in sources of imports, in import routing and in the introduction and strengthening of import licensing, the relationship between imports and domestic demand is remarkably strong. Indeed, so long as domestic and overseas demand moved in the same direction, imports appeared to be closely dependent on GDP. But in 1969, GDP rose because of a high copper price and a very high physical level of copper exports, partly out of accumulated stocks of copper concentrates. At the same time, *domestic* demand actually fell and so did imports. This can be seen in Figure 6.1, where imports move closely in line with GDP (which includes exports) from 1964 to 1968 but not thereafter.

As with non-copper taxation, it is necessary to remove the effect of copper price changes from the figures to see that imports are dependent on income *except* in so far as income is determined by changes in the copper price. This is shown in Figure 6.2 where imports are plotted against national income *minus* mining profits.

It would seem therefore that imports are determined by income, with an import function of the type

$$M=\overline{m}+mY$$

where M = imports
$\overline{m}$ = that part of imports unaffected by income
m = marginal propensity to import (or, more precisely, the marginal propensity for imports to change as a result of a change in income).

This function only holds, however, if the copper price is assumed constant, or if Y is defined to exclude the effect of changes in the copper price.

5 IMPACT OF CHANGES IN THE VOLUME OF EXPORTS AND IMPORTS

It is normally reasonable to assume that changes in production cause changes in employment. As explained in Chapter 3 (Section 8), the other factors of production remain constant in the short term. The amount

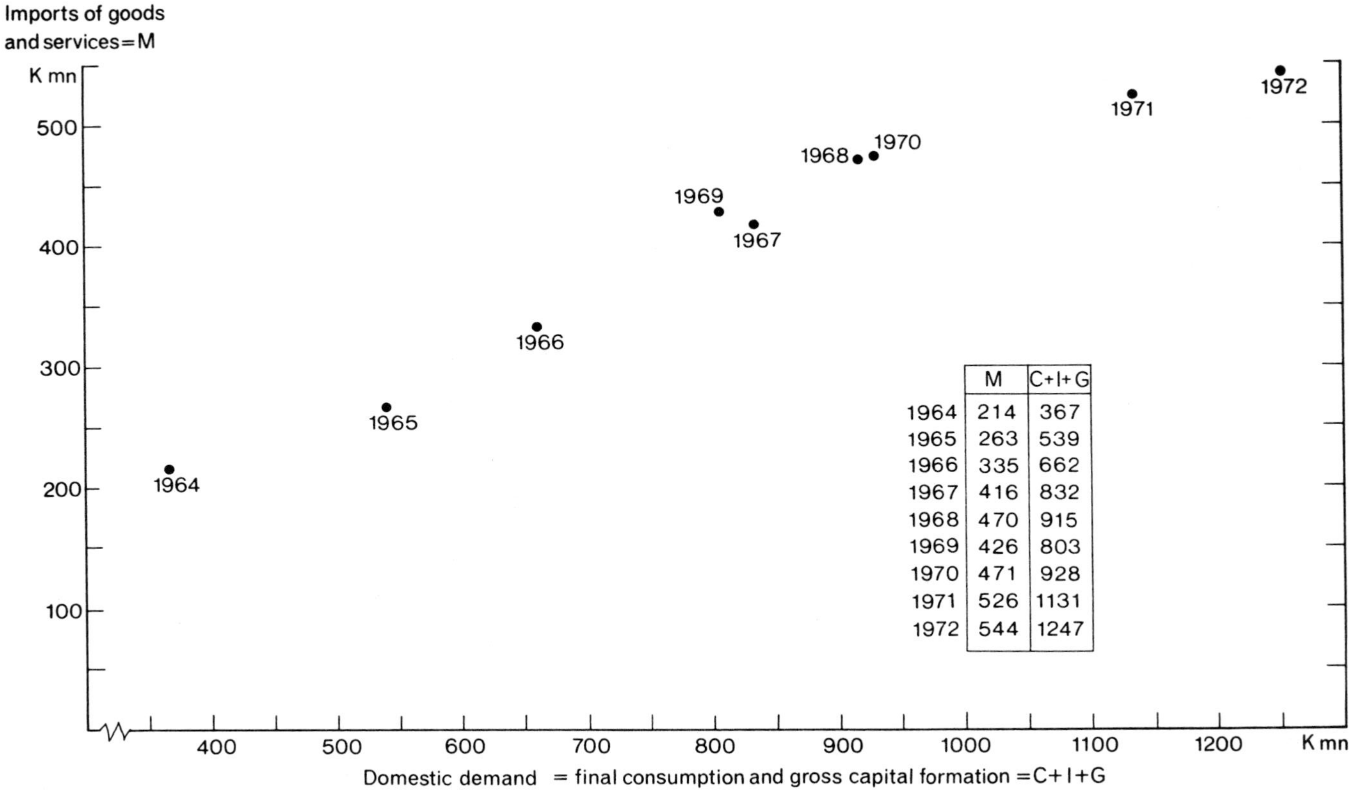

	M	C+I+G
1964	214	367
1965	263	539
1966	335	662
1967	416	832
1968	470	915
1969	426	803
1970	471	928
1971	526	1131
1972	544	1247

Note: 1971 and 1972 are not strictly comparable because domestic demand based on new SNA.
Source: *Monthly Digest of Statistics*.

Figure 6.2 Imports and domestic demand

of capital in the form of buildings and machinery, the technology used, the training and experience of the workers are all fixed in the short term. So changes in output are usually accompanied by changes in employment. It is possible for the same number of workers to work longer or shorter hours, but any big change should require the hiring or firing of workers.

Changes in the volume (the physical quantity) of copper produced and exported should therefore cause changes in mining employment. But this is not so. Table 6.4 shows changes in production and employment in copper mining, 1964–72.

TABLE 6.4

Changes in production and employment in copper mining: 1964–72

	Changes in production ('000 tonnes)	*Changes in employment*
1964	+49	+928
1965	+70	+1218
1966	−80	+1354
1967	+44	+767
1968	+24	−848
1969	+35	−184
1970	−36	+242
1971	−33	(+1279)
1972	+67	+1097

NOTE: Head office employees included in the figures in 1971 for the first time, so the increase in that year is overstated.

Source: *Mining Year Book of Zambia*, various years.

In only four out of the nine years in Table 6.4 do employment and output even move in the same direction. The year of the biggest fall in production (1966) was also the year of the biggest increase in employment. Nor is it possible to explain the table by pointing out that there was a long-term increasing trend in employment, since employment actually fell in 1968 and 1969 – at a time when production was increasing.

The explanation is that changes in mining output have mainly been the result of temporary problems and recovery from those problems, superimposed upon a slightly rising trend in capacity. The mining companies have therefore had an interest in maintaining the labour force (labour hoarding) when output fell temporarily, and even in continuing to increase it.

The fall in employment in 1968 and 1969 was probably because of the huge rise in wages in 1966 and possibly also because of political uncertainty in anticipation of some sort of takeover. A takeover occurred in 1969 and new expansion plans led to a renewed increase in employment – the fall in output immediately afterwards was because output was exceptionally high in 1969 and because of the Mufulira mining disaster in late 1970. Another reason for the rise in employment after 1969 may have been the relatively slow increase in mining wages.

What this amounts to is that large changes in mining output have had a very small feedback on the incomes of mining workers. This is confirmed by Table 6.2: total wages paid by the mining sector hardly changed at all from 1967 to 1969, despite a rise in output of 59,000 tonnes.

Other payments, to various sectors of Zambian industry, increased sharply, however, from K98 mn to K178 mn. Some of the individual changes between 1967 and 1969 are a little hard to understand and may be the result of errors in the statistics or changes in definitions; but it is probably correct that payments for inputs do increase and decrease with output. There is undoubtedly also a long-term increase in the proportion of inputs supplied locally, but changes in mining output do cause changes in demand for inputs about this trend. In other words changes in mining output cause demand for inputs to be higher or lower than it would otherwise have been.

Finally, changes in mining output affect profits. When the mines are forced to produce below their potential capacity, as by the shortage of coal in 1966 or the cave-in at Mufulira in 1970, a large part of cost is *not* reduced. Fixed costs in the form of interest on borrowing, local taxes, salaries (since workers are *not* dismissed) still have to be paid, while output is down. Even with an unchanged copper price, this reduces profit. For the same reasons, when output increases after such a setback, profits increase, since all costs do not increase proportionately with output. If output increases as the result of new capacity coming into operation (the opening of a new mine or the extension of an old one) profits normally increase as a result. Similarly if output falls because of a reduction in capacity (the closing of a mine or part of a mine) profits normally fall as a result.

Changes in mining profits have very little feedback effect, however. Tax revenue changes, but in Chapter 5 it was established that changes in tax revenue do not always get spent – certainly there is no systematic relationship between revenue and spending. Part of after-tax profit is sent abroad in the form of dividends which have no further impact on the economy. Since the takeover in 1969, 51% of the dividend is paid to Mindeco: some or all of this was used until 1973 to redeem the bonds issued in compensation at the time of the takeover, the remainder being retained by Mindeco. In August 1973, the bonds were redeemed by the government, partly out of foreign exchange reserves, partly out of government borrowing overseas. The whole of the Mindeco dividend is now available, therefore, to be paid over to government as part of current revenue (just like taxation from the government's point of view) or to be reinvested in the mining industry or to be held as a reserve. Similarly, the mining companies' post-tax, post-dividend, retained profits are available either to be invested in new production or to be held as a reserve.

The question that remains is thus whether an increase in retained profit, by Mindeco and the mining companies, as a result of an increase in production, causes an increase in spending. Clearly the cash available for investment may have *some* influence on investment. But in the case of Zambian mining, any potentially profitable investment can probably attract funds from abroad so that the availability of local funds would only affect mining investment if foreign finance were, for some reason, not available. It is also possible that a current change in output, and thus profit, could cause a change in investment *plans*, but that seems unlikely since it in no way affects the future profitability of new investment.[5]

In summary, changes in the *volume* of exports, as a result of changes in output,[6] are in themselves changes in GDP. Their feedback effect on other incomes and expenditure can occur in three main ways: via employment income, purchases from Zambian industry, and profits. Employment income is largely independent (in the short term) of output changes; and profits have little effect on spending. The effect of output changes is thus limited to changes in purchases from local industry (including the mining sector itself, see Table 6.2). This last effect is important, however, and has grown substantially in the long term as local industry supplies an increasing proportion of mining inputs.

Assume for the moment then, that the copper price is constant.[7] Imports are then dependent on income in such a way that

$$M=\overline{m}+mY$$

where M = imports of goods and services
$\overline{m}$ = a constant, being that part of imports independent of changes in income
m = the marginal propensity to import (as a result of changes in income)
Y = GNP (that is, output less profits remitted abroad).

A change in the volume of exports, and therefore in mining output, creates a change in income of ΔX plus the feedback effects. But the feedback effects are less than they would be if income generated by mining changed as well, and was respent. In order to derive a formula for this, we must first discover the 'normal' multiplier for the model enlarged by having an import function.

The equations are:

$$Y=C+I+G+X-M \qquad \text{(i)}$$
$$C=a+bY(1-t) \qquad \text{(ii)}$$
$$M=\overline{m}+mY \qquad \text{(iii)}$$

Substituting for M and C in equation (i)

$$Y=a+bY(1-t)+I+G+X-\overline{m}-mY$$

So
$$Y=\frac{a+I+G+X-\overline{m}}{1-b(1-t)+m}$$

Using the same algebraic method as before, this means that the modified multiplier for a change in investment or government spending is
$$k=\frac{1}{1-b(1-t)+m} \qquad \text{(iv)}$$

Since this new expression has $+m$ on the bottom line it is smaller than the expression derived in the last chapter
$$k=\frac{1}{1-b(1-t)}$$

The new expression, equation (iv), is smaller because an additional leakage has been introduced: some spending is on imports, so each successive round of spending out of increased income is less by the marginal propensity to import.

For example, an increase in government spendng, ΔG, will create new income of that amount. The marginal propensity for this new income to be spent and create new income will depend on the marginal propensity to consume (b) out of income remaining after marginal tax $(1-t)$ and after deducting the amount spent on imports. So the income created by the new spending, ΔG, is
$$(b(1-t)-m)\Delta G \qquad \text{(v)}$$

This new income will be spent, taxed, etc. creating new income
$$(b(1-t)-m)^2\,\Delta G, \quad \text{and so on.}$$

By the same algebra as used in Chapter 4, the final increase in income will then be as follows:

For simplicity, write $c=b(1-t)-m$, so
$$\Delta Y=\Delta G+c\,\Delta G+c^2\,\Delta G+\ \dots$$
$$=\Delta G\frac{1}{1-c}=\Delta G\frac{1}{1-b(1-t)+m} \qquad \text{(vi)}$$

using the same algebra as in Chapter 3.

Now consider an increase in exports of copper, at a fixed copper price. This must be the result of an increase in production. An increase in exports of ΔX creates new income of that amount. But because employment is not affected by short-term changes in mining output, and because profits do not induce new spending, the marginal propensity for new income to be spent and create new income can only be applied to *part of* ΔX, say $l\,\Delta X$ where l is a constant representing that part of an increase in mining output which creates additional demand for *local* goods and services. So the new income created will be
$$\Delta Y=\Delta X+cl\,\Delta X+c^2\,l\,\Delta X+\ \dots$$

Writing this differently, to separate that part of ΔX which creates new income ($l\Delta X$) and that part which does not $(1-l)\Delta X$, the equation becomes

$$\Delta Y=(1-l)\Delta X+l\Delta X+cl\Delta X+c^2 l\Delta X+\ \dots$$
$$=(1-l)\Delta X+l\Delta X\frac{1}{1-c} \qquad \text{(vii)}$$

In other words, the multiplier

$$k=\frac{1}{1-c},$$

only applies to that part of an increase in exports which creates new local income, $l\Delta X$. According to Table 6.2 roughly 20% of gross output is spent on local goods and services, so the multiplier can be applied to about one fifth of an increase in mining output. In the longer term, for example the opening of a new mine or the extension of an old one, creating new capacity, more miners would get jobs; but changes in output with unchanged capacity only have this limited feedback effect.

As usual there is no account in this analysis of changing domestic prices, so that it is only valid for variations in income which have their main effect on output and imports. An additional reason for not applying it to situations where demand for domestic output exceeds domestic capacity is that the import function may very likely not be the same under these conditions. As domestic output reaches capacity the economy will have to import not only the goods that cannot be produced at home, but also domestic goods for which demand exceeds domestic supply. In addition, if prices start to rise, or rise faster, imports become cheaper compared to domestic goods. It is likely therefore that the import function does not hold, or in other words that the marginal propensity to import is not constant but increases when there is no spare capacity in the economy.

6 EFFECT OF CHANGES IN THE PRICE OF COPPER

In the short term, fluctuations in the price of copper only affect mining profits. So long as fluctuations occur *above* the marginal cost of the highest-cost mine, no changes in output will occur as a result of price fluctuations. Even if the copper price falls below marginal cost in the highest-cost mine, the mine would almost certainly be kept in production for a while, in the hope that the copper price would rise above the break-even point within a short time. The cost of closing a mine, dispersing the labour force, reopening it, reassembling the old workers and (where necessary) training new workers, is high. In any case this has not occurred in recent years, nor is it likely under present conditions.

It is possible that under the right technical conditions the copper price could influence the marginal grade of ore mined. Thus a high price might induce a mine to hoist slightly lower grades of ore. However there is little evidence that short-term changes of this nature occur.

If only profits are affected, then changes in the price of copper have little or no short-term impact on the economy; the same arguments apply as in the previous section when the effect of output changes on profits, and the feedback effects, were being analysed. Mining investment and government spending are not usually changed quickly in response to copper price changes. There may, however, be an impact from a *rise* in the copper price if the economy has been suffering from a shortage of foreign exchange. A prolonged period of low copper prices and falling foreign exchange reserves, as in 1970–72, causes the government to restrict demand in several ways: higher taxes, import controls, severe restrictions on the growth of government spending. If the copper price then rises it may be possible to remove some or all of these restrictions quite fast.

The reverse is not true. If the copper price falls after a period of being relatively high, there will normally be enough foreign exchange reserves to allow a high level of internal demand (and thus of demand for imports) to continue for a while. In any case, it usually takes longer to impose restrictions on various types of spending than it does to remove them.

Changes in the copper price may have a very important impact on *expectations* – but on the other hand they may not. A rise or fall in the copper price may cause a change in expectations as to the long-term future price of copper; changed expectations will affect both mining investment and government expenditure plans. On the other hand, a rise or fall in the copper price may be regarded as temporary so that, provided enough foreign exchange exists in the case of a price *fall*, the price change will be ignored. Human expectations are very hard to predict, but as a first approximation it is probably true that price changes are usually regarded as temporary at first and have a gradually increasing effect on expectations the longer they are sustained. But the current level of the price of copper is only one of many factors affecting expectations. Others include the world demand and supply situation, which in turn is affected by known plans for investment in new capacity and forecasts of future industrial growth, and such technical factors as the level of stocks on the London Metal Exchange; new technical developments in both the production and uses of copper and its substitutes; even the international monetary situation affects the copper price. This is not the place to try and explain at length how the price of copper is determined since it is so largely outside Zambia's control; but it is important for the student to know that attempts to forecast the price, short or medium or long term, have all been very unsuccessful.

7 CONCLUSIONS

Two main conclusions emerge from this chapter. The first is that the Zambian economy is still surprisingly insulated in the short term from fluctuations in its most important industry, whether of output or of price, provided foreign exchange reserves are adequate. In the long term, shortages of foreign exchange can have a crucial impact on the economy. This is partly because of the 'enclave' nature of the industry. But the isolation of copper mining from the rest of the economy has gradually been reduced: by rising wages for Zambian miners and by Zambianization,[8] by increased domestic supply of inputs, by government participation in ownership, and most significantly of all by increased taxation of mining profits. However, because government revenue and mining profits are not automatically respent in the short term and because mining employment does not appear to depend on output, only a small proportion of changing output and virtually none of changing price have feedback effects on the economy. This conclusion is not much altered by the monetary impact of copper output and price changes, to be discussed in Chapter 8.

No distinction has been made between copper and other mining, mainly lead and zinc. Essentially the same arguments apply to other mining; in any case the size of other mining is very small compared to copper. The arguments used about mining may have some relevance to other industries however. Was it wrong to assume a high feedback from output increases in earlier analysis? After all, much of the non-mining industry is foreign-owned and may also hoard its labour. It is true for example that one of the main effects of the post-Independence boom was a huge increase in profits sent out of the country.

In general, the mining industry tends to maintain employment independently of output changes much more than other Zambian employers, for three main reasons. The mining union is probably the best organized and most militant in Zambia; the mining industry being by far the biggest and most important in the country it is also the most exposed to public and political pressure not to sack its workers; and labour costs are low as a proportion of total costs in a very profitable industry with a very high tax rate (73% compared with 45% for other industries) so that the mines can *afford* to maintain employment where other industries cannot.

Investment theory is dealt with later, but it is worth noting here that mining investment has to be based on very long-term considerations. It takes five years or so to develop a new mine (*after* the discovery of an ore body) and once developed it is useless for any other purpose – a hole in the ground cannot be sold to anyone unless what is at the bottom is worth having. Other industrial investment tends to be less long-term and less specific. Buildings and machinery are often saleable to other producers and for other purposes. So it may be that non-mining profits are more quickly respent. For the time being, though, we must assume that the marginal propensity to consume does take adequate account of the respending of profits while noting the dominant mining industry as an important special case.

NOTES

[1] Alternatively the Bank of Zambia as agent of the government may use an export surplus to pay off earlier foreign borrowing.

[2] Copper was 93% of visible exports in 1971, a year of much lower copper prices and lower copper production after the mining disaster at Mufulira.

[3] CIPEC stands for the French equivalent of 'Intergovernmental Council of Copper Exporting Countries'. OPEC is the equivalent group of oil exporters.

[4] Mainly in 1969; this was one of the reasons why production in that year was so high.

[5] This discussion is a little difficult coming, as it does, *before* the chapter on investment. The student may find it useful to re-read this part after reading that chapter.

[6] It seems sensible to ignore differences between output and export in this analysis. Since the copper fabrication plant came into operation in 1970, a small amount of copper is used locally. The main difference between output and exports, though, is the stock situation in Zambia, which changes because of transport and other difficulties.

[7] Variations in the copper price are considered in the next section of this chapter.

[8] Although Zambianization seems to have slowed down almost to a stop in 1970–72: Mindeco *Mining Yearbook of Zambia* 1972 gives the following figures for the number of expatriate employees replaced by Zambianization.

1968	178
1969	100
1970	24
1971	40
1972	7

7 *Investment*

1 DEFINITION

Investment is any sort of spending which makes more consumption possible in the future. So investment in the macroeconomic sense is spending on factories and machinery, the development of new mines, increases in herds of cattle, the building of roads, the building up of the national stock of maize, the building up of foreign exchange reserves, and so on.

Investment in people, through education and health services and improved nutrition, is not treated statistically as investment. Only the money spent on long-lasting equipment and buildings is treated as investment. There is thus a somewhat artificial distinction between current and capital spending on such services from the point of view of the long-term development of the country. This chapter, however, is concerned only with the short-term determinants of macroeconomic investment spending as conventionally defined.

In common speech the word investment is also used to mean the purchase (by an individual or an institution) of a second-hand asset, but this leads to no new investment overall because the purchase in one part of the system is offset by a sale in another. Only a purchase of something second-hand, for example machinery, *from abroad* is investment in the macroeconomic sense. The word investment is also used in common speech to mean the purchase of a financial asset, as, for example, investing in a savings bank or a building society. Although this is investment to the individual concerned, in that it enables him to increase his future consumption, it is not national investment since one man's financial purchase is a form of lending, offset by another man's borrowing. The only financial transaction that is a macroeconomic investment is the using of a balance of payments surplus to buy foreign financial assets.

Strictly speaking, not all investment makes more consumption possible in the future. Some investment fails to lead to greater future output. Furthermore, even if greater output *does* result from an investment, the increased resources may be further invested, putting off any increase in consumption still further in the future. A more generalized definition, therefore is that investment is spending which is intended to create a future flow of income which may in turn be either invested or consumed. This chapter is concerned with the determinants of investment spending rather than with its longer-term results.

In looking at the theory of investment it is *gross* investment that is important. Gross investment is actual spending on investment. *Net* investment is gross investment minus depreciation. Unfortunately, depreciation is not something that can be measured accurately, it can only be estimated.

In Table 2.5, where spending on GDP was shown, total investment was put at K529 mn, but this was gross investment; and the net export of goods and services was shown without any deduction for income paid abroad in the form of profits and expatriate savings. The figure of K529 mn is thus an overstatement of the amount of *national* income being invested for future consumption. Table 7.1 is a restatement of investment in 1970.

TABLE 7.1
Investment in Zambia: 1970

		K mn
Gross Fixed Capital Formation		327
Change in stocks		−13
Investment abroad:		
Exports minus imports	+215	
Income paid abroad:		
profits	−33	
expatriate savings	−105	+77
Gross national investment		391
Less:		
Depreciation (consumption of fixed capital)		−122
Net national investment		269

Source: *Monthly Digest of Statistics.*

According to this computation gross investment was 37% of GNP, and net investment was 29% of *Net* National Product (NNP) – when both GNP and NNP are calculated net of expatriate savings.

2 INVESTMENT AS A SOURCE OF FLUCTUATIONS

In more industrialized economies, private sector investment is the element of demand most likely to fluctuate. For this reason investment theory plays a particular key role in the explanation of national income fluctuations. But in Zambia there are several other major causes of fluctuations deriving from dependence on one commodity export, the impact of the weather on farm output (especially maize), the problems of being landlocked, etc.

Furthermore, as shown in Table 7.2, the fluctuations in gross investment between 1964 and 1970 were caused mainly by fluctuations in investment abroad and investment in stocks. Investment abroad affects the foreign exchange reserves and foreign indebtedness and has almost no domestic impact (except on bank liquidity, see the next chapter). Changes in stocks are dominated by changes in mining industry stocks (see Table 7.3) which also have very little impact on the domestic economy.[1]

Table 7.3 shows that changes in fixed domestic investment were of the same order of magnitude as changes in consumption in the period 1964–70; and in one year, 1967, it was consumption that changed by the largest amount because of the huge rise in wages that year. So although investment does fluctuate, it is wrong to assume that it is the most important source of fluctuations in national income.

TABLE 7.2

Investment in Zambia: 1964–70 K mn

	1964	*1965*	*1966*	*1967*	*1968*	*1969*	*1970*
Gross fixed capital formation	76	120	176	225	265	254	312
Changes in stocks	−19	+36	+50	+49	+56	−40	−13
Investment abroad	+76	+62	+53	+8	−3	+338	+77
Gross investment	133	218	279	282	318	552	376

NOTES: (1) Investment abroad shown net of both profits and savings sent abroad.
(2) Unrevised figures (pre-new SNA) are used for 1970 to facilitate comparison.

Source: *Monthly Digest of Statistics.*

TABLE 7.3

Changes in investment and consumption compared K mn

	1965	*1966*	*1967*	*1968*	*1969*	*1970*
Fixed investment	+44	+56	+49	+40	−11	+74
Mining industry stocks	+35	+16	−6	+9	−79	+12
Other stocks	+20	−2	+5	−2	−17	+15
Domestic investment	+99	+70	+48	+47	−107	+101
Private consumption	+50	+49	+94	+24	−10	+22
Government consumption	+24	+3	+28	+12	+4	+17
Consumption	+74	+52	+122	+36	−6	+39

NOTE: Government consumption is given here in its national income form, that is excluding transfers. Unrevised figures (pre-new SNA) are used for 1970 to facilitate comparison.

Source: National accounts and input–output tables.

3 THEORIES OF INVESTMENT

In industrial economies, two main theories of investment have been dominant: that investment depends on the rate of interest and that investment depends on the current level of income (or the rate of change of income).

Both of these theories are based on some assumptions about

ssmen's motives and the economic circumstances in which they . Most fundamentally of all, businessmen are assumed to invest in the expectation of making a profit. For example, a businessman will build a factory because he expects to be able to sell the factory's product for more than the costs of production; this future flow of profits must be enough to 'justify' the original cost of the investment. The truly logical way of making such a calculation is explained at length in a later section. It is enough at this point to grasp the basic idea.

Imagine a businessman thinking of building a shoe factory. He must estimate the demand for the shoes he will be manufacturing; he must estimate the cost of making the shoes, including the cost of buying raw materials, of labour, of power, etc.; he must find the finance, from his own savings, those of his relatives, from a bank, etc.; he must also pay for the finance, by paying interest, by promising a share of future profits, or (conceptually at least) by foregoing the interest he could have earned by investing his money elsewhere; he must also take into account the cost of the factory itself. He will also make some adjustment to his calculations to allow for the many uncertainties and thus the risk of being wrong. Either he will 'discount' (that is, reduce) his profit estimates to allow for risk, or he will only invest if his profit estimates are very high.

Within this general framework, investment theories have concentrated on just a few variables. Thus the theory that investment depends on the rate of interest requires that the cost of finance is the key variable, all other costs, all revenue estimates, the availability of finance, etc., being assumed unimportant.

The theory that investment depends on current income, or the rate of change of income, is really a theory about revenue expectations and the availability of funds. On the one hand, high or rising income is assumed to create expectations of high or rising income in the future and thus of profitable investment opportunities. This assumes, therefore, that one of the things that businessmen worry most about is their prospects of selling their product; and that recent trends in income are a good guide to those prospects. On the other hand, high or rising income is assumed to create high profits out of which investment can be partially or wholly financed. In addition, high profits make it easy to borrow (although it does not follow that banks, for example, have funds to lend even if they are willing to lend, as is explained in the next chapter).

Both of these theories are discussed in greater detail in later sections of this chapter[2] since they continue to dominate economic textbooks. But in Zambia, as in other African countries, only some types of investor fulfil the underlying assumptions of these theories. These assumptions include:

(1) that investors expect to sell mainly on the home market, so that their sales estimates depend on what is expected to happen to home demand;

(2) that investors are primarily interested in making a profit out of future production from their investment, and spending that profit on consumption or further investment within the domestic economy;

(3) that when profitable investment opportunities exist, there are investors with adequate access to finance, know-how, inputs, markets for outputs, and knowledge of the opportunities;

(4) that investment takes place within the general framework of the market and government rules and regulations.

Several important categories of investor in Zambia do not fit these assumptions, for example:

(1) most exporters (of minerals and agricultural products) sell almost entirely to overseas markets, where demand is independent of local economic conditions;

(2) foreign investors are frequently more interested in getting their profits out of the country than in local investment opportunities, however profitable; more interested in making a profit out of selling machines or intermediate inputs (produced abroad) than in using them for profitable local production; more interested in protecting or increasing their share of the import market than in local production; expect concessions, especially on tariff protection, peculiar to their own particular investment;

(3) small-scale farmers tend to have poor information about investment opportunities in the market economy, poor access to credit, know-how, markets, inputs, etc., because of physical remoteness, illiteracy, poor communications, etc.;

(4) small-scale farmers investing in order to increase production for their own consumption, that is, 'subsistence' investment, are relatively little affected by conditions in the market economy;

(5) individual investment in housing is constrained by problems of legal access to urban land as well as by lack of access to credit and other inputs;

(6) parastatal firms can run at a loss financed by the government, and borrow money for investment from the government, both of which allow them to ignore profitability (as normally defined) when deciding to invest.

In short, it would be quite wrong to assume that all types of investor in Zambia (and in other African countries) are similar and make investments for the same reasons. As a minimum one should distinguish between foreign and domestic investors; between those who plan to produce mainly for the domestic market, for the export market or for their own consumption; between those who do and those who do not have access to inputs such as finance; and probably also between large companies, small companies and individuals. Further subdivisions are also necessary, especially in the case of foreign investors, as will be seen in the next two sections.

4 NEW FOREIGN INVESTORS: 'MARKET-PROTECTORS'

The most important type of new foreign investors[3] is the firm seeking to protect or increase its share of the domestic market, previously supplied by overseas production in the form of imports. Such a firm is not therefore new to the country in the sense of having no previous experience of it. On the contrary it has been supplying the market for some time, typically progressing from using a local agent to setting up its own distribution facilities (this may already involve a form of investment, although not in manufacturing).

Most foreign firms regard African countries as risky and unprofitable areas for investment. African governments are regarded as unstable, likely to nationalize foreign firms without 'adequate' compensation, likely to impose discriminatory taxes on foreign firms or to impose restrictions on the remission of profits. Furthermore, African national markets are typically small so that local manufacture will not benefit from the cost-saving advantages of large-scale production (economies of scale).

As a result, a foreign firm with a share of the import market will normally prefer to continue to manufacture in its own country and export the product to Africa. It will only decide to manufacture in an African country *either* if it is threatened with losing its share of the market *or* if local manufacture offers an opportunity of greatly increasing its share of the market.

Threat of market loss comes either from government putting heavy tariffs on imports or from a rival supplier of imports investing in local manufacture and seeking tariff protection against imports of competing products. This latter strategy is of course the way in which firms seek to increase their share of the market. But even when such an investment is decided upon, the investor will try and minimize his risks by investing as little of his own money as possible, and by transferring as little as possible of the manufacturing process to the African country.

> Accordingly, they spent their time looking for ways to reduce the exposure of the company's capital to a situation they conceived to be risky and uncertain. For example, they looked for assurances of repatriation of capital, and they negotiated for higher customs protection and guarantees against devaluation. They further investigated various means to reduce the size of the dollar investment. A search for loans in local currency and negotiations aimed at reducing the percentage of local value added by production in the proposed factory were two important factors in this respect.[4]

Thus it is quite usual for a 'factory' to be set up which does little more than assemble and package imported inputs. The inputs are now treated as 'intermediate products' and come in free of import duties, while rival products continue to carry duty as 'finished products'. The investor will usually attempt to secure from government a *higher* tariff on competing imports[5] in order to protect what is now a local 'industry'. This enables him to charge a higher price than before and, so he hopes, to capture a bigger share of the market. A few rather low-skill jobs are created for local people; some expensive assembly and packaging machinery is imported; maintenance of the machinery and management of the operation requires highly paid expatriates to be employed; meanwhile the consumer pays in the form of higher prices, and reduced choice of product if rival products are no longer available.

A further problem for the African government is that the firm is now in a position to manipulate the price of its intermediate product supplies. If local tax rates are increased or exchange controls imposed on profit remission, then by raising intermediate product prices the firm can make higher profits at home and lower profits in Africa. This process is an example of 'transfer pricing' and effectively avoids local taxes and exchange controls.[6]

In practice, firms often succeed in taking advantage of tax holidays and guarantees of profit remission (or succeed in bargaining for them at the time of the investment). Yet these additional advantages are largely irrelevant to the original investment decision if the main reason for investing is to get maintained or increased sales of intermediate products and so increase profits in the country of origin.

This description of a typical 'market-protecting' investment does not mean that there is no potential gain from it for African economies. Tough requirements on training and localization of the labour force, on the increasing use of *local* rather than imported inputs, taxes on concealed forms of profit remission, can increase the local gains. The most difficult form of control is over transfer pricing because it is often so difficult to find out what prices *ought* to be. However, many products which are traded between associated companies are also traded at 'arm's length' – that is, between companies which are not associated – so that it is possible (although difficult) to check on some transfer pricing.

An alternative strategy is part-ownership by government. This has advantages and dangers for both sides. The main advantage for government is increased control of a type not obtainable from 'external' methods of control such as taxation and exchange control; ideally part-ownership should enable government interests to be cared for by means of increased *knowledge* of the running of the business. Part-ownership, whether majority or minority, does not necessarily give control however[7] and requires the government to put up some of the cost of the investment. Many private firms do not at first like the idea of being in partnership with the government, but often find that it alters very little and can have considerable advantages in the form of political acceptability and the additional privileges of being a parastatal – mainly protection in various forms from competition but also such benefits as access to government finance.

Where a government, as in Zambia, insists on all major new industrial investments being in partnership with the state, it may be that the availability of government money becomes an important determinant of new foreign investment. This would mean in Zambia's case that the price of copper has an important influence on industrial investment since the biggest variations in government revenue are the result of copper price variations. State participation in major new industrial investments may also affect the *type* of investment that is undertaken – perhaps taking more account of social needs, using local raw materials, etc. However, Zambian policy is distinctly ambiguous, requiring parastatal businesses to 'show a greater consideration for social benefit than would normally apply to privately owned companies. They ... must operate in a business-like manner....'[8]

Another way of looking at this question of state participation is to note that putting money directly into industrial investment may be a better way of 'spending' state money than by offering tax concessions and having generous rules on the remission of profits. Concessions may not even attract any additional investors (those that do invest would have invested anyway in order to protect their markets); meanwhile they lose the country a lot of money from the profits of existing investors.[9]

This discussion has not produced a theory which would succeed in predicting the amount of market-protecting investment. It is *not* a sufficient condition for investment that the local market should have grown by enough to justify a local plant, since import suppliers prefer to continue to supply from abroad unless their market is threatened (by government or by a rival supplier). Indeed Kilby has shown that in Nigeria there was typically no local manufacture for many years after the market had grown big enough to justify such an investment; then within a very short period several factories would be set up by rival firms, each determined to prevent the others from capturing the whole market even though this meant that huge amounts of excess capacity were created.[10] It might be thought that excess capacity would lead firms to seek export markets; but small scale of production and newness leads to high costs and anyway many foreign investors prohibit exports that might threaten their other markets supplied from their countries of origin.[11] Also, industrial investments in Africa tend to be in the same products which reduces the possibility of intra-African trade.[12]

The discussion *does* suggest that market-protecting investment will take place as a result of threat; but what causes the timing of the threat, or how much investment it will induce, is not apparent. Profitability is not relevant, since it is determined by the concessions obtained from government, especially on tariffs and the degree of monopoly. Even if firms do *not* succeed in obtaining sufficient concessions from government to guarantee local profitability the investment may still take place because of the profits to be obtained from supplying inputs (possibly at favourable transfer prices) or in the hope of obtaining concessions at a later date.

The discussion also suggests that the government can induce market-protecting investment by threatening to exclude a firm from the import market; furthermore, the government is in a much stronger bargaining position than has often been suspected, since the investor has something important to lose. However, the investment may be of little or no benefit to the economy unless the government *uses* its bargaining power; otherwise consumers as a group may lose far more than is gained by those who get jobs; and the manufacturing operation may be a mere assembly and packaging affair, creating few jobs and few skills.

Alternatively, the availability of government revenue may determine the amount of participatory parastatal investment that takes place – but this is a tenuous connection because governments can borrow for this purpose, or even insist on a 'free ride' (a free allocation of shares, in return for tax concessions, or even in simple recognition of government's bargaining power). Sometimes 'aid' is available to help finance such projects since aid donors can see the advantage to their own economies of expanded exports of intermediate products and of machinery. Tied aid, that is aid tied to donor country products, is specifically aimed at this objective. It is, of course, as much aid to donor country export industries as to the industrialization of the recipient's economy.

5 NEW FOREIGN INVESTORS: NON-MARKET-PROTECTORS

In the previous section, two reasons for foreign investment were identified, namely protection of or increase in a firm's share of the local market by setting up local production facilities. The question to ask in this section is what other reasons an investor might have for risking his money in small underdeveloped African countries, of which he has no previous experience, and which are apparently therefore (to him) highly unstable politically. It is an unfortunate fact that only bad news about Africa appears in most foreign newspapers and that bad news about one African country tends to create a bad impression about others, to those who have no first-hand experience of the countries involved.

The 'classic' answer to this question, that is, the answer given in a lot of academic writing and implied by the sort of concessions frequently offered to foreign investors, is that investors will appear, attracted by the size of the market and comforted as to the security of their profits (and being allowed to remit them out of the country) by the promises of governments and the speeches of presidents, ministers and ambassadors. But African countries do not have large markets, and anyway the obvious investor in this case is the market-protector of the last section who already supplies the market from abroad and so has several advantages over the complete newcomer to the local scene. It is difficult, therefore, to see what sort of investor could possibly be interested in such a remote and apparently risky investment.

In his investigation of foreign investors in Nigeria (which is very much larger than most African countries and potentially could be a very large market indeed) Kilby found only one 'classic' investor. He divided what he called the non-market-protectors into five types.[13]

(1) The 'classic' investor, attracted by the size of the Nigerian market, looking for a profitable investment opportunity.
(2) Individual investors (including crooks) seeking the backing of government agencies on favourable terms.
(3) Manufacturers trying to sell redundant machines.
(4) Machinery manufacturers seeking a profit by selling their machinery.
(5) Machinery merchants seeking a profit by selling other people's machinery.

Only the first type did not require Nigerian public capital – all of the remainder were not prepared to back the investment entirely with their own money. In the case of the machinery merchants their contribution was typically very small indeed.

The most important point about types (2) to (5) is therefore that they expect somebody else to put up the money and take the risks; and in the case of types (3), (4) and (5) the firms had little or no interest in successful *production* since their profit came from selling *machinery*.

Redundant machines are not necessarily 'wrong' for countries like Nigeria and Zambia; indeed second-hand machinery may be cheaper and more suitable to local conditions if, for example, it is easier to maintain and uses more labour than more modern machinery. In buying second-hand machinery it is important to ask why it is being sold. If it is worn out, or if it is being replaced by more efficient machinery which would also be more efficient in, say, Zambia – then it is almost certainly poor value. If it is available because a firm has gone bankrupt, or if it is being replaced by a machine less suitable to Zambian conditions, then buying second-hand may be a sound policy. Nevertheless, there remain considerable difficulties in using second-hand machinery successfully.[14]

The worst form of investment for Nigeria was by machinery merchants. None of the firms ran profitably and so they required subsidies out of public funds. They absorbed over £30 mn of public investment money. The reasons for failure were that investments were made for political rather than economic reasons, machines were often of the wrong sort and badly matched with each other, and the quality of the management was poor. Most fundamentally, the machinery merchants had no interest in successful production, not even for the sake of the reputation of the machines since they were selling other people's machines. The UNCTAD study quoted above found a similar situation in Ethiopia, where the risks were taken by the Ethiopian government and eleven out of a sample of twelve firms made losses.[15]

Management is very important. Buying a complete factory and then trying to hire management on the international market is seldom successful. On the other hand a firm investing in order to manufacture its own product (usually a market-protector) with foreign personnel supplied from its own operations elsewhere, clearly has a real interest in successful *production* and a much better chance of achieving it because of the people it can use and the technical back-up of its world-wide operations. Such a firm also has an interest in the reputation of its product. On the other hand such firms have greater opportunities for transfer pricing.

For all types of non-market-protectors (as for market-protectors) profitability depends very heavily on government decisions. The most important government decision is usually on the level of tariff protection, but others include price control over both inputs and outputs and the degree of monopoly or competition permitted. In any case, profitability is not a sufficient condition for investment, since even the existence of an opportunity to make profits is not certain to induce investment if potential investors consider the situation to be too risky. Even if a government is correct in believing that its own country is politically stable and a low-risk area for foreign investment, it may be unable to persuade foreign firms that that is the case. Nor is profitability a necessary condition for investment since profit may be made out of selling machines, selling intermediate products or buying output rather than out of local production.[16]

One type of non-market-protecting investment remains to be discussed, namely investment in producing raw materials for export – this is so important that it is dealt with in a separate section.

6 INVESTMENT IN MINING

Mining investment is a special case. It is both extremely risky and, potentially, extremely profitable. Mining companies thus need large amounts of finance to carry the risks of prospecting and the cost of developing mines, often in places without any previous modern development. Mineral ore bodies are seldom located conveniently near to existing railways, towns, water supplies, skilled workmen, etc. At the same time the very large profits that can be made encourage such investment.

There are thus two obvious determinants of, say, copper mining investment. One is the expected future price of copper (for which the present price of copper may be a guide); the other is anything which reduces the risk of prospecting for copper and then developing a mine, or which reduces the risk of not being able to make a profit once a mine has been developed. Taking price expectations first, there are unfortunately a number of reasons why the current copper price is not a very good guide to investment.

Some copper mining investments are so obviously profitable that they take place regardless of expectations as to the future price of copper. In addition, as was pointed out in Chapter 6, Section 6, the current price of copper is a poor guide to copper price expectations. Thirdly, international mining companies are in a good position to use international sources of finance and so are not necessarily dependent on a high current copper price to generate investment funds. Fourthly, political expectations affect profit expectations. Fifthly, it takes a long time to develop a new mine (typically, five years) so that once begun, investment is likely to continue despite price fluctuations, unless price expectations fall so low that it seems worthwhile to cancel an investment when it is half-developed. Thus mining investment in Zambia in the period 1964–9 was inhibited by a tax system which discouraged investment and which the mining companies expected would be changed, and investment was also inhibited by the growing uncertainty about whether a takeover would occur and if it did, what form it would take. As a result, mining investment was almost certainly lower than it would otherwise have been, at a time of high prices. After the takeover, large increases in investment were announced, both as a result of the removal of uncertainty as well as of the tax reform which accompanied the takeover.[17] These investments continued despite low copper prices in the period 1970–72.

Yet another reason why mining investment may take place independently of short-term price movements is that the need to secure a regular supply of the metal may be more important than making a profit from mining. Thus Japan, having industrialized later than Western Europe and North America and having a very rapid rate of growth in the 1960s, actually invested in copper mining in Zaire, then Congo (Kinshasa), when the political risks were very high, certainly high enough to prevent any other sort of foreign investment. Japan was unable to buy enough copper through the London Metal Exchange (LME) because relatively little copper is actually sold through the LME. Zambia's copper, for example, is sold at prices based on the LME prices, but most of it is sold on long-term supply contracts to particular customers. The only way, therefore, for Japan to secure increased supplies of copper was to invest in mining with the promise of long-term supply contracts.

Despite all the above arguments that investment *can* be independent of prices and price expectations, they obviously have *some* influence. It has been argued that there is in fact an investment cycle. High prices induce investment; after a time-lag for the development of the new mining capacity, additional supplies bring the price down; investment is then neglected and a new shortage develops, driving prices up again.

Furthermore, the sort of world shortage of the metal that induced Japanese investment in the Zaire in the 1960s, normally coincides with high prices and therefore with high profit expectations.

The point, as far as any individual country is concerned, is that other considerations are frequently more important, even if this investment cycle explains investment world-wide. In modern Zambia, non-price factors have been dominant; and before Independence some at least of the periods of heavy investment can also be explained by non-price factors: for example, the granting of exclusive prospecting licences in the 1920s, and the setting of a thirty-six-year limit on the BSA Co.'s enjoyment of the mineral royalty in 1950.[18] Both of these were in fact risk-reducing factors.

Another aspect of mining investment is that it has to be relatively long-term in nature. Prospecting takes time; the development of a new mine, once an ore body has been identified, takes an average of something like five years, as already mentioned; the life of a mine is seldom less than ten years, often more than twenty. Furthermore, there is no question in mining of a minor investment in assembly and packaging; mining requires a massive investment in fixed capital (very fixed in the case of the mine itself, the investor cannot take a hole in the ground away with him).

Mining can also create a very large investment compared with any single industrial investment. Manufacturing investment tends to be limited by the size of the local market, at least initially, whereas the size of a mining investment is determined more by the size of the mineral deposit and can be very large in relation to the local economy. Size and relative permanence create both strengths and weaknesses in the bargaining relationship between governments and mining companies.[19] Most importantly, both sides know that ultimately they have to reach agreement on how the mining industry is to be run and owned. In other sectors of the economy there are examples of foreign firms closing down their operations or being closed down by the government, rather than reaching agreement.

Finally, mining, and also foreign investment in agricultural raw materials for export, creates a conflict between the investor and local interests in the development of further processing. If the foreign investor has refining plant with spare capacity in his country of origin he will be unwilling to invest in refining capacity in the country where the mine or plantation is. The local government must then use what bargaining power it has to increase the proportion of value added locally. This is the counterpart of the problem of increasing the proportion of value added locally by import-substituting firms.

7 FOREIGN INVESTMENT: EXPANSION OF EXISTING INVESTMENT

Foreign investors with an existing investment in the country (provided that they have an interest in production) are affected by some of the same factors as locally owned businesses. Thus some (gross) investment is necessary in order to maintain a business as depreciation occurs, and most businesses try and expand with the market. On the other hand foreign-owned business may have additional or alternative objectives not shared by locally owned firms, for example:

(1) To get profits out of the country.
(2) To maximize the purchase of intermediate inputs from associated companies (also a way of getting profits out).
(3) To invest in areas not reserved by law for local citizens (or expected to be reserved by law in the future).

As a result, the reaction of foreign-owned businesses to a profitable investment opportunity could be quite different from that of a locally owned business – namely to get profits (and capital too, where possible) out of the country rather than to invest in expanded capacity. Similarly, a foreign firm with a profitable opportunity to increase the proportion of value added locally, by extending the local production process, would not necessarily do so, but might prefer to continue importing as much as possible from the parent company. Thirdly, African governments have been reserving an increasing number of business opportunities for their own citizens; non-citizens must react to or avoid these new laws and may also try and react to the way such laws are likely to develop in the future.

The *nature* of investment may well also be affected by whether investors are foreign or local. Basically, the foreign investor is less sure of having a long-term future in the country – that is why he is often more interested in profit abroad than profit locally – and so prefers investment in short-term projects. As a result, the foreign investor may avoid investments with a longer-term pay-off, even when that pay-off is very high. A fairly minor example is the way foreign investors prefer to rent office accommodation and executive houses, rather than buying, even when rents are very high. Local institutions, faced with the same relative costs tend to buy (or build) because they *do* have a long-term future in the country.

Not all types of foreign investor have the same opportunities for pursuing their particular objectives. Thus the long-term resident foreigners to be found in many parts of Africa (Asians, Southern Africans and sundry Europeans in Zambia; Italians, Greeks and Lebanese in Ethiopia, etc.) are less likely to be buying intermediate inputs from associated companies than branches of multinational companies and other companies with non-resident ownership. For the same reason, resident foreigners find it more difficult to get money out of the country – transfer pricing by collusion with suppliers is more difficult to organize than transfer-pricing within the same group of companies.

It is not possible to say which type of foreign investor has the shorter time-horizon. Resident expatriates may wish to get their money out, but some of them may believe in a long-term future for themselves in the country and some may have nowhere to go – or prefer the risk of staying to the risk of going. Foreign companies with non-resident ownership might appear to have longer-term prospects: many have been encouraged to invest by the government and they can survive (as corporate bodies) the complete localization of personnel, for example. But foreign firms may have a very short-term view of their likely profitable life in an African country, because government policies may change, because of the risk of expropriation, etc. Where they are essentially in the business of selling management expertise or some other form of technology their exclusive knowledge may be short-lived as local people acquire it. In the extreme cases of those foreign investors who are not interested in production, having made their profit out of selling machinery before production starts, it is unlikely that an expanding market will induce investment – most of such firms run at a loss anyway.[20]

Attitudes to investment in Africa probably change over time. Thus in Zambia immediately after Independence some of the locally resident foreign businessmen left as fast as they could despite the enormously profitable opportunities created by the post-Independence boom. Of those that now remain presumably most are relatively confident of the short- to medium-term prospects. Their attitudes are fairly sensitive to government policy changes, however, not only as regards Zambianization of various sectors of the economy but also in such matters as how they are treated in the queues for credit, import licences, etc.

Similarly, the attitudes of companies owned by non-residents are adversely affected by such events as takeovers and changes in government; but over time investor confidence tends to recover as investors discover they can survive and make profits. For example, in South Africa, normally regarded as the safest haven for foreign investment in Africa, investor confidence was badly shaken by the changes taking place in the rest of Africa in the late 1950s, and by Sharpeville, so that there were large net outflows of investment finance in the years 1959–65; a net inflow recurred in 1966.

Summarizing this section, then, it would seem that foreign investors with an existing stake in the country, whether resident or non-resident, *may* respond to profitable opportunities in much the same way as domestically owned businesses. But although a profitable opportunity is a *necessary* condition for the expansion of a foreign-owned business, it is not a *sufficient* condition since the business may have alternative objectives to that of making profits on local production. Secondly, a foreign-owned business may be unwilling to commit itself to a project whose profitability will only be realized over a relatively long period, whereas locally owned business (especially parastatals) is more likely to be able to take a longer view.

Where a parastatal is in partnership with foreigners, investment behaviour depends on who is the dominant partner, how the contracts were written, whose money is invested in expansion. Clearly the motive for government participation is precisely to change foreign investor behaviour in the direction of local interests, but in practice this objective is not automatically achieved simply by participation. On the one hand, government participation should give foreign investors greater security, better access to government services (import licences, credit) and other government-allocated benefits (tariff protection, monopoly). On the other hand, state participation reduces foreign investor's freedom of manoeuvre, and may create an increased obligation to fall in with government policy (price control, recognition of unions, local purchasing of inputs). The relationship between the partners is thus essentially a bargaining one whose outcome depends on their relative strengths and weaknesses and is therefore difficult to predict.

8 LOCALLY OWNED INVESTMENT

In the previous sections, foreign investment was discussed on the implicit assumption that there was a domestic counterpart with which it could be compared. It is important to ask, for African countries, whether there *is* really a significant class of domestic businesses which is comparable to the class of foreign businesses – in being capable of using modern technology (and having access to it), in having access to bank credit, to urban (and overseas) markets, etc.

The answer to the question in Zambia is that there is a small but rapidly growing group of Zambian citizens owning and running 'modern' businesses in such sectors as farming, transport, retailing, etc., but that large-scale industry and commerce are still dominated by foreign investors, increasingly in partnership with the government; and that the purely capitalist, purely domestic sector is still *mainly* made up of businesses which do *not* have very good access to technology, bank credit, markets, etc.

This means that investment opportunities may not be taken up, when local investors do not have the means, and foreign investors do not regard the opportunities as profitable enough to allow for the risks as they perceive them. This would suggest that government could induce investment either by providing technical assistance to local investors, or by reducing the risks as perceived by foreign investors. The policy of trying to induce foreign investment has already been discussed; trying to help local investors is just as difficult – for all sorts of fairly obvious reasons it is very hard indeed for the small-scale local business to change its whole nature so that it begins to use modern technology and large-scale modern manufacturing methods.

The maker of buckets from old corrugated iron sheet in the corner of some local market is not easily transformed into a metal-processing manufacturer employing hundreds of men, using precision machine tools and a production line. It is much more likely in fact that he will be put out of business by imports or by the local assembly (or last-stage manufacture) of imported inputs by a foreign investor. The competing foreign investor also has the advantage of being able to advertise his product and its alleged superiority, even though the locally produced product may be more suitable for local people and their needs. In fact the small-scale local business is often discriminated *against* by government policy. Restrictive licensing of taxis, retail stores, hawkers, etc., reduces opportunities. Legal requirements regarding land use, building regulations, etc., have the same effect and also make it difficult to get credit. There are many other examples.

Small-scale agriculture is really only an example of locally owned and operated business. The constraints are particularly severe, because of remoteness, lack of information and know-how, etc. Farmers do, however, respond to profitable opportunities when these constraints are not operative or when they are overcome by a sufficiently well-organized and efficiently delivered package of services. For example, the opportunity provided by the growth of copper mining and urban demand for food in the 1930s produced a very rapid response from Zambian farmers in the products which they already knew how to produce – maize and beef.[21] New technologies have been successfully adopted in Zambia since Independence for instance in cotton growing and poultry farming, as a result of a combination of attractive prices and a well-organized extension programme.[22] As with other forms of business, though, apparently attractive investment opportunities may not be taken up because local farmers do not have the means and because those who do have the means are not interested (because the profit will be spread over too long a period or because they are simply more interested in getting their money out of the country).

Investment in subsistence farming is a special case. It may take place entirely without reference to the market economy. More frequently in modern Africa it competes for the farmer's time with the alternatives of investment in cash crop production, and with non-agricultural employment. The large-scale migration of people from the remoter areas of Zambia is a fairly clear demonstration that investment opportunities in farming, for cash crop production or for own consumption, have been relatively unattractive. Unfortunately not much more is known about subsistence farming investment; even the guesses as to the size of the 'traditional' cattle herd are only very rough guesses indeed, and even less is known about other forms of investment.

What this discussion amounts to therefore is that a period of rising income, which creates all sorts of profitable investment opportunities, and of freely available investment funds (whether from high profits or bank credit being available), will not have a uniform effect on every sector of the economy. Where local people already have the means to take up investment opportunities, investment is likely to occur. Where local people are not able to invest and foreigners are unwilling, investment will not take place and either imports will increase or goods and services will simply not be provided. Meanwhile, high foreign-owned profits will be remitted abroad, legally or illegally.

9 THE CALCULATION OF EXPECTED PROFIT

Some investment is determined mainly by expectations of profit rather than by government decisions. Of course all investment decisions are affected by broad government policy – on taxation, the cost of such government-supplied inputs as electricity, coal and railway transport, and many other policies. But these policies tend to apply to all firms indiscriminately. It is reasonable to assume these various policies unchanged while examining the impact of purely economic variables on investment, provided that the investment decision does not depend on a change or concession in government policy *peculiar to that investment decision*. For example, if an investment decision depends on the granting of a protective tariff or a change in a government-controlled price then 'pure' economic factors cannot be considered independently of government decisions.

An investment decision made on the assumption of unchanged government policy (or simply allowing for the general possibility of favourable or unfavourable changes) will normally be based on expectations of profit – that is, the difference between expected revenue and expected cost. Even some of those investment decisions dependent on a particular government decision can be included in this framework since investors can be assumed to calculate the effect on the expected returns of the government action.

Suppose, for example, a transport operator is planning to buy another lorry. In principle he should estimate its useful life, what he can sell it for at the end of its useful life, how much revenue it will earn and the running costs. The timing of each cost and each receipt is also of great importance. This is because an expense now of K100 costs the investor more than an expense of K100 in a year's time. If the money has to be borrowed then interest must be paid on an immediate payment; if the investor has cash, then spending it now means he cannot put the money in a bank or building society to earn interest. In either case, the spending of cash now costs more than the spending of cash later.

The same argument applies to the receipt of revenue now, which is worth more to the investor now than the receipt of revenue at a later date. Receipt of cash now enables the investor to reduce his borrowing and pay less interest, or to put more money into a financial institution and receive more interest.

The variation in value of costs and receipts according to their timing is especially important in investments with a long 'gestation' period, that is, a long time from when costs start to when receipts start. Hydroelectric schemes are a good example of an investment with a long gestation period: building a dam and installing hydroelectric machinery can take years, during which expenses are high, while no revenue is received until the project is complete. If money has been borrowed to build the dam interest must be paid during the construction period; if investors put in their savings to finance the scheme, they must forego alternative earnings on their savings until the scheme begins to earn a profit.

In principle, an investor expecting to sell a product for K100 should not mind whether he receives K100 now or K100$(1+r)$ in a year's time, if r is the annual rate of interest obtainable on savings. If he receives K100 now he can put it in a savings account so that in one year it will be worth K100$+r\times$K100, or K100$(1+r)$.

Another way of expressing this is to say that the 'present value' of K100$(1+r)$ receivable one year in the future is K100. By the same process, K100 becomes K100$(1+r)^2$ in two years' time if it remains invested in a savings bank. So the present value of K100$(1+r)^2$ receivable two years in the future is K100.

Generalizing this into a formula, the present value of a sum $x(1+r)^n$, receivable n years' time in the future, is x. Writing

$$x(1+r)^n=y$$

then the present value of y, receivable n years in the future is x. But

$$x=y/(1+r)^n$$

In other words, a sum y receivable n years in the future is worth less in present terms, and the lesser amount is given by this formula.

Similarly, if a cost of K100 can be put off for a year, the investor should not mind if it costs K100$(1+r)$ in a year's time since he can earn $r\times$K100 in interest on the cash, or save that amount in borrowing costs.[23] So the present value of a cost of K100$(1+r)$ in a year's time is K100. Generalizing as before, a cost of y in n years' time has a present-day equivalent of x, where

$$x=y/(1+r)^n$$

If the investor, whether a private investor or the government, does not make such calculations, then there is no way of distinguishing between investments where costs are immediate or postponed to a later date, or between investments with early or delayed receipts. The process of calculating the present value of future costs and receipts is called 'discounting to present value', and the interest rate used is sometimes called the 'discount rate'.

The estimated present value of an investment is the difference between the present value of estimated benefits and the present value of estimated costs. The 'rate of return' on an investment is the interest rate which would have to be used to reduce the present value to zero. The example of a lorry should help to make this clear.

Suppose the lorry has a life of three years (quite generous for some parts of Zambia), costs K3,000, and is expected to have costs and revenue as shown in Table 7.4.

TABLE 7.4
Investment in a lorry

	Start of year 1	*End of year 1*	*End of year 2*	*End of year 3*
Purchase of lorry	3,000	—	—	—
Running costs	—	1,200	1,300	1,400
Receipts	—	2,500	2,500	2,500
Net revenue	−3,000	+1,300	+1,200	+1,100

NOTE: Assumption is that all running costs and receipts are met simultaneously at year-end. This makes little difference to the calculation. It would occur if the lorry was leased to a subcontractor who simply paid over the net revenue at the end of each year. It is also assumed that the lorry has a scrap value of nothing at the end of three years.

The present value of the flow of payments and receipts, discounted at 10%, is

$$\text{Present value} = -3000 + \frac{1300}{1+0{\cdot}1} + \frac{1200}{(1+0{\cdot}1)^2} + \frac{1100}{(1+0{\cdot}1)^3}$$
$$= -3000 + 1182 + 992 + 826 = 0$$

In other words the expected rate of return on this investment is 10%. Although the total of net receipts is K600 greater than the original investment of K3,000, these receipts are expected in the future while the K3,000 must be paid at once.

Another way of putting it is to say that if the investor had to borrow K3,000 and pay 10% on the loan, he would end up with exactly nothing – no profit, no loss – at the end of three years. This can be seen from Table 7.5.

TABLE 7.5
Investment in a lorry: borrowing at 10%

	Start of year 1	*End of year 1*	*End of year 2*	*End of year 3*
Net revenue (from Table 7.4)	−3,000	+1,300	+1,200	+1,100
Interest due on borrowing	—	−300	−200	−100
Balance outstanding	−3,000	−2,000	−1,000	—

NOTE: Assumption is that all interest is paid in one payment at year end, on the borrowing outstanding at the beginning of each year.

Yet another way of putting it is to say that if the investor had cash, he would be just as well off investing in a savings account yielding 10% as investing in the lorry. It is assumed that interest on the savings account is reinvested, and that net receipts from operating the lorry are also reinvested at 10%. This can be seen in Table 7.6.

TABLE 7.6
Investment in a lorry or a 10% savings account

	Start of year 1	*End of year 1*	*End of year 2*	*End of year 3*
Savings account:				
amount invested	3,000	3,300	3,630	3,993
interest received	—	300	330	363
Lorry:				
receipts	—	1,300	1,200	1,100
interest	—	—	130	263
Cumulative total	—	1,300	2,630	3,993

In real life, most investors would prefer a safe 10% in a savings account to the very risky business of running a lorry for the same prospective rate of return. These figures, though, oversimplify the decision. The amounts of net revenue from running the lorry are only estimates. If, for example, the investor guesses that the earnings shown are the *minimum* he can expect, and that there is a good chance of much higher earnings, he may well prefer to gamble on buying the lorry.

The discussion in this section has been about the private investor who takes existing prices as beyond his control and seeks to make a profit within that framework. But in small, underdeveloped African economies, in which governments have interfered in many ways with the price mechanism, prices do not necessarily indicate to investors what would be to the greatest benefit of the country as a whole. It is thus open to government to try and alter the prices used by private investors – by subsidies, taxes and direct price control. For its own investments the government can use 'shadow prices' – these are the prices which government thinks reflect more accurately the 'social' costs and benefits of its investments. For example, if high wages make it unprofitable to employ a lot of labour, yet unemployment exists, then government could use a lower, shadow wage rate in calculating the social return on an investment. Once shadow prices have been established by government planners, the calculation of the rate of return proceeds in the same way. Of course if the government business then makes a loss, because it must operate in a world of real prices, then the loss must be made up from other revenue sources. There is not space here to go into the whole area of social cost benefit analysis, but the student should be aware of the possibility.

10 INVESTMENT AND INTEREST RATES

Another investment theory, which deserves only limited attention, is that investment depends on 'the' rate of interest.[24] The reasoning is roughly that because there is an expected rate of return on an investment, which logically investors should calculate, then if that expected rate of return is greater than the cost of borrowed money (or than the rate obtainable on the best alternative use for the funds) the investment should be undertaken. In the example of investment in a lorry, if the rate of interest were less than 10%, the investment would be profitable.

This theory focuses attention on the financial process by which savings reach investors and are spent. This process is indeed important – it will be given a great deal of attention in the chapter on money. But the *cost* of money to investors is no more important than any other cost, such as the cost of labour or of capital equipment. Indeed there are a number of reasons why the cost of money may be considerably *less* important than other costs.

The rate of interest has received an excessive amount of attention partly because of the logical neatness of comparing rates of return with rates of interest; and partly because of the attractions of a macro-economic model in which the rate of interest provides an equilibrating mechanism between savings and investment. As explained in Chapter 3, it is rather misleading to concentrate on savings and investment rather than on aggregate demand and supply; and savings are *not* in any case determined by the rate of interest. Because investment theory in basic textbooks still gives great attention to this idea, some space must be given to the reasons why it has little relevance in developed economies and even less relevance in underdeveloped ones.

Interest rates have the smaller influence on costs (and so on profitability) the shorter is the life of the investment. This is easily shown by arithmetical examples; it is necessarily true that present value is affected more by the interest rate the greater the number of years involved, since present value is derived by dividing by $(1+r)^n$, where n is the number of years in the future. Clearly the larger is n, the greater is the influence of $(1+r)^n$ on present value. Another way of expressing the same idea is to note that the shorter the life of an investment the greater is the depreciation charge as a proportion of costs and, therefore, the smaller are other costs as a proportion of costs, including borrowing costs.

There are a number of reasons why investors assume a short life for investments, shorter perhaps than is indicated by the physical life of machinery and buildings. Technical change and changing consumer tastes shorten the life of investments; political uncertainties, especially strong in underdeveloped countries, reduce investors' time horizons; foreign investors discount especially heavily for political risk. The foreign investor is also more likely to be using foreign funds, in which case any influence on the investment decision is of a foreign interest rate.

Another way of expressing the importance of uncertainty is to note that investors expect a very high rate of return in order to allow for risk. Thus if investors expect a 30% return on investment and the interest rate is, say, 8%, then even quite large variations in the interest rate will be very unlikely to affect the investment decision.

Investment takes place not only out of borrowed funds but out of retained profits, the investors' own savings and the savings of close relatives and friends. Although there is a theoretical opportunity cost to using one's own funds, it can be ignored since it is not a cost that has to be met by making a cash payment. Furthermore, the interest rate on funds lent is usually less than that on funds borrowed and so has less influence. Some investors are unwilling or unable to borrow, so that borrowing costs are irrelevant to them.

A great deal of investment in Africa is undertaken by people on their own account, using their own labour and therefore independent (or nearly independent) of the financial system. Such investments include the building of huts, the building up of herds of cattle, self-help urban housing, the clearing of new land, and so on. In such investments the rate of interest is so remote that it is clearly absurd to consider it.

The monopoly or tariff-protected position of many investors in Africa would enable them to pass on any increase in interest costs, in the form of higher prices; or to compensate by paying higher transfer prices, licence fees, etc., to foreign associate companies.

As has already been argued, very long-term investments are more influenced by interest rates than short-term investments. Easily the most important example is housing. Housing investment is also peculiar in that the returns from housing are often very much more certain than the returns from other forms of investment. The reasons are that in most countries there is a gross shortage of housing, especially in towns; the shortage is usually so great in relation to the rate of building of new houses that excess demand is certain to exist for the foreseeable future; housing is such a basic need that demand for it is certain to continue. As a result the 'risk premium' in housing is very low, so that the expected rate of return does not need to be as much greater than the cost of borrowing (assuming the funds to be borrowed) as in other more risky investments. For these reasons it is argued that of all types of investment housing must surely be most influenced by interest rates. But precisely because housing is so necessary, and because there is never enough of it, demand is very inelastic (that is, unaffected by price changes) so that higher costs can very easily be passed on in higher prices. So housing investment is no more likely to be affected by interest rates than any other sort of investment. In any case, in Zambia as in many parts of Africa, most modern sector housing is provided by employers or by public authorities, so that interest rates are of minor (if any) importance.

One final point: interest rates in Zambia hardly varied at all in the period 1964–74. Investment did vary. Interest rates are therefore of no value in explaining investment changes in Zambia for that period of ten years.

11 THE AVAILABILITY OF FINANCE

In discussing the influence of current income and current changes in income it was pointed out that they both had an influence on retained profits and therefore on investment. More generally, the *availability* of finance for investment has some influence on investment, certainly a much greater influence than the *cost* of finance.

The other main source of finance for investment is bank credit. The availability of bank credit will be explained in the chapter on money and banking. Suppose for the moment that, for whatever reason, banks have money to lend. Does this make it more likely that investment will take place? Rephrasing the question: in what circumstances does a shortage of bank credit hold back investment?

Firstly, many investors do not have access to bank credit – small farmers, small urban businessmen, poor urban people building their own houses, etc. Secondly, few investments are financed wholly out of bank credit; bank credit tends to be available for working capital, with fixed investment financed by other means. Thirdly, foreign investors may have access to alternative, foreign credit.[25] Fourthly. availability of bank credit does not of itself create profitable investment opportunities, it merely makes it more possible to pursue them. There are circumstances in which availability of credit is associated with low interest rates, but this makes little difference if interest rates do not influence investment very much.

The circumstances in which increased availability of credit affects investment are these: an unsatisfied demand for credit, from people to whom the banks will lend, for the sort of investment normally financed by banks such as building up stocks and working capital, or improvements with a quick pay-off period. For example, the building up of stocks in large-scale retail and wholesale trading, improvements to large-scale commercial farms which lead to rapid increases in output, are the sort of investments most likely to be held up by lack of credit.

Putting it another way, bank lending in Africa developed in order to finance international trade. The banks were (and still are in Zambia) foreign-owned and lent to the foreign-owned trading concerns that handled the import–export trade. To a very considerable extent bank credit is still used in Zambia to finance imports (it is seldom needed in the export trade, at least at the high copper prices of the last ten years) so that changes in the aggregate of bank lending have more impact on imports than anything else. Secondly, bank lending makes possible the greater *use* of existing investments, by providing working capital for stocks and work-in-progress. To the extent that imports and working capital are used to increase stocks then bank credit is used for investment. Thirdly, only to a minor extent is bank credit used for fixed capital formation.

The unwillingness of Zambian banks to lend for longer term investment[26] has led to various attempts to provide long-term finance through government-sponsored institutions. The earliest was the Land Bank, which later switched to mainly short-term lending under its new name, Credit Organisation of Zambia, and was wound up in 1970 with an enormous amount of bad debts.

Indeco began as a sort of development bank, that is, an institution for providing development (or long-term) finance; this function was gradually superseded by its role as a government holding company. It was then used to buy up shares in existing foreign businesses and to go into partnership with new foreign businesses. Indeco's funds have partly been provided directly by government, and partly from retained profits; it also borrows from the banks. The level of Indeco's retained profits is less a function of current demand than those of other private sector businesses because parastatal firms are more subject to price control over their products.

Other institutions trying to fill the need for long-term finance are the Development Bank which was started in 1974, the building society which lends for house purchase, the state insurance company and the Zambia National Provident Fund. All three depend mainly on the current level of income for funds, and the building society depends also on how its interest rates paid to savers compare with alternatives, mainly bank savings accounts. The other major financial institution, the Post Office Savings Bank, invests entirely in government debt – in recent years it has attracted very small amounts of savings anyway.

It is important that new ways of providing investment finance be made available, since (in a market economy) it would be a waste if investment were held up for lack of finance. But the main thrust of the argument in this chapter has been that other constraints are usually more important. The main exceptions are that the government investment programme may be held up for lack of funds, and that investment generally may be held up for lack of foreign exchange. Export earnings, and the availability of aid and other types of foreign finance for government, may therefore be important determinants of investment.

12 CONCLUSION

This long chapter has reached very few conclusions. Zambia's investors vary so much in their motives, their access to information about investment opportunities, their access to technical know-how and their access to different types of finance that a general theory of investment behaviour is not likely to be found. The only common thread running through the discussion has been that the current level of income affects both investment opportunities and investment funds for *most* types of investor. Even then one must make major exceptions. Most agricultural investment depends heavily on government-controlled prices; new foreign investment depends heavily on government action of several sorts; investment in copper mining, the country's biggest industry by far, depends on expectations about the externally determined copper price.

In short, it would be odd if more than a tenuous relationship between income, or changes in income, and investment could be traced. Unfortunately, official investment statistics are available for sectors of the economy rather than for the categories of investor used in this chapter, so that much research remains to be done on their usefulness.

Appendix: capital stock adjustment and accelerator principles

The factor most likely to increase the return on investment is high and rising aggregate demand. This enables lorries to earn money for more hours per day and factories to run nearer capacity, so that returns on investment increase. Unfortunately there is no obvious way of guessing what businessmen's expectations are. It has been suggested that the current level of income is a good guide. If income is high, profits will be high giving both an incentive to invest and some of the means of investing, since retained profits are an important source of investment funds. If income is low the reverse will be true. This hypothesis assumes, however, that businessmen use the present level of income as a guide to future levels of income (and thus demand for their products). It also assumes that businessmen do not have any spare capacity – a situation which is quite likely at high levels of income, but not necessarily true.

A more elaborate hypothesis, taking into account the possible existence of spare capacity, is that investment varies positively with income in the previous period (there being a time-lag as investors react to income levels) and negatively with the existing capital stock. This is called the 'capital stock adjustment principle' and can be expressed thus

$$I_t = aY_{(t-1)} - bK_t$$

where I is investment, Y is income, K is the capital stock, a and b are positive constants, and the subscripts t, $t-1$ refer to time periods.[27]

A special case of the capital stock adjustment principle is where $b=1$. Then

$$I_t = aY_{(t-1)} - K_t$$

and $$I_{(t-1)} = aY_{(t-2)} - K_{(t-1)}$$

Subtracting the second equation from the first gives

$$I_t - I_{(t-1)} = a(Y_{(t-1)} - Y_{(t-2)}) - (K_t - K_{(t-1)})$$

But $$K_t - K_{(t-1)} = I_{(t-1)},$$

since the change in the stock of capital *is* investment. So

$$I_t = a(Y_{(t-1)} - Y_{(t-2)})$$

Investment, according to this hypothesis, is determined by the rate of change of income in the previous period. This theory is known as the 'accelerator principle' since a rising income would generate rising investment which, through the multiplier, would generate yet higher income.

Because businessmen's expectations are determined by other things besides current income and the existing capital stock, neither theory is particularly useful in explaining investment. In Zambia, where an increasing amount even of manufacturing and other commercial investment is being undertaken as a result of government initiative and where foreign investors are predominant, these theories could at best only explain part of investment. Nevertheless, since businessmen are no better at foreseeing the future than economic theorists, it *is* quite useful to remember that high and rising income is quite likely to generate a high and rising desire to invest.[28]

NOTES

[1] For example, in 1969 the fall in stocks nationally of K40 mn was more than accounted for by a fall in stocks of copper of K69 mn which was in turn due to the smelting, refining and exporting of accumulated copper concentrates with only minor effects on domestic employment and income.

[2] See Appendix for investment and changes in income; see Section 10 for investment and the rate of interest.

[3] 'New' here means an investor new to the country, i.e. making a first investment in Zambia.

[4] Y. Aharoni, *The Foreign Investment Decision Process*, Harvard University Press, 1966, p. 84, referring to a particular foreign investment decision by an American firm.

[5] Or even the total exclusion of competing imports, in the extreme case.

[6] Other ways of getting money out are through licensing agreements, management agreements, interest on loans from the parent company, all of which count as 'costs' and so reduce profits in Africa and increase profits in the country of origin. Transfer pricing can also occur through the underpricing of exports to an associated company. For some gross examples of both, see UNCTAD, *Major Issues arising from the Transfer of Technology: a case study of Ethiopia*, UN, 1974, pp. 57–9.

[7] This is further discussed in Chapter 11, Section 8. Government acquisition of 51% ownership in the Zambian copper mines in 1970 did not increase government control

at all in fact, control on all matters of substance being retained by the minority shareholders by means of the management and other agreements reached in 1969.

[8] ZIMCO, Chairman's statement for 1970/71.

[9] See A. Young, *Industrial Diversification in Zambia*, Praeger, 1973, pp. 198–204, for a more extended discussion of this point in the Zambian context.

[10] See Peter Kilby, *Industrialisation in an Open Economy: Nigeria 1945–66*, Cambridge University Press, 1969, Chapter 3, especially Table 16, p. 54.

[11] See, for example, C. V. Vaitsos, 'Bargaining and the distribution of returns in the purchase of technology by developing countries', *Bulletin of the Institute of Development Studies*, Vol. 3, No. 1, 1970. Vaitsos found 85% of contracts, in a sample of foreign-owned Colombian firms, specifically prohibited exports.

[12] Thus by 1971 Zambia was already producing more than 70 of the 75 or so products which had been imported from Rhodesia to a value of K200,000 or more in 1964.

[13] Kilby, op. cit., p. 75. As Kilby's book was about industrialization he omitted investment in raw materials – this is discussed separately in Section 6 below.

[14] For a successful example see Kilby, op. cit., pp. 76–7; for an unsuccessful example see C. Cooper and R. Kaplinsky, *Secondhand Equipment in a Developing Country: jute processing in Kenya*, ILO, 1973, which also has a discussion of the general principles underlying the use of second-hand equipment in developing countries.

[15] UNCTAD, op. cit., pp. 48–9.

[16] One should also note here that a profitable investment opportunity is not sufficient to induce investment by *domestic* investors, even though they may regard the situation as less risky and are not usually so concerned to expatriate their profits. Domestic investors suffer rather from not having the know-how, especially if they must compete with imports.

[17] See M. Bostock and C. Harvey (eds.), *Economic Independence and Zambian Copper*, Praeger, 1972, Chapter 7.

[18] Bostock and Harvey (eds.), op. cit., pp. 56–61 (chapter by A. Drysdall) and pp. 42–6 (chapter by P. Slinn).

[19] See, for example, the section called 'Bargaining powers' in J. Potter's essay 'The 51% nationalisation of the Zambian copper mines', in M. Faber and J. Potter, *Towards Economic Independence*, Cambridge University Press, 1971, pp. 103–8.

[20] Some never even start producing. One company whose plant was established in Ethiopia in 1968 was still not operating four years later (UNCTAD, op. cit., p. 49).

[21] See R. E. Baldwin, *Economic Development and Export Growth*, University of California Press, 1966, pp. 146–59.

[22] See C. S. Lombard and A. H. C. Tweedie, *Agriculture in Zambia since Independence*, NECZAM 1972, especially p. 10.

[23] This statement ignores the fact that the interest rate paid on borrowing is always *higher* than can be obtained on putting savings on deposit in a financial institution. An investor with cash in hand should therefore use a lower rate of interest in calculating present value than an investor who has to borrow.

[24] 'The' rate of interest does not exist, as there are many rates of interest. It is arguable though that any particular investor can reasonably use one rate, or at most the weighted average of his borrowing rates and the rate he could otherwise get on his own funds.

[25] But foreign investors frequently *prefer* to use local borrowing rather than committing their own money; the availability of local credit may therefore encourage some types of foreign investment.

[26] The reasons for their unwillingness are discussed in the chapters on money and banking.

[27] See R. C. O. Matthews, *The Trade Cycle*, Cambridge University Press, 1959, Chapter 3.

[28] The accelerator theory has received far too much attention from economic theorists

because it leads to an attractively neat theory of investment (or business) cycles; *see* Matthews, op. cit., especially Chapter 2. Matthews' book is in fact a very useful review of a lot of macroeconomic theory even if business cycle theory is of relatively little importance in Africa.

8 *Money*

1 DEFINITION

The definition of money is very simple: it is anything that people will accept as money. In the modern world there are only two sorts of money: bank notes and coin on the one hand, bank deposits on the other. These modern forms of money have great advantages over some of the items that have been used for money in the past – for example cowrie shells, copper rings, cows, cigarettes – because modern forms of money are more easily divisible, more easily stored and more precisely comparable. Money needs to be used as a medium of exchange, as a store of value and as a unit of account or measurement.

No type of money is perfect. Although bank notes and coin are acceptable everywhere in Zambia, they are quite expensive for the banks to shift around the country and notes can be burnt or eaten by ants. Notes and coin are also inconvenient for very large payments. Bank deposits are safer but much less convenient. Not everyone will accept a cheque in payment, banks are often not open when cash (in the form of notes and coin) is needed and in some parts of Zambia there are very few banks. As a result, those who have bank accounts try and keep a convenient amount of notes and coin in their pockets with the remainder of their money safely in a bank account.

If bank cheques are not always acceptable, for example by shops, then it might seem that bank deposits do not fit the definition of money – that it be widely acceptable as money. The point is that the person to whom a cheque is offered in payment is not always sure that the payer has enough money on his bank account to 'honour' (or pay) the cheque. If the cheque has a bank guarantee on it or if the payee (the person receiving the cheque) *knows* that there is enough money to pay the cheque, then there is no reason why he should not accept it. The point is, therefore, that even though cheques are not money, bank deposits are. In general, large payments, payments involving companies and governments tend to be by cheque; small payments, especially those between individuals, tend to be by notes and coins.

One minor problem remains: there are two sorts of bank deposit. *Demand* deposits can be withdrawn 'on demand' and can be used for payments by cheque. Holdings of demand deposits are often called 'current accounts'. Normally no interest is paid on current accounts. It is also possible to deposit money in banks on *time* or *savings* accounts, which earn interest. These deposits cannot be used for making payments, nor can they be converted into cash immediately – normally withdrawals of cash can only be made of a limited sum or after a specified period of time. Strictly speaking, therefore, time and savings deposits are not money.

Nevertheless, it is sometimes useful to count time and savings deposits as money because *in practice* it is so easy to transfer them to a demand deposit account. Various other types of 'near money', that is forms of investment that can quickly and easily be converted into money, can be included in calculations of the total money supply if it seems helpful to do so. For most of this chapter the definition used will be that the money supply equals currency outside the banks plus demand deposits at banks.[1]

2 THE CREATION OF MONEY

The absolutely vital point about bank deposits as money is that banks can create more of them. Bank deposits are thus quite different from other types of money like cows, copper rings and cowrie shells. Bank deposits are just figures on a sheet of paper, with no intrinsic value, and more of them can be created simply by the process of granting credit. Few people understand how this can happen, so it is necessary to explain in considerable detail.

Suppose a man wishes to buy a new car for which he has no money. Suppose also that he is lucky enough to be able to get credit from his bank – Bank B. He then writes a cheque even though he has no money on his bank account. He gives the cheque to the car dealer, who accepts it in payment for the car because he knows that the buyer's bank will honour it. The car dealer pays the cheque into *his* account at Bank S, where his account rises by the amount of the cheque.

Bank S then sends the cheque to Bank B for payment, since Bank B owes Bank S the amount of the cheque. Payment is made between banks by means of their accounts at the *central* bank. Commercial banks all have accounts at the central bank, and settle debts between themselves by authorizing transfers from one account to another. Bank B then debits the car buyer's account, creating an overdraft,[2] since he has nothing on his account.

If the buyer and the seller both happen to have accounts at the same bank, then the process is much simpler: the bank debits the car buyer's account, creating an overdraft (or negative balance) and credits the car dealer's account. That is all.

From the point of view of the money supply, the result is the same. Bank deposits have gone up by the amount of the cheque, so the money supply has increased by that amount. Bank advances to the public have also increased; and if the two people banked at different banks, there has been a transfer from one commercial bank balance at the central bank to another. The creation of new money is at the same time the creation of new spending power. A new car has been bought out of borrowing, not out of income; and the new money created, namely the addition to the car dealer's bank account, can in turn be spent.

In practice a bank does not go round to other banks each time a cheque drawn on another bank is paid in to the credit of one of its customers. What happens is that each bank collects together all the cheques paid into the accounts of its customers, and sorts out those drawn on other banks; at the end of the day it takes them to some agreed place used as a 'clearing house' and exchanges them with the other banks for cheques paid in by *their* customers, drawn on itself. Any differences in the totals (which are usually small in relation to the total sums on the cheques) are settled by an adjustment of the banks' accounts at the central bank.[3]

Coming back to the central point once again, however, if a bank grants an overdraft to a customer then the money supply goes up. The commercial banking system as a whole can create money simply by giving credit, which results in a rise in overdrafts (bank lending to the public) and a rise in deposits. The people who are granted credit use it by writing cheques and handing them over to people from whom they are buying goods; these sellers then deposit the cheques in *their* bank accounts, thus causing a rise in deposits. This new money can of course be spent.

Bank money is simply a series of entries in bank ledgers showing how much money has been deposited at the banks by each of their customers. It is unique in that it can be created by the banks themselves.

The banking sector is therefore not just another sector of the economy, like the manufacturing sector or the transport sector. It has this unique property, that bank deposits are accepted as money. Because banks can create new bank deposits simply by granting credit, they can create money. They cannot, however, create new money in unlimited amounts. The various factors which limit the creation of new money by banks are explained below.

3 LIMITS ON THE CREATION OF NEW BANK DEPOSITS

Although, as already described, commercial banks can create money by lending to their customers, they are constrained by the fact that customers *may* want to have some of their funds in the form of currency,[4] rather than keeping it all on deposit in banks. For example, the car dealer, who pays into his bank a cheque received from selling a new car, may draw out some of this new money in notes and coin in order to pay his employees or to spend on his own needs. Some of the new money will be spent in paying for new cars ordered from the manufacturer, or in paying such things as his electricity bill. Such payments, being made by cheque, merely result in transfers from one bank deposit to another, so that the money remains as bank deposits.

In general, as the level of bank deposits rises, so does the amount of money held by the public in the form of notes and coin. Even when the demand for notes and coin is not rising, banks must keep some notes and coin available for their customers. But banks know, from long experience, that they do *not* need to keep 100% of demand deposits available in notes and coin, since it is very unlikely that all their customers will want to draw out all their money at once. So banks try and keep a proportion of demand deposits, which they are liable to repay to their customers on demand, in the form of 'cash' (notes and coin) and in the form of their accounts at the central bank. Just as people can convert their bank deposits on current account into notes and coin, so commercial banks can draw on *their* bank accounts at the central bank for more notes and coin. If the *central* bank needs more notes, to supply the demands of its commercial bank customers, it simply orders more from the printers (and more coins from the coin manufacturers or Mint).[5]

Over the years, banks discovered how much cash they needed to keep handy in order to meet withdrawals by customers. In England, where banking first developed in its modern form, it became customary to regard 8% as a safe 'cash ratio'. The cash ratio is the proportion of demand deposits held by banks in the form of notes and coin and money deposited at the central bank. In Zambia, when the Bank of Zambia was created soon after Independence, it was made compulsory for commercial banks to hold 8% of their demand deposits in the form of bank deposits at the Bank of Zambia.[6]

Now the process of money creation by banks, as described in the previous section, did *not* result in the creation of any new 'bankers' cash', that is, commercial bank deposits at the central bank. There was a *transfer* from the account of Bank B (the car buyer's bank) to the account of Bank S (the car seller's bank), but no change in the total of bankers' cash.[7] If both the car buyer and the car dealer banked at the same bank, there was similarly *no* increase in commercial bank deposits at the central bank. On the contrary the granting of credit and the creation of additional bank deposits is likely to lead to an increase in the public's holdings of notes and coin. So as advances increase the banks are likely to have to draw down their balances at the central bank in order to supply their customers with more notes and coin.

As a result, banks will only be able to grant more credit and create more money when they have spare cash. This was the position in Zambia in the years immediately after Independence. In 1965, bankers' balances at the Bank of Zambia averaged about K8 mn. In addition, the commercial banks had, at their head offices in London, balances which averaged nearly as much again, K7·8 mn. The balances required to be held at the Bank of Zambia, namely 8% of demand deposits and 3% of time and savings deposits, averaged about K5 mn. So the banks had about 60% more cash at the Bank of Zambia than they needed in order to satisfy reserve requirements; and because they were then branches of British international banks, they had in London an additional source of cash, which was itself more than one and a half times the amount required by cash ratios.[8]

In conditions like these, banks can create new credit and new money without worrying about their cash ratios. It is nevertheless important to ask why the commercial banks had so much spare cash. In general, banks prefer to invest money and earn interest on it, rather than leave it on an account at the central bank where it earns nothing. In fact the most profitable way of using money deposited with the banks is for them to lend it to customers.

Commercial banks do not, however, lend money if they do not expect to be repaid. So even when they have cash in excess of their reserve requirements they may not expand their lending. *Either* there may be a shortage of creditworthy customers, *or* their normal borrowers may be unwilling to borrow because of poor economic conditions. In short, banks will only expand their lending if people whom the banks regard as creditworthy are demanding credit and if the banks' reserve position makes additional lending possible. In general an expanding economy creates a rising demand for credit as firms require more working capital to finance increased output; in a stagnant or declining economy firms do not want to borrow and banks do not want to lend. An expanding economy also creates profit opportunities, and increases the profits of existing activities. So an expanding economy not only increases the demand for credit but makes that demand more likely to be successful with the banks. In contrast, even very respectable businesses may not succeed in getting more credit at a time of falling demand and falling profits.

After Independence in Zambia there was very rapid economic growth and a rapidly growing demand for bank credit. Because the commercial banks were very liquid they were able to supply this demand. In the first half of 1968, lending to the private sector had risen from an average of K35 mn in 1965 to an average of K107 mn, and from 43% to 74% of total deposits. At the same time bank balances at the Bank of Zambia were barely enough by 1968 to meet cash reserve requirements, while the banks were overdrawn (i.e. net borrowers) on their overseas head office accounts.[9]

The question remains as to whether the Zambian commercial banks could have continued to borrow from their head offices. This question is a bit hypothetical since in April 1968 the Zambian government introduced direct controls over bank lending as part of the first set of economic reforms. There is strong reason to believe, however, that bank credit would have been reduced in 1968 even without direct controls.

Basically, the international banks do not like lending except for very short periods, to their branches and subsidiaries in particular countries. They did not like doing so even in the 1950s when the colonial system in Africa was still intact and there was thus little or no risk of nationalization, expropriation or currency devaluation. All of these risks have now increased, so that it seems likely, and this likelihood is supported by the evidence, that international banks are not likely to lend to their overseas branches or affiliates[10] for more than short periods.

It seems therefore as though the level of commercial bank deposits at the central bank, and the ratio that this must be to total deposits, are in fact of key importance in determining the banks' ability to expand the money supply only if overseas cash is not freely available. If the banks have easy access to cash overseas, which they can quickly add to their local cash balances, then, as has been explained, they can expand credit and the money supply if there is a demand for credit from suitable borrowers. If, on the other hand, the commercial banks have no spare cash at overseas head offices, or are overdrawn, then the local cash position becomes the key factor in controlling monetary expansion.[11] The fact that bank head offices will lend to overseas affiliates for short periods may prevent the local cash ratio from having an immediate restraining effect; but the unwillingness of head offices to lend for long periods means that shortage of 'local' bankers' cash will eventually force the banks to reduce their lending and therefore growth in the money supply.

Banks also hold 'liquid assets' consisting mainly of Treasury Bills and government stock.[12] These assets are less profitable to commercial banks than lending to their customers, but can be sold for cash. Any commercial bank that is short of bankers' cash can therefore sell some liquid assets *provided that* it has some liquid assets to spare and can find a buyer. The point is that commercial banks have to maintain a certain ratio of liquid assets to deposits, a 'liquidity ratio' as well as a cash ratio.

In order to expand lending, therefore, commercial banks need to have not only spare bankers' cash, but spare liquid assets as well. As deposits rise, the required amount of liquid assets (28% of deposits in Zambia at present) also rises. If the banks do not have any liquid assets to spare, some of their spare cash must be used to buy more.

In practice, the Zambian commercial banks always try and keep a substantial amount of liquid assets in excess of the required liquidity ratio – they aim at having roughly 10% to spare, giving a minimum liquidity ratio of 38% rather than 28%. If their liquidity ratios fall below 38% they try to push them up again, even though there is no legal necessity. This spare margin of liquid assets protects the banks from having to make very abrupt changes in their lending policy. As will be explained in the next section, bank liquidity is subject to very sudden changes in Zambia, mainly because of external economic forces. It would be very damaging to longer-term economic development if the commercial banks had to make very sudden changes in lending policy in response to sudden changes in the copper price, for example.

The central bank, as agent of the government, decides on the cash ratio and the liquidity ratio. These ratios have only once been changed in the ten years since Independence, however, so it is essential to know what determines the level of bankers' cash and bank holdings of liquid assets. Since banks use bankers' cash to buy liquid assets from the government,[13] the really basic need is to know what determines the level of bankers' cash. Commercial banks' ability to create new money is ultimately limited by this, in the absence of any change in the cash ratio.

4 CHANGES IN BANKERS' CASH

In theory it is possible for the central bank to exercise complete control over 'bankers' cash' (commercial bank balances at the central bank) and thus over commercial banks' ability to expand the money supply. In practice, events outside the control of the central bank cause changes in bankers' cash and the central bank is left with the urgent task of trying to ensure that the monetary consequences are not too damaging to the economy.

There are three *main* ways in which bankers' cash can alter: deficits or surpluses on the balance of international payments, deficits or surpluses on the government budget, purchases or sales of government debt by the central bank. Firstly, it is essential to understand just how these three events affect bankers' cash; then it should be possible to understand just how the monetary system affects the economy and how the central bank tries to exercise control.

(*a*) *Changes in the Balance of Payments*

Consider an increase in the price of copper, or an increase in the volume of copper exports, or a fall in the volume of imports, or the purchase of a Zambian firm by a foreign investor. All of these events can occur quite suddenly; all of them cause a sudden increase in Zambia's holdings of foreign exchange (over what they would otherwise have been). The mechanism is essentially the same in all the examples so consider for simplicity the purchase of a Zambian firm by a foreign investor, since that is a purely financial transaction without income multiplier effects.

The foreign investor has foreign exchange, for example US dollars. The owner of the Zambian firm wants Kwacha. The buyer tells his bank in America to transfer dollars to the American branch of (say) Barclays Bank, for the credit of the owner of the Zambian firm. The dollars are then sold to the Bank of Zambia (since all foreign exchange owned by

Zambians must be sold to the central bank). Barclays' account with the Bank of Zambia is then credited with the equivalent Kwacha, and the seller's account at Barclays is credited with the same amount. As a result of these transactions, therefore, the money supply (in the form of bank deposits) has gone up, the foreign exchange reserves have gone up and, most importantly from the monetary point of view, bankers' balances at the Bank of Zambia have also gone up.

Now if the money is used to buy imports, or otherwise transferred back into foreign exchange and out of Zambia, then a reverse process takes place. The Zambian uses his Kwacha to buy foreign exchange. Barclays buys the dollars for him, debits his account and debits Barclays' account at the Bank of Zambia to pay for the dollars. The foreign exchange reserves, the money supply and bankers' cash all go down. So clearly the monetary impact of foreign exchange transactions occurs only when there is a *net* change. A rise in exports offset by a rise in imports has no direct monetary impact, since bankers' cash is not affected.[14] Similarly a rise in imports financed by the receipt of a foreign loan (or aid, for example) has no direct impact on bankers' cash.

(b) Changes in the Government's Budget Deficit

Consider a decision by the government to spend an extra K1 mn, without any offsetting extra taxation. The ministry involved writes a cheque for K1 mn on its account at the Bank of Zambia. This cheque is given to a member of the public, say a building contractor who has built a school. He pays it into his account at a commercial bank. The bank pays it into *its* account at the Bank of Zambia. The ministry has no money, so the Bank of Zambia has to 'lend' the government K1 mn in order to be able to debit the cheque to the ministry's account. The government now 'owes' K1 mn to the Bank of Zambia. But the government owns 100% of the Bank of Zambia, so the 'debt' is just a paper transaction creating no real obligation. It is of no significance that the government owes money to itself. Bankers' cash has been created simply by writing figures in a ledger, as a result of the unfinanced budget spending.

As in the case of an export surplus, if the government spending is financed by taxation or by borrowing from the general public, the direct monetary effect does not occur. If, for example, the government spends K1 mn on nationalizing a private sector firm and the owners use the money to buy government stocks or development bonds, there is no change in bankers' cash.

In a modern economy governments can always 'finance' their spending even though they do not increase taxation and even if nobody wants to lend them money, since central banks can simply create money. This process not only creates additional *demand* and the income multiplier effects that follow, but it also creates additional bankers' cash and the possibility of an expansion in the money supply as well. Modern governments do not, therefore, have to use the printing press in order to spend money they do not have; they simply 'borrow' from the central bank, an even simpler process than printing notes and the purest form of money creation.

(c) Central Bank Purchases and Sales of Government Debt

As part of its financing, the government sells debt to the general public. Most of this government debt is sold to financial institutions. For example, the Zambia National Provident Fund buys government debt so that most wage-earners are indirectly lending money to the government. Other buyers of government debt include the commercial banks, the state building society and the state insurance company. Government debt is of two main forms: Local Registered Stock and Treasury Bills.[15] Before Independence stock was also issued in London; since Independence the government has continued to borrow abroad, but not by issuing stock to be bought in foreign markets.

If the central bank *does* buy some government debt from a financial institution then new bankers' cash is created. The central bank pays with a cheque drawn on itself. The seller pays the cheque into his bank account at a commercial bank. The commercial bank pays the cheque into *its* account at the central bank. As a result, therefore, the money supply and bankers' cash have risen.

Exactly the same process occurs when a government loan matures. That is, when the due date for repayment arrives, the central bank pays out cash on behalf of the government in exactly the way described above, and with the same result. For this reason, the central bank normally hopes that it will be able to sell a new stock to replace the old maturing one so that no new bankers' cash is created. The process of selling new loans to replace old maturing ones is sometimes known as 'funding'.

Clearly, the reverse process takes place when the central bank *sells* government debt. Payment is made by cheque, which is given to the central bank. The cheque is paid into the government's account, thus reducing a deficit or adding to a surplus. The commercial bank on which the cheque is drawn has its account at the central bank debited, and in turn debits the customer's account. Bankers' cash and the money supply go down by the amount of the cheque.

If the central bank buys government debt from a commercial bank the process is even simpler. The central bank pays with a cheque drawn on itself which the commercial bank credits to its account at the central bank. Bankers' cash increases by the amount of the cheque. Alternatively, the central bank may lend directly to the commercial bank, with the same effect on bankers' cash.[16]

The process of buying and selling government debt by the central bank has traditionally been known in industrialized countries (more precisely, in the textbooks written for students in industrialized countries) as 'open-market operations'. This is because the central bank in an industrialized country operates through a well-established stock exchange, with an active market in government debt. Even in such a market, the central bank cannot necessarily buy or sell as much government debt as it would like, certainly not without causing large movements in the prices of government stocks, and thus of course in interest rates.

In an underdeveloped country, with an underdeveloped market in government debt, central bank buying and selling is even more constrained. Basically, the central bank reacts to *demand* for government stock by making stock available when required. There is a fairly steady demand from institutions that invest other people's savings such as the National Savings and Credit Bank of Zambia (formerly the Post Office Savings Bank) and the Zambia National Provident Fund. When these institutions require cash and wish to sell stock, the central bank acts as residual buyer in the absence of other buyers. If the central bank did *not* act as residual buyer, the financial institution might have real difficulty in meeting its obligations, which would be to nobody's advantage. Furthermore, it would be impossible to sell government debt in future if it was not 'marketable' in this sense.

Where the commercial banks are concerned, the central bank sells government debt on demand. If the commercial banks want to sell, and cannot find private sector buyers (as is very likely), then the central bank will buy. But because the central bank is the residual buyer, it can decide the price paid. If the central bank wants the commercial banks to reduce their lending to customers, then it can inflict *losses* on the commercial banks by paying a low price for their liquid assets. Alternatively the central bank can offer to lend to the commercial banks at such a high rate of interest that they prefer to reduce their lending to customers in order to repay the central bank loan. These possibilities, of inflicting financial penalties on the commercial banks, greatly add to the central bank's ability to control bank lending and the money supply, *but only when* the commercial banks have no spare cash.

5 THE MULTIPLIER EFFECTS OF A CHANGE IN BANKERS' CASH

The practical importance of an increase in bankers' cash, whatever the reason for it, is that it allows a *multiple* increase in the money supply.

Suppose that demand deposits are K200 mn and that commercial bank deposits at the central bank are K24 mn; and suppose that the required ratio is 12% (as at present in Zambia) so that the banks have no spare cash. Ignore time and savings deposits for the moment – they complicate the analysis, but do not really alter it.

Now suppose the government spends K1 mn, for which it has no tax revenue, and which it is unable to borrow. The government has to 'borrow' from the central bank, that is, the central bank credits the government account with K1 mn. The money supply rises by K1 mn and so does bankers' cash. Demand deposits are now K201 mn, bankers' cash is K25 mn. The commercial banks only need K24·12 mn in cash (12% of K201 mn), so they have spare cash.

If there is a demand for new credit, which is quite likely since additional unfinanced spending by the government is expansionary and has *income* multiplier effects, then the money supply can expand. The question is by how much.

As bank advances and bank deposits expand, the public's demand for notes and coin will rise. This has to be met out of bankers' cash. So the additional K1 mn in bankers' cash is needed for two purposes: to pay for the rise in notes and coin held by the public (and by the commercial banks as till money, but this is very small) and to meet the 12% cash ratio requirement of the rise in demand deposits. Recently, notes and coin in circulation in Zambia have been about 50% of demand deposits. So if demand deposits were to rise by the maximum amount possible, writing D for demand deposits and ΔD for the increment, then 50% of ΔD plus 12% of ΔD must equal K1 mn.

This gives 62% of $\Delta D = \text{K}1\text{ mn}$

or $\Delta D = \text{K}1{\cdot}6\text{ mn}$ (approximately).

The total change in the money supply equals the change in deposits, K1·6 mn, plus the change in note circulation, K0·8 mn; so the money supply rises by K2·4 mn approximately if the banks lend as much as the increase in bankers' cash makes possible. In other words the money supply can expand by nearly 2½ times the original expansion of bankers' cash, assuming that the banks take maximum advantage of the situation – and assuming that nothing else occurs in the meantime to affect the level of bankers' cash.[17]

Generalizing this, if

c = bankers' cash ratio
c' = ratio of public's cash to public's bank deposits
ΔB = change in bankers' cash
ΔD = maximum change in demand deposits
ΔM = change in the total money supply

then
$$c\,\Delta D + c'\,\Delta D = \Delta B$$
or
$$\Delta D = \Delta B/(c+c') \qquad (1)$$

The total change in the money supply is equal to the change in demand deposits *plus* the change in the public's note holdings, so

$$\Delta M = \Delta D + c'\,\Delta D = \Delta D(1+c')$$
$$= \Delta B(1+c')/(c+c') \qquad (2)$$

These two formulae, (1) and (2), are general in the sense that they hold for a decrease in bankers' cash as well as for an increase. But of course the commercial banks would only be forced to reduce their lending (and thus the money supply) by a reduction in their cash if they had no spare cash in the first place. If bankers' cash *is* reduced below the amount required by the cash ratio, then formula (1) shows the *minimum* by which demand deposits must be reduced in order to restore the cash ratio. When bankers' cash is increased, in a situation where the banks have no spare cash, formula (1) shows the *maximum* by which demand deposits can increase – whether it actually occurs or not depends on the reaction of the banks and their customers. In *both* cases, of a reduction or an increase in bankers' cash, it clearly makes no difference if the banks already have spare cash; the change merely alters the *amount* of spare cash.

However, the cause of a change in bankers' cash makes a difference. An unfinanced budget deficit stimulates demand without any compensating reduction in demand through taxation, so that one would expect (other things being equal) that bank lending would also increase in response to the increase in demand and its multiplier effects. In contrast, a purely monetary transaction, such as the purchase (in the 'market') of government debt by the central bank, does not of itself stimulate demand; lending will only increase in this situation if there was already an unsatisfied demand for credit which the banks were unable to meet because of a shortage of cash.

If, in the situation already described, the commercial banks had no spare *liquidity*, that is, their liquidity ratio was at the legal minimum, then some of the new bankers' cash would be needed to buy additional liquid assets. This would reduce the possible expansionary effect of an increase in bankers' cash. In the Zambian case, where the banks try to keep spare liquid assets (that is, in excess of the minimum required by the legal liquidity ratio) an expansion of deposits could reduce their liquidity ratio below their 'target'. The banks would then expand their lending (and the money supply) by less than would otherwise be the case.

If cash ratio is 12% and the 'target' liquidity ratio is 38%, then 26% of ΔD would have to be applied to buying new liquid assets if the banks had no spare liquid assets and adhered strictly to their target. This also assumes that the commercial banks are unable to buy liquid assets from anyone except the central bank. In other words, there is a ceteris paribus assumption about the demand for liquid assets from other financial institutions. If the banks could buy, say, Treasury Bills from the Provident Fund, then the latter would deposit the cheque with a bank and bankers' cash would not be affected. On the figures quoted above, deposits could only rise by K1·1 mn rather than the K1·6 mn derived earlier when it was assumed that no cash was needed for buying liquid assets. Similarly the money supply would rise by only about K1·7 mn[18] rather than K2·4 mn. So a tight liquidity situation added to a tight cash situation greatly reduces the expansionary effect of an increase in bankers' cash.

6 FOREIGN TRADE AND BANK LENDING

The formulae derived in the previous section take no account of the extreme 'openness' of most African economies, that is, the importance of foreign trade.

Suppose bankers' cash increases because of a budget deficit and that bank lending also increases – because of the stimulus to demand and the existence of additional bank liquidity. Because of the high propensity to import, bankers' cash will be *reduced* by paying for the additional imports. Indeed, a great deal of bank lending is actually used to finance imports. Banking was originally developed in Africa in order to finance foreign trade and only gradually extended to other sectors. Even where banks lend to domestic producers, the money is used indirectly to finance imports because so many inputs into, say, industry and agriculture are imported.[19]

The propensity to import is therefore a sort of leakage from bankers' cash, reducing the multiplier effects of an increase. Similarly, taxation acts as another leakage. As the economy expands, tax receipts increase thus reducing the budget deficit or increasing the surplus. If the improved budget position is used to reduce the amount of government 'borrowing' from the central bank, that is, to reduce the amount of pure money creation caused by an unfinanced budget deficit, then bankers' cash is reduced and bank liquidity is reduced with it. In most African countries the bulk of taxation comes from foreign trade. Economic expansion leads to high imports, which in turn increases tax receipts.

As an extreme case, consider an increase in the price of copper. When the proceeds are sold to the Bank of Zambia, bankers' cash increases. But 73% of the increase is due to the government in taxation; some of the remainder will be paid out in dividends to foreign shareholders and to Mindeco. Only the Mindeco dividend and retained profits remain within the banking system. There are, of course, time-lags in this process since taxation is not immediately payable and dividends are even further delayed. But the commercial banks are unlikely to expand their lending on the basis of an increase in bankers' cash which they know to be temporary. In short, the economy is protected to a very great extent from the *monetary* effects of fluctuations in export prices. Some effect remains however so that if for some reason the government wishes to prevent a monetary expansion, the excess bank liquidity will have to be neutralized in some way – for example by increasing the statutory cash ratio or by persuading the copper companies to buy government debt rather than leaving their money with the banks. On occasion, the Bank of Zambia has simply required the copper companies to deposit their surplus cash at the Bank of Zambia, in the form of 'Special Deposits'.

The close links between bank lending and imports mean that the government has to co-ordinate monetary management very closely with management of the balance of payments. For this reason the central bank is normally in charge of both.

7 TIME AND SAVINGS DEPOSITS

If a bank customer converts his spare cash from a demand deposit to a time deposit it presumably means that he is not planning to spend that money in the short term. It releases a small amount of bankers' cash since the official Zambian requirement is that 8% of time (and savings) deposits must be kept in bankers' cash, compared with 12% of demand deposits.[20]

Time and savings deposits have tended to grow faster in Zambia than demand deposits; in 1965 time and savings deposits together were roughly half demand deposits, whereas by 1973 they were roughly equal. Most of the growth has been in time deposits which are mainly used by the larger firms; savings deposits are used by individuals.

Suppose that an unfinanced budget deficit of K1 mn, as discussed in Section 5, results in equal increases in demand deposits and in time and savings deposits. Writing demand deposits as Dd and savings deposits Ds, t then the bankers' cash required to meet cash ratios is

$$12\% \text{ of } \Delta Dd + 8\% \text{ of } \Delta Ds, t$$

In addition, currency in circulation will increase by 50% of ΔDd. If Dd and Ds, t are roughly equal, as in 1973, then

$$12\% \text{ of } \Delta Dd + 8\% \text{ of } \Delta Ds, t + 50\% \text{ of } \Delta Dd = \text{K1 mn}$$
$$\text{so } \Delta Dd = \text{K1·43 mn}$$

In total therefore, demand deposits can rise by a maximum of K1·4 mn, currency by K0·7 mn, and time and savings deposits by another K1·4 mn. So the money supply defined as currency and demand deposits only can rise by about twice the original budget deficit; and money supply defined as currency plus both sorts of deposit can rise by about three and a half times the original budget deficit. Both conclusions must be modified, as before, by any leakage through an increase in imports and by the amount of any cash that has to be spent on buying liquid assets from the government.

8 ALTERNATIVE SOURCES OF BANK LIQUIDITY

Commercial banks do not rely entirely on their cash for liquidity. As already discussed, they also invest in Treasury Bills and short-dated government stock. These assets are attractive to commercial banks because they carry some interest but can be converted into cash at short notice and at relatively little risk of loss.[21]

Banks also invest in bills of exchange. Essentially these are ways of lending money in a way that yields a marketable asset. If a bank lends money to customers in the form of an overdraft it cannot sell the overdraft to another bank or to the central bank.[22] A bill of exchange is a promise to pay in the future. The borrower instructs his bank on a piece of paper to pay a debt some months in the future. If the borrower is regarded as creditworthy he can sell the piece of paper or bill of exchange to someone who has spare cash. The bill sells at a 'discount', or less than the amount promised in the future, so that the investor makes a profit equivalent to the interest rate. In this way the borrower gets cash now and banks, for example, acquire a liquid investment on which they earn some income.

Bills of exchange were devised to finance foreign trade and are still used almost exclusively in that field. Thus an importer in Africa wishing to buy something in, say, Germany does not wish to pay for it until it arrives. The German exporter however wants cash when the product leaves his factory. If he is paid by bill of exchange he can sell the bill to a bank and get his cash straight away, while the importer does not have to pay until the due date on the bill, by which time (he hopes) the goods will have arrived.

Bills of exchange are thus a way of financing the time-lags caused by international transport. Shipping is usually the cheapest sort of transport, especially for heavy bulky goods, but it is slow and so requires financing. The Treasury Bill is a special sort of bill of exchange, used by governments to finance the gap between spending and receipt of tax revenue.

If a commercial bank discounts (buys) a bill of exchange, it pays a cheque to a customer. The customer's account increases and the bank's account at the central bank is not affected. The commercial bank thus acquires a liquid asset and the money supply has increased. If the bill is bought from someone with an account at another bank there is a change in the relative cash and liquid asset position of the two banks, but overall the banking system acquires a liquid asset and the money supply has risen by the amount of the bill.

Buying bills of exchange is thus a way for commercial banks to lend more while adding to their liquid assets. Because deposits (and probably the public's demand for currency) rise, such lending puts the same strain on *cash* resources as lending by way of granting overdrafts, but clearly it is attractive to banks in need of more liquid assets.[23]

On the other hand, the central bank can control the *type* of bills of exchange bought by commercial banks. Since bills of exchange are only really liquid if the central bank is willing to buy them, the central bank can announce which bills it will buy – for example bills to finance imports of agricultural inputs but not bills to finance imports of luxury consumer goods. Alternatively, the central bank can discriminate by offering a better price for favoured bills (that is, discounting them at a lower rate of interest).

The final source of liquidity for commercial banks is borrowing from the central bank. Sometimes it is simply convenient for the central bank to provide cash to the banking system in this way; or the central bank may impose conditions on its lending in order to try and get the commercial banks to comply with official policy. For example the central bank may impose a high interest rate and short repayment date, in order to get the banks to slow down their lending.

In addition, however, the central bank stands ready to lend in a real crisis. Banking depends very much on confidence. If all depositors asked for their money at once, no bank would be able to pay since a proportion of deposits has been advanced to customers who cannot all repay at once. If, then, a bank is basically sound (that is, it has not been lending money foolishly to people who cannot repay) the central bank will lend it cash until confidence is restored. The very existence of a central bank makes a crisis of confidence, a 'run' on a bank when all the depositors try and get their money out at once, less likely. But it could still happen.[24]

In Zambia the banks are either subsidiaries of large international banks or government-owned, so that a crisis of confidence is unlikely. The foreign head offices would probably provide short-term finance to the expatriate banks if it were needed, as would the government to the parastatal commercial banks. But in Nigeria, for example, where a large number of small private banks were founded in the early 1950s, a great many bank failures occurred, with consequent losses for their depositors. There was also a loss of public confidence in indigenous banks which 'caused many Nigerians to decide to keep their savings in expatriate banks'.[25]

There is a slight paradox, then, in the functioning of a central bank as 'lender of last resort'. Banks which are basically sound do not usually need such support, although they may borrow from the central bank sometimes as an alternative to selling (to the central bank) some of their marketable assets. Banks which are basically unsound should not have access to central bank lending. Nevertheless, the soundness of the 'good' banks depends partly on the willingness of the central bank to lend to them, even if that willingness is seldom seriously tested.

9 ALTERNATIVE METHODS OF CONTROLLING BANK CREDIT[26]

Zambia has tried a number of alternative ways of controlling bank lending (and therefore the money supply) – alternatives, that is, to action affecting bank liquidity.

The first set of economic reforms in April 1968 included a rule that all non-Zambians and non-Zambian companies would in future have to apply to the Bank of Zambia for 'exchange control' permission to borrow from a commercial bank.[27] As it was presented publicly, the main motive behind the new rule was to channel more bank credit to

Zambians and to prevent foreign companies making large profits out of local borrowing. The *effect* of the rule, however, was to give the Bank of Zambia direct control over the total volume of bank credit, since the Zambian sector at that time only accounted for about 15% of total bank credit.[28]

As it happened, the Mulungushi speech of April 1968 coincided with the first shortage of bank liquidity since Independence. The commercial banks had virtually no spare cash at the Bank of Zambia, were net borrowers from their overseas head offices and their liquidity ratio had fallen to 27% which left them with only a tiny margin of liquid assets over the minimum. In these circumstances it is not really possible to say whether the fall which occurred in bank lending was a result of the new regulation or whether it would have occurred anyway as a result of the banks' extreme shortage of liquidity. The regulation did, however, give the Bank of Zambia power to try and favour sectors within the economy which it was felt should have priority, for example, agriculture.

In August 1969 the force of the new rule was considerably reduced by redefining 'Zambian' to mean any business with majority Zambian ownership. The new 51% parastatals, including the copper companies whose takeover was announced at the same time, were therefore excluded from direct credit controls.

In 1970 and 1971 bank credit to the private sector continued to expand very fast (and the balance of payments position was deteriorating rapidly) so in January 1972 a new rule was introduced: non-Zambian companies could only borrow up to 50% of their equity capital and Zambian companies up to 100% of their equity capital, without Bank of Zambia permission. This new control did not work fast enough, partly because of the large amount of 'unused facilities' – that is, arrangements to borrow from banks which had not yet been used. To be more quickly effective the rules would have had to prevent unused facilities from being used even though this would (in a formal sense) have amounted to enacting retrospective legislation on a contract between a bank and its customers.

So later in 1972 yet more new rules were introduced. Cash ratios were raised (from 8% and 3% for demand and other deposits to 12% and 8%), the liquidity ratio was raised from 25% to 28% and bills of exchange and promissory notes could not exceed 10% of liquid assets (after a short adjustment period). At the same time government also made changes in the definition of liquid assets.[29] The reasons for the changes were not only to reduce bank lending but also to improve the balance of payments. The two are of course closely connected because of the amount of bank lending that finances imports and because of the high propensity to import which Zambia shares with most African countries.

Zambia is still experimenting with the right balance between direct controls over bank lending and control over cash, liquid assets and the ratios that they are required to bear to deposits. It is probably true to say however, that controls are much harder to operate when the banks have spare liquidity; that is 'direct controls need, in order to be effective, the additional support of a tight liquidity situation'.[30]

Certainly, in the Zambian situation it makes rather more sense to use the indirect method of operating on bank liquidity, since good administrators are scarce. Secondly, the greater the financial importance of administrative decisions, the greater is the risk of corruption.[31] Thirdly, central bankers are not really able to make good decisions on individual loan applications: that is what bank managers are for and taking the decision out of their hands is in a way a waste of their expertise. There may be a case for controlling the *direction* of credit in line with national priorities but that is different in principle from controlling each individual loan.[32]

10 SUMMARY OF CENTRAL BANK FUNCTIONS

The discussion so far has, in passing, already covered a large part of the most important central bank functions. Thus the central bank acts as banker to the government and to the commercial banks, and holds the country's foreign exchange. As a result changes in the government's cash position, the commercial bankers' cash position and the balance of payments are all reflected immediately and directly in accounts at the central bank – with the effects on bank liquidity and the money supply that have been discussed. The central bank thus has the opportunity to try and control bank lending by buying and selling bank liquid assets or by changing the rules – altering cash and liquidity ratios or altering what the banks can count towards those ratios.

In most countries it is illegal for anyone to hold foreign exchange without permission from the central bank, whether in the form of foreign currency or as bank accounts abroad. If exporters keep their earnings overseas (as the copper companies in Zambia did before 1968) rather than selling to the central bank in exchange for local currency, they can pay for imports, dividends, foreign loan interest and repayments, etc., without the knowledge of the central bank. Fluctuations in export proceeds result, in such circumstances, in fluctuations in foreign exchange holdings of private companies without any impact, monetary or otherwise, on the domestic economy. Most governments prefer to perform the reserve-holding role themselves, through their central banks, and exercise equal control over the foreign payments of exporters and others. Having to deal with the domestic monetary impact is considered a minor price to pay for this control. Incidentally, the government then receives the interest on foreign exchange holdings invested abroad, paying local currency for the matching local investments of the exporters.[33]

The central bank handles the note issue, ordering (or performing, as in the case of the Bank of England which has its own printing works) the printing of notes, and distributing them to the commercial banks on request, either in exchange for a reduction in their accounts, or in exchange for old, dirty notes. Increases in the note issue are a theoretical liability of the central bank, against which it holds government debt. But the central bank can always meet its liability by printing more notes.

Central bank holdings of government debt against the note issue are thus pointless – the government pays the central bank interest on its holdings of debt, and the central bank, being owned by the government, pays this straight back to the government (after deduction of expenses) as its profit – or lends it back as part of its 'reserves'. What this all amounts to therefore is that increases in the note issue are effectively interest-free loans to the government, the only expense being the relatively very minor one of printing the notes and administering their issue. Increases in the note issue to meet the normal increasing demand for them by the public as the economy grows (and becomes monetized, in the case of underdeveloped countries) are a useful and cheap form of finance, which every government should plan for, and use gratefully.

The central bank also acts as lender of last resort to the banking system; and it provides finance to the government if nobody else will, by what is called lending but is in fact money creation. The central bank also exercises some influence over interest rates, but other factors are also important in this, as will be explained in the next chapter.

There remain two other functions which are rather more vague, but nonetheless important. Central banks act as advisers to government on the management of the economy. A great deal of information passes through central banks simply as a result of their acting as bankers to the government and the commercial banks, and as managers of the national debt and foreign exchange. Central banks are therefore in a particularly strong position to gather and analyse up-to-date information.

The remaining function of central banks, especially in underdeveloped countries, is to try and stimulate the development of financial markets and institutions. The logic of this is to make more efficient the flow of savings into investment on the assumption that market forces are the best way of achieving this, and that where markets do not exist they must be stimulated or new institutions created – for example the development bank.

This process of financial development is a rather artificial one in Zambia because the government has participated in the ownership of most major companies – except the banks themselves. As a result some of the major buyers and sellers in the market for government debt are in fact partly or wholly owned by government. The rather elaborate process of financial independence for these parastatal institutions, requiring them to maintain liquid assets, etc., could therefore simply be replaced by government guarantees of some sort. For example, the State Insurance Company and the ZNPF could simply be guaranteed borrowing rights at the Bank of Zambia, in order to ensure their ability to meet short-term crises; instead of 'investing' in government stock they could deposit money at the central bank and be paid interest. Historically, the issue of marketable debt occurred in order to encourage *foreign* institutions, especially the banks, to invest in local assets rather than foreign ones. This had the enormous advantage that Zambian money deposited in banks was made available to the Zambian government rather than being invested in London and used to finance the needs of the British government.

The system continues, although in Zambia a parastatal 'money market' now exists in which short-term money is borrowed and lent within the parastatal sector. One parastatal company which is short of cash will borrow from another which has a surplus, by-passing the banking system. Such financing ignores 'market' criteria, to some extent, on the assumption of an implied government guarantee of the solvency of parastatals. Subsidies to cover parastatal losses and some funds for capital spending are provided through the government's budget.

The logic for some financial markets continuing to develop and market criteria continuing to be applied is presumably that management of parastatals is more efficient if separated from direct control by the civil service and made subject to the scrutiny of bank managers. It will be interesting to see how this develops in practice. There is no way of telling at present whether the balance will tip towards allocation of resources by planners or by the market, in Zambia as in many African countries.

A good illustration of this dilemma is the history of the Zambian Stock Exchange. Its creation was announced in the Mulungushi speech in 1968, in the context of Zambianizing the economy. Certainly if foreign-owned companies sold shares to Zambians there would be some increase in Zambian ownership of domestic economic resources, although Nigerian experience suggests that share ownership would be limited to a very small group of people.[34] A Stock Exchange Act was duly passed and a secretary actually appointed. In the meantime, however, the government bought into the major existing companies and participated in the major new ones. The viability of the Zambian Stock Exchange now depends, therefore, on whether shares in parastatal companies (presumably from the parastatal portfolio) will be traded. A decision on this point has long been delayed with the Stock Exchange remaining inactive as a result. In short, Zambia appears to have chosen a different path towards Zambian ownership of the country's industry, without quite closing the door on the alternative.[35]

11 CONCLUSION

Even in an open economy, with commercial banks foreign-owned, the central bank can exercise considerable monetary control. But the large fluctuations in export earnings plus the importance of the public sector mean that the central bank can be presented with much bigger changes in the liquidity of the banking system than it is likely to be able to deal with by buying and selling government debt. Nevertheless, the central bank can also alter liquidity requirements (as it has in Zambia, by a very large amount) and has other weapons to hand, notably exchange control and import licensing.

Central banks are also supposed to be able to influence the banking system by 'moral suasion' – which is supposed to mean by simple request. There is some scope for pointing out to the commercial banks that the national interest and their interests coincide. But the real power behind any central bank request derives from the fact that the central bank can inflict losses on the commercial banks – by squeezing their liquidity in such a way that they have to either sell liquid assets to the central bank (at a price chosen by the central bank) or borrow from the central bank (at an interest rate chosen by the central bank). Ability to borrow from abroad slows down but does not eliminate the central bank's powers, since head offices will lend for short but not for long periods.

Fortunately, the heavy taxes on exports mean that export price fluctuations produce offsetting effects on liquidity. Thus a rise in the copper price increases bankers' cash but the resulting budget surplus reduces it. This offset is not complete however; nor is it immediate.

A large budget deficit is more difficult for the central bank to manage; but here again the openness of the typical African economy reduces the monetary impact. A high propensity to import drains away some of the cash created by a budget deficit, as imports rise in response to the income multiplier effects of the deficit. Of course if import controls are used to prevent imports rising then the monetary expansion must be controlled in some other way – for example by raising cash or liquidity ratios, or by finding some other way of forcing the banks to buy government debt.[36]

There remains the possibility that the economy has unemployed resources to the extent that a rise in demand will lead to a rise in domestic output without any pressure on prices. In these circumstances, it is highly unlikely that increasing bank liquidity will lead to an expansion of lending. The banks will probably have spare liquidity already, and in any case there is not likely to be an excess demand for credit (from bankable borrowers) in a slump. The correct policy measure is thus a budget deficit financed by money creation; domestic borrowing would reduce spending power and bank liquidity. These circumstances are however rare in modern Africa – and assume that the balance of payments can stand the strain, which is even rarer.

Appendix: Definitions

1 GOVERNMENT STOCK

One of the ways in which the government borrows money is by issuing 'stock'. Essentially, members of the general public, and institutions, are invited to lend money (on certain terms) to the government. The government promises to pay a stated rate of interest on the loan, for a stated number of years. For example if the government announces a new stock in 1975 called '5% Local Registered Stock 1985' the investor can buy say K1,000 of this stock; he will receive 5% (K50 on K1,000) annually for 10 years; in 1985 he will receive back his K1,000.

If the investor wants his money back *before* 1985 he can try and sell his stock to someone else. The price he gets will *not* necessarily be K1,000. If the 'market' interest rate has risen in the meantime to 10%, an investor wishing to get 10% on his money will pay less than K1,000 for the stock which yields only 5% at a price of K1,000. Suppose the year is 1984 and the stock has just one year to 'maturity' (that is, the date on which the government has promised to repay the money). The investor will pay roughly K955 for the 'nominal' K1,000 of stock. He will then receive K50 in interest (that is fixed by the 5% 'coupon' or interest promised at issue by the government) and on maturity he will make another K45 'profit' since he will receive K1,000 for stock for which he paid only K955. Altogether he will therefore receive K95, which is roughly 10% of his original investment of K955.

This example illustrates three very important principles: firstly, that the value of a fixed-interest stock changes in the *opposite* direction to changes in the rate of interest. Thus if the interest rate goes up, the market value of fixed-interest government stock goes down; and if the interest rate falls, the market value of fixed-interest stock rises.

Secondly, if there are very few buyers of government stock and the central bank acts as the residual buyer of stock it can have a very big influence on the price of stock. By offering a low price, thus lowering the value of stock, it can effectively push up the interest rate. By offering a good price, it can keep interest rates down.

Thirdly, the nearer to maturity a stock is, the nearer the market price will be to its repayment (or nominal) value and the less is the variation in its market price. That is why banks prefer short-dated stock.

2 TREASURY BILLS

Treasury Bills are simply very short-dated government debt. In Zambia they are a way of borrowing money for three months. Thus if a copper company buys a Treasury Bill, it is lending money to the government for three months. Because Treasury Bills have such a short life, the government does not 'pay' interest on them: instead it sells them at a discount, that is at less than their 'face' or nominal value.

For example, a K50,000 Treasury Bill is offered for sale on 1 March for K49,500. On 1 June the government will pay out K50,000 to the owner. The investor thus invests K49,500 and earns K500 in three months, which is roughly 1% on his money. The rate of interest is therefore roughly 4% calculated at an annual rate, as is usual.

3 MARKETABILITY

An investment is marketable if you can sell it. Thus a deposit in the Post Office is not marketable; to get your money back you *withdraw* your money, you do not sell the deposit to a friend. Government stock and Treasury Bills are marketable; the investor is issued with a piece of paper which entitles him to receive a fixed annual payment of interest (in the case of stock) and repayment of the full nominal amount (in the case of stock and Bills) on the due date (at maturity).

An investment is *more* or *less* marketable according to how easy or difficult it is to sell it. In turn this depends on how many buyers and sellers are active in the market and how well organized the market is in bringing them together. In the case of government debt, marketability is of course greatly increased if the central bank acts as a residual buyer and seller. As already noted the central bank has great control over the price of government debt because it acts as residual buyer and seller. The central bank has an interest, however, in maintaining a steady price for government debt in order to make it easier to sell government debt in future. If big fluctuations occur, and in particular if big and sudden rises in the interest rate (equal to falls in the price of government debt) occur, investors will be less willing to put their money into government debt in future.

Marketability of government debt, and a fairly steady price, is not just useful because it enables governments to spend more money without levying higher taxes. Some financial institutions have a real need for marketable long-term securities. For example the insurance company and the provident funds have future liabilities to pay pensions, etc. But in the meantime they have *unknown* short-term liabilities: people have accidents, die, lose their jobs and so make claims. As a result the institutions need 'liquid' investments, which give an income in the form of interest but which can be sold quickly if short-term liabilities suddenly increase. Marketability thus has an important social function.

In an economy where the major financial institutions are publicly owned, it would clearly be possible for the government simply to make money available when needed, rather than to issue stock and then make it marketable in a rather artificial way by means of the central bank. The reason why the latter method is still used in Zambia is partly historical – that is the way it was done when financial institutions were privately owned and the full adjustment to nationalization has not yet been made – and partly because not all financial institutions are owned by the government (notably the banks) and possibly partly because it is believed to be more efficient to give parastatals considerable independence in day-to-day management and control them indirectly through the 'market'.

4 LIQUIDITY

Money is perfectly liquid. Thus cash in the form of notes and coin is 100% liquid by definition – it can be spent at will. Bank deposits are to all intents and purposes liquid since they can be converted into cash on demand – hence the term 'demand deposits'.

Investment in, say, a house is very illiquid since it takes considerable time to sell a house and thus convert it into cash. Furthermore, the price to be obtained on selling a house is uncertain, especially when the sale is made in a hurry (a 'forced sale').

Liquidity is thus made up of two elements

(a) the *speed* with which an investment can be converted into cash
(b) the degree of certainty about the *amount* of cash that will be received.

Thus *marketable* securities, for example government stocks and Treasury Bills, are very liquid in the first sense, since they can be sold for cash in the market (if there is one, or to the central bank in the absence of an active market). They are less liquid in the second sense, since their prices vary with variations in interest rates. Treasury Bills are more liquid than government stocks, in the second sense, because their price varies less. In general, the shorter-dated a stock, the less risk is there of variations in its price.

Illiquid investments can be used as security for borrowing. Thus a business with its money tied up in machinery and stocks of raw materials can usually borrow money – unless it is regarded as inefficient and on the verge of bankruptcy. One of the functions of banks is to provide liquidity for individuals and firms who do not wish to sell their longer-term investments just because they (temporarily) have no cash.

In Zambia, the official definition of liquid assets was:

gold
notes and coin of Zambia
balances at the Bank of Zambia
Zambia Government Treasury Bills
bills of exchange and promissory notes eligible for discount at the Bank of Zambia
Zambian Local Registered Government Stock of maturity not exceeding six years
balances in the UK
UK Treasury Bills
UK call deposits[37]

In 1972 the external assets, namely the last three in the above list, were excluded; Zambian Local Registered Stock with more than six years to maturity was included; not more than 10% of liquid assets could be bills of exchange and promissory notes.[38]

5 FINANCING A BUDGET DEFICIT BY BORROWING FROM COMMERCIAL BANKS

It has already been explained that financing a budget deficit by 'borrowing' from the central bank is in fact money creation and enables commercial banks to expand their lending. Financing a deficit by taxation or by borrowing from the 'non-bank' public creates no new money nor any new bankers' cash. Finance from the commercial banks is somewhere between these two extremes.

Suppose the government has an unfinanced deficit of K10 mn. Bank deposits rise by K10 mn; so does bankers' cash. Now suppose the commercial banks buy government debt – stock and Treasury Bills. Presumably they will keep K1·2 mn (12% of K10 mn) in bankers' cash, and buy K8·8 mn of government debt, unless they already have K1·2 mn of 'spare' cash. The result is then that the money supply has risen by K10 mn, but the commercial banks have no additional spare cash.

If the central bank actually succeeds in selling the full K10 mn's worth of debt to the commercial banks, then this will absorb K1·2 mn of their spare cash. The money supply will have risen by K10 mn and the capacity of the banks to expand their lending will have been reduced.

In both cases, the commercial banks' holdings of liquid assets will have risen. Suppose initially that demand deposits were at K200 mn, bankers' cash K24 mn (12% of demand deposits) and liquid assets K56 mn (28% of demand deposits) – in this case the banks have no spare cash or liquid assets. Now suppose the government has an unfinanced deficit of K10 mn, the commercial banks buy K8·8 mn of debt and bankers' cash rises by K1·2 mn. The liquidity ratio then becomes nearly

31% (K64·8 mn of liquid assets, divided by K210 mn of demand deposits). In theory the banks can expand lending if they can sell some of their liquid assets. In practice, the expansionary effect of the budget deficit would probably cause a rise in non-bank note holding, requiring the banks to use their liquid assets to get cash to supply notes to their customers. The central bank might also try and prevent advances from rising by use of direct controls – this would be consistent with a policy of trying to sell government debt to the commercial banks.

In Zambia, the commercial banks try not to allow their liquid assets to fall as low as the minimum percentage of 28% (25% before 1972), but keep an additional safety margin of roughly another 10% of demand deposits (making approximately 38% in all). The central bank knows this and so can affect bank lending by causing liquidity to fall below 38%. The additional safety margin gives more flexibility which has some advantages for all concerned. It would be disruptive and damaging in most circumstances if very sudden changes had to be made in bank lending.

By preventing bank lending through direct controls, by raising the liquidity ratio, or by changing the definition of the liquidity ratio, the authorities (the central bank and the government) can reduce the monetary effects of a budget deficit unfinanced by other sources. By forcing the commercial banks to buy government debt with additions to their cash, the authorities ensure that only the money supply goes up, not bank lending to the private sector.

NOTES

1 Bank of Zambia's *Quarterly Statistical Review* and *Monthly Digest of Statistics* use this definition. Time and savings deposits are referred to as 'quasi-money'.

2 Traditionally, banks used to write overdrafts on bank statements in red figures – hence the expression 'in the red' for being in debt.

3 This practice of 'clearing' cheques with each other is the origin of the name 'clearing banks' for the biggest English banks.

4 Currency means notes and coin. Notes are much more important than coin – in Zambia at the end of 1973 of K71·7 mn currency in circulation K67·9 mn (95%) was notes, K4·7 mn (5%) was coin.

5 The coin manufacturer in the UK is called the Mint, hence the expression 'minting money'.

6 In some countries, the cash ratio *includes* notes and coin held in commercial bank tills ('till money'). In Zambia till money is excluded from the calculation of cash ratios. This detail makes no essential difference to the analysis. The Zambian cash ratio was raised to 12% in 1972.

7 To bankers, 'cash' is what they can count towards their cash ratio, and use to meet customer withdrawals. In common speech, 'cash' means money (notes and coin) in one's pocket.

For this reason, when discussing the banking system, the reader should be careful to note the specialized meaning of 'bankers' cash'.

[8] Figures derived from those published in the *Monthly Digest of Statistics*. Averages are given to eliminate month-to-month fluctuations. The averages are in fact for the last nine months of 1965, as figures for the full year are not available. See Table 5.3 in my chapter 'Financial constraints on Zambian development' in C. M. Elliott (ed.), *Constraints on the Economic Development of Zambia*, Nairobi, OUP, 1971, p. 124, for the commercial banks' cash position, expressed in monthly averages, for the years 1965–8.

[9] Tables 5.1, 5.2, 5.3, pp. 123–4 in Elliott (ed.), op. cit.

[10] The two big expatriate banks in Zambia are now locally registered companies rather than just branches as they were at Independence. But they are still 100% foreign-owned and still have accounts overseas. Even nationalization would be unlikely to affect this particular issue; see my paper 'The control of credit in Zambia', *Journal of Modern African Studies*, 1973.

[11] The 'liquidity' position is also important, as explained below.

[12] For definitions of Treasury Bills, government stock, marketability and liquidity see Appendix at the end of this chapter, Sections 1 to 4. Section 4 also lists the assets officially allowed to be counted towards liquidity ratios in Zambia.

[13] Bills of exchange and promissory notes are also liquid assets and are a form of lending to the private sector rather than to the government. This refinement is of relatively minor importance; it is dealt with in Section 8.

[14] In practice, the rising level of economic activity caused by equal rises in exports and imports would probably lead to a rising demand for notes and coin – the banks would have to pay for this by drawing *down* their central bank balances.

[15] Government stock and Treasury Bills, and the concept of marketability, are defined in the Appendix to this chapter.

[16] Central bank lending to commercial banks is further discussed in Section 8.

[17] This is a rather unrealistic assumption; the effect of relaxing it is discussed below, later in this section and in Section 6.

[18] Currency would increase by half of K1·1 mn, namely K0·6 mn approximately, giving a rise in the money supply of K1·1 mn + K0·6 mn = K1·7 mn.

[19] But bank lending has penetrated ever more deeply into the domestic economy. For example bank lending in Zambia increased by 238% from 1965 to 1970 while imports increased by only 62%.

[20] Until 1972 only 3% of time and savings deposits had to be kept as bankers' cash.

[21] See Appendix to this chapter, Section 4, for a discussion of liquidity and a list of the assets that Zambian banks are allowed to count towards their liquidity ratios.

[22] In some countries loans made to certain favoured industries, for example agriculture, may be discounted, i.e. sold, to the central bank. This occurs in Jamaica, see A. Ally in P. Selwyn (ed.), *Development in Small Countries*, Croom Helm, 1975.

[23] For this reason restrictions on the use of bills of exchange as liquid assets may be introduced – see below, Section 9.

[24] It happened in Britain in 1973, to one of the smaller banks, and the threat of a world trade recession in 1974 caused many rumours of bank failures in Europe.

[25] See C. V. Brown, *The Nigerian Banking System*, London, Allen and Unwin, 1966, especially pp. 25–6.

[26] This section is based on my article 'The control of credit in Zambia', *Journal of Modern African Studies*, 1973.

[27] Exchange control is normally used as a way of controlling foreign payments, so that this new rule was an extension of the normal meaning of the expression.

[28] See Bank of Zambia, Annual Report 1968, p. 29. 'Non-Zambian' was defined in the new rule to mean any business not 100%-owned by Zambians so that even the new parastatals, created by the 51% takeovers announced in the Mulungushi speech, counted as non-Zambian.

[29] See Appendix to this chapter, Section 4.

[30] See my article 'The control of credit in Zambia', op. cit., p. 388.

[31] One might almost say, the greater is the certainty of corruption.

[32] The question of directing lending to the indigenous sector and away from the foreign sector is discussed in the next chapter. Achieving sectoral targets may come back to controlling individual loans if a sector is dominated by one firm – as is common in Africa.

[33] The Zambian copper companies have objected, not surprisingly, to receiving relatively low Zambian interest rates instead of relatively high British interest on their short-term investments.

[34] D. Gustafson, 'The development of Nigeria's Stock Exchange' in T. J. Farer (ed.), *Financing African Development*, M.I.T., 1965.

[35] W. A. Lewis, *The Theory of Economic Growth*, London, Allen and Unwin, 1954, pp. 266–9, has a good version of the argument for a stock exchange.

[36] See Appendix to this chapter, Section 5, for an analysis of the impact on the money supply of a budget deficit financed by the commercial banks.

[37] Call deposits are deposits with the 'Discount Market' – essentially part of the banking system. This refinement does not exist in most African countries – Rhodesia and South Africa are exceptions. See R. A. Sowelem, *Towards Financial Independence in a Developing Economy*, London, Allen and Unwin, 1967, Chapter 4, for the Rhodesian case. The book relates to the federal period.

[38] Bank of Zambia, Annual Report 1972, pp. 56–7.

9 *Theories of Money and Monetary Policy*

1 INTRODUCTION

The last chapter stuck as closely as possible to the *mechanics* of money creation, although in discussing the role of the central bank some policy issues inevitably appeared. Thus money is created by banks granting credit, by unfinanced government budget deficits and by balance of payments surpluses. The two last *also* create bankers' cash so that multiple expansions of the money supply may ensue. The 'natural' limitations upon multiple expansions of credit and money supply are the public's desire to increase their currency holdings and the need for banks to maintain stocks of cash and liquid assets. Furthermore, increases in payments of tax to the government (after a delay) and increases in imports (if they are not prevented) also reduce bankers' cash, and thus restrain monetary expansion. The central bank can impose additional restrictions, for example by changing the official rules regarding cash and liquid asset ratios or by direct controls on bank lending.

Implied in all this were some theories about the demand for money and the supply of money. The next task, therefore, is to make these theories explicit and to see whether they throw any further light on how the macroeconomy works and how governments can and ought to react.

2 THE DEMAND FOR MONEY

There are three main motives for holding money. The first is called the 'transactions demand' and is partly implicit in assuming that the public's demand for currency increases with income. In fact, as national income increases all types of money owners increase their demand for both currency and bank deposits, the split between them being decided entirely by convenience. As it happens, historical evidence tends to show that the demand for money increases *faster* than income – as people become richer they can afford to maintain higher money balances as a proportion of their income. When people are very poor their average money balances tend to be very low in proportion to their incomes since they spend most of their income soon after receiving it.

Closely allied to the transactions demand for money is the precautionary motive for holding money. Essentially this reflects the desire to be prepared for abnormal spending. Like the transactions demand, the precautionary demand for money tends to rise with income. It can also be satisfied, however, by holdings of liquid assets and by the ability to borrow. In the rural areas the precautionary motive is partly or wholly satisfied by ownership of cattle, goats, chickens, maize stocks and the like, which provide against crop failures, visits from relatives, the need to reward work parties and so on. As the rural economy comes increasingly in contact with the use of money, and the supply of goods for money, there is a tendency for the precautionary motive to be satisfied by holding money rather than goods,[1] just as transactions increasingly use money rather than barter.

These general propositions are born out by the Zambian figures. As shown in Table 9.1, the money supply has grown much faster since Independence than money national income; and this is true whether one defines the money supply as currency plus demand deposits or includes other bank deposits as well.

TABLE 9.1

The rise in money supply and national income: Zambia 1965–70

		1965 *K mn*	*1970* *K mn*	*Increase* %
1	Notes and coin with the public	19	43	+126
2	Demand deposits	58	143	+147
3=1+2	Money supply	76	186	+145
4	Other deposits (quasi-money)	31	104	+234
5=3+4	Money supply (wider definition)	107	290	+171
	GDP at current prices	650	1,143	+76
	National disposable income at current prices	562	908	+62
	GDP at fixed prices	650	872	+34
	Consumer price index	112	149	+33

NOTE: The choice of years may be slightly misleading since notes and coin with the public failed to increase 1968–70 see Appendix to this chapter) but the broad picture presented by the figures is undoubtedly correct.

Source: *Monthly Digest of Statistics.*

It may be that people also hold money for 'speculative' reasons. If there is a choice between money and some alternative asset, then it is logical to hold money if the value of the alternative asset is expected to fall. Equally, if alternatives to money are expected to increase in value then people should prefer to spend their 'asset' money and gain from the rise in price – always assuming that enough money is retained for other needs, that is, for transactions and precautionary purposes.

The practical significance of the speculative demand for money is that in some circumstances an increasing supply of money may not result in an increasing amount of spending. For example, if business prospects are poor then businessmen may prefer to hold cash balances rather than spend them in the form of investment. Similarly, banks will not normally wish to increase their lending when business prospects are poor, so that adding to their cash will not necessarily result in increased spending by bank customers.

As explained in the previous chapter, most of the ways in which the money supply can expand – budget deficits, increased bank lending, export surpluses – are themselves a stimulus to demand. In expansionary conditions, prices of goods are unlikely to be falling so additions to the money supply are unlikely to be added to speculative balances. If, on the other hand, the money supply increases because the central bank or the government buys an asset, at a time of depressed business conditions and falling prices, then there is a possibility that the new money will not be spent.

Even an export surplus may not result in increased spending. In Zambia, a rise in the copper price may not stimulate increased economic activity if the price rise is expected to be temporary. All the parties concerned – the government, its holding companies, the copper companies – may simply add to their reserves. If the banks take the same view they will not increase their lending. This could perhaps be described more accurately as an example of the precautionary motive, but the name is not vital. What is important is to understand that not all increases in the money supply result in increased spending.

A particular and rather peculiar example of the non-spending of increased money holdings occurred in Zambia in 1968 and 1969, when the copper companies were forced to keep half their after-tax profits in the country. Despite high copper prices relatively little investment was taking place, probably because of uncertainties over the political future. Essentially the companies preferred not to commit themselves to more investment than they needed until they knew whether and on what terms they would be nationalized. Put another way, they preferred to hold money rather than investing in assets whose future value was highly uncertain.

In contrast, price increases for agricultural exports produced by small farmers are much more likely to be spent, provided that they reach the farmer. Marketing boards in West Africa have sometimes failed to pass on price increases, for example of cocoa, to farmers, adding to reserves instead.

In practice, if money holdings increase, they tend to be invested in savings accounts or Treasury Bills (for large companies). In both cases the money ends up being lent to the government, directly in the case of Treasury Bills, indirectly if banks increase their holdings of government debt rather than increasing their lending to their customers. In order therefore for a rise in the money supply not to be spent, it is not only necessary that holders of increased money balances refrain from spending but also that banks do not increase their lending (to the extent that the money is held in banks) and that government does not increase its spending (to the extent that the money is lent to the government).

3 THE QUANTITY THEORY OF MONEY

Some of these ideas can be expressed in terms of the quantity theory of money. This theory, one of the oldest ideas in economics, is based on the 'equation of exchange'

$$MV = PT$$

where M = the average quantity of money
V = its velocity of circulation, i.e. the speed with which it gets spent on average
P = the average price of each monetary transaction
T = the number of transactions

all the symbols referring to a period of time.

The equation is in fact an *identity*, that is, it is always true with the definitions given. The quantity *theory* is that variations in M *cause* variations in P, so that V and T are assumed not to vary (or to vary in ways that cancel each other out).

In its crudest form, the quantity theory states that P varies directly with changes in M so that a 10% increase in the money supply, for example, causes prices to rise by 10%. Essentially this assumes that output (as represented by the number of transactions) is unaffected by changes in the money supply. It also assumes that the velocity of circulation of money does not change. Put differently, this last assumption is that people spend increases in their holdings of money in much the same way as before, that is, they *do not* increase (proportionately) their holdings of money as an asset.

An alternative version of the quantity theory is rather more flexible in its assumptions. This version is based on the equation

$$M = kP'O$$

where M = the average quantity of money
k = the proportion of their income that people choose to hold as money
P' = the average price of transactions included in the measurement of national income
O = output of 'final products', i.e. those included in national income.

Changes in M can then cause changes in k (which roughly represents the speculative demand for money), in prices or in output.

In the theory as developed in industrialized economies, a rise in k would occur if *interest rates* were expected to rise, by almost everybody. Because interest rates and the price of marketable fixed interest loans ('bonds') move in opposite directions, if everyone expects interest rates to rise, by definition everyone expects the price of bonds to fall. So if the choice is between holding bonds or holding money, people will choose money in order to avoid losses as bond prices fall. If people hold money rather than bonds then borrowers, that is those who want to spend, will not get hold of the increase in money.

Even in an industrialized economy relatively little spending takes place through borrowing by the issue of marketable bonds. In the underdeveloped economies of Africa, with their underdeveloped or non-existent capital and money markets, the whole idea of the speculative demand for money depending on interest rates is thoroughly irrelevant.[2]

It remains important, however, to explain what *does* happen to any increase in the money supply that does not get spent. The holder of the increase in money will either leave it on a demand deposit account, or more likely deposit it in some fixed interest savings account, at a bank or some other financial institution. Other possibilities are buying Treasury Bills or government stock, and the holding of notes; the latter is quite likely among small businessmen, especially farmers.

If the money remains with a commercial bank, then if no additional spending is to occur, it must be assumed that the banks have no unsatisfied demand for credit. The same argument applies to other financial institutions that lend to the private sector such as building societies. If the money is lent to the government by buying government debt, for there to be no spending as a result one must assume that government spending is not affected by this additional inflow of finance. Buying of government debt may also drive down the rate of interest on that debt, or prevent it from rising. This happened in Zambia in 1969 and 1970 when the copper companies put increased cash holdings into Treasury Bills and drove the rate right down. Other interest rates were not affected though; nor was the rest of the economy.[3]

If an increase in the money supply is held in the form of currency it is a form of interest-free loan to the government. Suppose for example a rising price for agricultural exports produced by small farmers is partly saved in the form of notes buried in boxes in the countryside. The government buys the foreign exchange from the domestic marketing board (or other intermediary). The farmer receives cash in the form of notes from the marketing board, which drew notes from its bank, which in turn obtained them from the central bank by drawing down its balance there. The government has therefore acquired foreign exchange (which it can invest in money markets overseas) in exchange for notes which it simply has printed. The commercial banks have no additional liquidity as a result of these transactions, so they cannot increase their lending. So there is no additional spending to offset the non-spending of income by the farmers, *unless* the government decides to spend.

There is thus an argument that government should spend to offset saving in the form of notes, since such saving is not 'matched' by spending elsewhere in the economy – as is, for example, saving in a building society which makes available money to be spent on houses. In reality, though, governments should match their spending to the capacity of the economy as a whole, taking into account total private sector spending, rather than thinking in terms of one or other type of saving. It *is* valid to argue that increases in the note issue are *not* an inflationary form of financing a budget deficit.

It is possible for both *output* and *prices*, O and P' in the revised quantity theory equation, to rise following increases in the supply of money, M. Output will rise to the extent that unused capacity exists in the domestic economy and prices will rise where excess demand develops and imports cannot supply the difference or are prevented from doing so (for example, by import controls). But it is not necessarily correct that these changes in output and prices are *caused* by an increase in the money supply.

The main ways in which the money supply can increase are by budget deficits, increased bank lending in a situation of spare liquidity and export surpluses. All of these are themselves the result of increases in demand and spending, so that any consequent rise in output or prices can just as plausibly be put down to the increase in demand, which in turn causes *both* the increase in money *and* the increase in output, prices or both. Any *multiple* increase in the money supply that occurs because, say, a budget deficit is financed by pure money creation, only occurs because bank customers demand credit. Bank customers do not demand credit simply because it is available but because they have unsatisfied demand which they are willing to satisfy by borrowing – and paying interest on that borrowing.

An increase in the money supply caused by a central bank purchase of government debt (from banks or other holders) is not of itself an increase in demand, and it does increase the money supply. But if the seller wants cash in order to increase spending (or lending in the case of a bank) then any increase in output or prices can be attributed to demand. Similarly, a reduction in officially required reserve ratios *permits* an increase in bank lending but only has this result if there is excess demand for credit. It seems reasonable to say, then, that monetary policy can result in an increase in output or prices (or both) if it is in the form of taking the brakes off at a time of excess demand.

In the case of a *fall* in the money supply the sequence of events is somewhat different. The money supply can be deliberately reduced by raising cash and liquidity ratios; or by sales of government debt by the central bank.[4] In these two cases the central bank is not directly affecting demand but is reducing part of the means of satisfying demand, by reducing the money supply and at the same time reducing bankers' cash. If, then, prices or output fall, one can perhaps say that it is the reduction in money supply that is the cause. If on the other hand the money supply falls because of reduced demand for bank credit, leaving the banks with excess liquidity, or because of a reduction in the export surplus, or because of reduced budget deficit: then it is a reduction in demand which is causing a reduction in the money supply and also any fall in output or prices.

The point really is that the results of changes in the money supply can only usefully be analysed by looking at what causes them. It is usually unhelpful to try and explain events by looking at the money supply alone.

4 THE DETERMINATION OF INTEREST RATES

Where there is an active market in some form of debt then changes in price imply changes in the interest rate of that debt. For example in 1969 and 1970 the copper companies greatly increased their holdings of cash in Zambia; this cash was invested in Treasury Bills and drove down the interest rate from an average of $4\frac{1}{2}\%$ in 1968 to an average of $2\frac{1}{2}\%$ in 1970. But other interest rates were unaffected. Commercial banks paid the same rates to depositors and charged the same minimum rate to borrowers; building societies and the Post Office Savings Bank (as it then was) made no changes in their rates. Even the rate of interest on government stock, in which there is a rather inactive market, did not appear to change.

Clearly, then, market forces are not the only determinants of interest rates. The other determinants are government decisions, interest rates in other countries and decisions made within financial institutions.

A lot of lending is done directly by government, to local authorities and parastatal institutions or by parastatal institutions themselves. Interest rates in this lending are under the direct control of the government; they can, as a matter of choice, be linked to other rates. In addition 'Bank Rate', the official lending rate of the central bank, has a considerable influence on other interest rates. The mechanism by which Bank Rate affects other interest rates is not entirely clear, however. Where there are developed money markets interest rates may rise if the commercial banks are forced to borrow from the central bank at Bank Rate. But even when no borrowing from the central bank is taking place, a mere announcement of a change in Bank Rate can cause other interest rates to change. This must be because everyone concerned with the money market (the market in short-term debt) knows that the central bank has the power to enforce a change in interest rates, by acting as residual buyer or seller. If, on the other hand, it is no longer believed that the central bank can or will enforce its will through the market, then announcement of a change in Bank Rate may not have the desired effect. In such circumstances the central bank would *have* to enter the market in short-term debt in order to achieve its objectives.

Where money markets are underdeveloped or non-existent the impact of Bank Rate on other interest rates presumably depends on an implied threat. In announcing a change in Bank Rate the central bank is in fact saying that it wishes other interest rates to change as well; if banks, building societies and other financial institutions *do* in fact change their borrowing and lending rates, it must be because they believe that the central bank is in a position to get its way somehow – if not by buying and selling marketable debt, then by changing the rules regarding liquidity, or even by seeking new legislation. In the situation where financial institutions are foreign-owned they may be especially anxious to oblige the authorities and avoid new legislation or nationalization.

The importance of interest rates in other countries is that some borrowers may have a choice of where to borrow and some holders of liquid assets may have a choice of where to invest. Thus before the introduction of exchange control in Zambia the copper companies kept most of their liquid assets abroad, partly because it appeared safer but partly also because they obtained higher interest rates abroad. More generally, importers and exporters have (theoretically) some choice as to when to buy or sell foreign exchange. For example, an importer with cash available can choose to buy foreign exchange before payment is due and invest it in an overseas asset. This has the effect of reducing the official foreign exchange reserves and may therefore be officially discouraged. In practice, the purchase of foreign exchange by importers is now so heavily controlled, by import licensing and exchange control, that very little choice remains. Where this is the situation, local interest rates can remain effectively isolated from foreign rates since the 'leads and lags' (as changes in the timing of foreign exchange transactions are called) cannot operate.

Where borrowers have a choice between borrowing locally or overseas, differing interest rates may have some influence. But, as was explained in Chapter 7 on investment, foreign investors choose to borrow locally for mainly strategic reasons, in order to avoid committing their own funds. Alternatively they may borrow (from affiliated companies) as a way of transferring profits out of the host country. On the whole, such strategic factors are likely to be more important than interest rate costs, especially when costs can be passed on in higher prices. Local investors do not normally have the opportunity of foreign borrowing, although very large companies may do so. With very large-scale borrowing the *availability* of funds may be as important as their cost, in deciding where companies borrow.

In summary, it seems as though interest rates in Africa are mainly determined by the government and its central bank, with minor influence from market forces where debt is marketable and some discretion in the hands of institutional lenders;[5] at the same time the authorities must pay some attention to interest rates overseas if their controls over foreign transactions are not very complete or not very effective.

5 THE IMPORTANCE OF INTEREST RATES

Interest rates play a key role in the macroeconomic theory that has been developed in industrialized countries. In particular the link between monetary theory and national income analysis depends very heavily on the part played by interest rates. The argument runs thus: a rise in national income causes an increase in the demand for money; this causes interest rates to rise; this causes a reduced demand for money;[6] higher interest rates also cause reduced investment; the rise in national income is thus slowed down, and a new equilibrium is reached in monetary supply and demand, and in the supply and demand for real goods and services. A similar argument is used for tracing the effects of a rise in the supply of money: it causes a fall in interest rates (unless they are already so low that all the additional money is added to speculative balances); this stimulates investment demand; income rises, causing a rise in transactions demand for money and slowing down the fall in interest rates until a new equilibrium is reached in both money and national income.

Without examining the whole of this model, it is clear that it depends crucially on two functions which include the rate of interest: firstly, the demand for money is supposed to vary inversely with the rate of interest; secondly, investment is supposed to vary inversely with the rate of interest. Both hypotheses are highly dubious even in countries with highly developed capital markets and industrial sectors; in underdeveloped countries they are demonstrably irrelevant, as has already been argued.

Thus a rise in the supply of money *may* reduce some interest rates, but *not* the interest rates paid by investors (where they pay interest rates at all) because very little borrowing for investment is done, in Africa, by means of marketable debt. Even if a rise in the money supply *did* reduce the interest rates actually paid by investors, there is little likelihood that it would have any influence on investment.

Interest rates do have some importance however, even in countries like Zambia. Firstly, to the extent that investment is undertaken out of borrowed money, the interest rate is part of its cost. A low interest rate thus reduces the cost of capital relative to other inputs: so it encourages the use of capital-intensive methods of production and fails to ration scarce capital to those who can make best use of it. Secondly, low interest rates are a sort of subsidy to those borrowers who are lucky enough to have access to cheap credit. Normally such lucky borrowers are the rich and the powerful, whether companies or individuals. The poorer potential borrower, the emergent businessman, the emergent farmer, generally comes last in the queue (or never even gets as far as becoming part of the queue) and in any case is an uneconomic proposition at low interest rates, from the lender's point of view. Thus even if there is enough credit for everyone at the existing rate, a higher rate might make it economic for a larger number of borrowers to get credit. These points are especially important where large borrowers are mainly foreign and small ones mainly local, since most African countries are trying to encourage local business to compete more successfully with foreign business. Where large-scale business is mainly parastatal, wholly or partly owned by government, motives become more mixed; but the argument that cheap credit over-encourages the use of capital-intensive techniques remains valid.

Little is known about interest rates in the informal monetary sector, or 'unorganized money markets' as they have been called.[7] Some borrowing goes on between friends and relatives and from traders, mainly for unforeseen consumption such as funerals, but also to a small extent for production purposes. This type of lending and borrowing is less developed in Africa than in Asia and Latin America – where it has been much criticized for charging high interest rates and creating dependence of small farmers on landlords, traders and professional money-lenders. In Africa there has been the alternative of temporary migration to the towns to earn a cash income; in Zambia high urban wages and an unusually large urban sector make this possible for an exceptionally high proportion of people. Certainly there are almost no rural money-lenders or rural landlords so that this particular form of exploitation is absent.

The informal monetary sector tends not to be connected very directly with the formal monetary sector, so that the sort of central bank policy measures discussed in this and the previous chapter have little impact on it.

6 MONEY AND NATIONAL INCOME DETERMINATION

Although models depending on a key role for interest rates seem inapplicable to African conditions, the working of the monetary system does have some influence on changes in national income. Most of the points have already been made: this section will bring them together.

Consider a change in income which is stimulated by something which does not *of itself* alter the money supply or bank liquidity. For example, national income might be increased by an upsurge in business confidence, causing in turn an increase in investment demand. If spending takes place and is financed by local sources (as opposed to an inflow of foreign finance, which would increase bankers' cash) then income will increase, with the usual multiplier effects. As income increases, so will the public's holdings of currency, bank lending and bank deposits. In addition, increasing imports and tax receipts will reduce bankers' cash, although after some delay. The banks will thus have an increasing *need* for liquid assets while at the same time a diminishing supply of cash to satisfy that need. If the banks do not have enough spare cash they will be unable to satisfy the increasing demand for bank credit.

Putting this slightly differently, increasing income will increase the demand for money. If the supply of money is not able to increase then the expansion will be slowed down – *not* because of a rise in interest rates and the supposed effect on the demand for money and investment demand, but because of the commercial banks' inability to expand credit (and therefore the money supply) if they do not have enough cash. If the banks *do* have enough cash, the expansion can continue unhindered, if the banks are willing to lend, to those who need credit.

The reverse situation does not produce a symmetrical argument. If national income is reduced by a falling away of investment demand, this reduces the demand for money, the banks have spare cash and thus have the financial strength to increase their lending. This is added to after a time by reduced demand for imports and reduced tax receipts. But in a situation of falling demand and income, there are unlikely to be many borrowers wanting to take advantage of spare bank liquidity; and there is a strong possibility that the banks, far from wanting to increase their lending, will want to reduce it even further because of fears about their customers' ability to repay. It is possible therefore that the monetary factor will *reinforce* the fall in income rather than offset it, as in the case of an increase.

It is possible, however, that if investment demand simply increases rather less fast in a situation of continuing expansion, then some bank lending capacity will be released to borrowers who were previously unable to get credit. The monetary factor would in these circumstances be an offset to the reduction in demand. Both arguments depend, as always, on the banks having no spare cash – when they have plenty of spare cash they can lend as much as they want, regardless of changes in their cash position.

Now consider a change in national income stimulated by something which of itself *does* change the money supply and bank liquidity – for example an unfinanced increase in government spending or an increase in investment financed from abroad. In this case the demand for money will increase with national income, but the banks' ability to increase the supply of credit (and therefore the money supply) will also have been increased. If the demand for money created by rising national income increases faster than credit can be supplied, then the monetary factor will slow the increase down a little; if the demand for money increases more slowly than credit can be increased then the monetary factor makes no difference.

In the reverse situation, for example where a reduction in government spending is not matched by a reduction in taxation, bankers' cash will be reduced, thus forcing the banks to slow down their lending if they have no spare cash. At the same time falling demand will reduce the demand for credit. If the banks are forced into reducing their lending faster than the demand for it is falling, it may reinforce the fall in income. In this case the monetary factor *reinforces* falling demand; otherwise the monetary factor makes no difference.

Although other possible variations could be explored, the essential point should be clear by now. The *availability* of finance is an important factor, even if its cost is not. It is also important to remember that the banks are not always *willing* to lend, even when they have spare liquidity and there is unsatisfied demand for credit; if the potential borrowers do not normally have access to bank credit, or are considered uncreditworthy because of general business conditions, or want long-term credit when only short-term credit is available, then a potential rise in income may be frustrated even though it looks as though the monetary factor should be no obstacle.

7 MONETARY POLICY

In the previous section it was assumed that the central bank takes no positive action, but merely allows events to take their natural course. 'Monetary policy' is a general term for central bank action to affect monetary variables, of which no action at all (a 'neutral' policy) is only one example. Most of the possible forms of central bank action have already been discussed: the following is again a summary.

If the central bank does not want to see excess liquidity used for additional lending, it can

(a) increase the official reserve ratios, cash or liquid assets or both;
(b) alter the definition of liquid assets in such a way that some assets previously counted as liquid can no longer be included in the official ratio;
(c) require 'special deposits' from the banks, that is, require them to deposit a certain sum, or percentage of liabilities, at the central bank, such special deposits *not* to be counted as liquid;
(d) require special deposits from other institutions – this has the same effect since the deposits have to be switched from commercial banks to the central bank;
(e) force government debt onto non-bank holders, or onto bank holders provided that it does not then count as liquid assets;
(f) impose direct controls, for example aggregate or sectoral ceilings on lending.

If the commercial banks do not have enough liquidity to meet the demand for credit, then the central bank, if it does not wish expansion to be slowed down, can

(a) lend money to the banks
(b) lend money to non-bank institutions
(c) buy assets from the commercial banks (assuming the banks' problem is lack of cash and not lack of marketable assets)

(d) encourage the private sector, bank or non-bank, to borrow abroad
(e) release special deposits (if there are any)
(f) reduce cash reserve and liquid assets requirements
(g) remove direct controls.

In an economy with an active market in government debt the central bank can enter the market as a seller in order to reduce bank liquidity, but at the risk of lowering the price of stock and thus raising interest rates; or enter the market as a buyer in order to increase bank liquidity, but at the risk of increasing prices and reducing interest rates. The point is that in order to sell or buy significant amounts the central bank may have to influence prices by enough to encourage buyers or sellers to come forward. More often in practice the central bank finds itself buying and selling stock in order to maintain an orderly market, when nobody else will do so – regardless of the needs of monetary policy. In economies like those in Africa with very inactive markets, the central bank is very seldom in a position to pursue monetary policy by open-market operations; it simply has to act as residual buyer and seller and use other methods (of which there are plenty) to achieve the objectives of monetary policy.

So far only central bank reactions to an existing situation have been discussed. It is also possible to 'remove the brakes' in a situation of excess demand for credit; but where there is no demand for credit or the banks already have spare liquidity purely monetary action will not succeed in expanding the economy. Similarly, action to reduce liquidity will succeed in restraining demand if the banks have no spare liquidity and there is excess demand for credit. Altering interest rates probably has little direct effect on investment demand or the demand for money, but it may influence where depositors choose to invest their spare cash and where borrowers choose to borrow. Thus a rise in interest rates should in theory cause an inflow of cash from abroad and a reduction in local borrowing in favour of foreign borrowing. So many other factors are at work however, especially fears of exchange controls and devaluation, that interest rates are unlikely to be a major factor in this sort of way.

It remains to compare monetary policy with other ways of controlling demand. In a situation of excess demand, which is when monetary policy can most often be effective, there is a danger of cutting off finance to industry for increases in working capital and thus preventing increases in output that could take place very quickly. Clearly, if large amounts of money have been spent on the fixed capital for a new factory or mine or railway, it would be very damaging to starve the new enterprise of finance for working capital. Spending on fixed capital creates demand with no matching supply so that there is a particular need to avoid any delay in the start of production. The same is true of finance for imports:

if domestic output cannot increase in the short term then imports are the only way of increasing supply rapidly.

On the other hand, monetary policy does not demand the large numbers of skilled administrators required by a new tax, nor is it as politically unpopular as a tax increase or a cut in government spending. Monetary and fiscal policy both cause distortions and disincentives, although of different kinds.

So the choice between monetary and fiscal weapons is a matter of judgement. Normally they must be used together. Certainly it makes no sense to have the budget pushing one way and monetary policy another way because of a lack of co-ordination in government policy. Although central banks are government agencies, it is not as rare as it should be for the Ministry of Finance and the central bank to be pushing in opposite directions, or for the one type of policy to be left to try and mitigate the damage caused by the other. It *could* be sensible to increase taxation and allow bank lending to expand, if it is thought that taxation will reduce consumption and increased borrowing will be spent on investment; but it would not be sensible if the objective was simply an overall reduction in aggregate demand rather than a shift of resources from one use to another.

Appendix: The effect on the money supply of depositing currency in a bank

In normal times there is no reason to suppose that the public will alter its payment habits in such a way that the relation between holdings of currency and holdings of bank deposits will change suddenly. Salary earners paid by cheque draw out cash, as do employers to pay their cash-paid labour. Retailers pay in currency received from shoppers. Over the long term one would expect a rise in the use of currency as the subsistence economy becomes monetized and the wage labour force increases; over an even longer period of time one would expect a greater use of banks to cause a relative fall in the use of currency.

It is odd therefore that currency with the public in Zambia increased very slowly from 1968 to 1970 after increasing very rapidly up to 1968. Rapid growth resumed after 1970. This pattern is true of both the absolute amount of currency with the public and currency as a proportion of GDP (with copper price fluctuations removed).

The explanation is probably that the currency was changed at the time of decimalization in January 1968. Many members of the public would simply have paid in old notes and coin to a bank and used new notes and coin instead. But some of those who kept their savings in currency, hidden in their houses or buried in the ground, must have decided to start a bank account instead of replacing old currency with new. The very fact of having to enter a financial institution in order to change their currency would have given them an opportunity to start an account, or indeed to increase an existing one. It is also possible that in the remoter parts of the country the trend to increasing use of money was temporarily halted by suspicion of the new currency.

After 1970, the public's currency holdings resumed their growth, both in absolute terms and as a proportion of income. Indeed the use of currency increased so rapidly that it appeared to catch up on the 'missing' growth of 1968–70.

The effect of this phenomenon was that in 1968–70 rapidly growing deposits were not matched by public demand for currency, so that bank liquidity was greater than it would otherwise have been. In 1971, when there was an exceptionally large increase in currency held by the public, bank liquidity fell by more than it would otherwise have done.

Perhaps surprisingly, a similar phenomenon was observed in Britain in the early 1960s when the note issue was changed. The public's holdings of notes fell by £90 mn more than expected at that time, suggesting that saving in the form of currency continues even in a highly industrialized economy. The effect was much shorter-lived in Britain than in Zambia, however, presumably because of the relatively slower adaptation of Zambians to their new currency. Certainly some shops in Lusaka were still quoting prices in pounds as well as Kwacha as late as 1970.

NOTES

1 But the tendency is a weak one: for example, holding cattle can be profitable (because they breed) whereas cash earns no interest; food stocks are better protection against physical shortages than cash.

2 The student who wishes to study the demand for money (also known as 'liquidity preference') derived from this idea can find it in any developed-country textbook. The theory may have little relevance to industrialized economies, as suggested above, but if the theory is not worth explaining here it is even less worthwhile to criticize it.

3 The interest rate may have some impact on whether people keep their cash in Zambia or elsewhere – this point is dealt with below in Section 5.

4 Where there is an active market in government debt the central bank may be able to sell additional debt by lowering the price, which in turn implies an increased rate of interest. Where there is not an active market, as in most African countries, additional sales of government debt can probably only be made by making it compulsory in some way.

5 Commercial banks can decide, for example, who qualifies for their minimum lending rate, and who should pay more.

6 The speculative demand for money is supposed to be the less the higher are interest rates (and the lower are bond prices) because fewer people will expect rates to go higher and thus more people will switch to bonds. This is another example of using a proxy variable for expectations, the proxy variable being the current level of interest rates. Expectations are just not that simple.

7 See U. Tun Wai, 'Organised and Unorganised Money Markets' in G. M. Meier (ed.), *Leading Issues in Economic Development*, 2nd edition, Oxford University Press, 1970.

10 *Inflation*

1 SOME DEFINITIONS: DEMAND AND MONETARY INFLATION

In a very general sort of way, inflation simply means rising prices. Although prices do not always change together, the interdependence of different parts of the economy does tend to push up all prices together. Thus it is interesting that in Zambia the two consumer price indices, for those with higher and lower incomes, tend to move quite closely together, despite the different consumption habits of the two groups. On the other hand, those farmers in Zambia who consume mainly their own production are obviously only affected to a limited extent by movements in prices in the money economy, and all farmers can be affected quite differently by price changes as compared with either the high or low income urban groups.[1]

The main purpose of this chapter is to examine some of the theories of inflation and to see if they are applicable in an African situation. In earlier chapters two causes of inflation have already been considered implicitly. Firstly, an excess of aggregate demand over aggregate supply, when output cannot increase, will cause a rise in prices – provided the excess demand cannot be satisfied by running down stocks, increasing imports, postponing demand or diverting supplies from the export market. This sort of inflation is called 'demand inflation' (sometimes also 'demand-pull') for obvious reasons. In practice, in a situation of excess demand it is not usually a case of 'either-or' since some or all of the possible effects will occur simultaneously, of which inflation is only one. But the scope for running down stocks and postponement of demand is limited; and few countries can allow imports to increase and exports to decrease for very long. In Zambia's case there has often been limited capacity on import routes even when there has been enough foreign exchange to pay for imports. For these reasons, inflation is usually an important element in an excess demand situation.

The second type of inflation already considered is what might be called 'monetary' inflation, that is, rising prices caused by increases in the money supply. As was argued at length in the previous chapter, however, the conditions in which an increase in the money supply can be said to cause prices to rise must be carefully identified. If the money supply rises because of a budget deficit or an export surplus then excess demand is *combined with* additional liquidity in the banks. If output cannot increase, then prices probably will, with the inflation made worse by additional bank lending if (as is likely) there is excess demand for credit. This is not a 'pure' case of monetary inflation. If bank liquidity is increased independently of demand (by reducing reserve ratios, for example) then in a situation of excess demand for credit, prices will probably rise. This may reasonably be called monetary inflation – although since it depends on the existence of unsatisfied demand for credit there is an element of excess demand as well as of monetary factors in its causes.

It is an oversimplification to distinguish too neatly between situations where output can or cannot increase. There is a genuine difference between the two extremes, and between the effects of changes in demand and changes in the money supply when, for example, there is widespread spare capacity in domestic industry. But intermediate situations are more common. As spare capacity in the economy begins to be eliminated there will be increases in prices *and* increases in output. Some industries will reach capacity production first, while other industries are still capable of increasing output. Some goods, for example radios, can easily be imported when domestic production is at full stretch, but others, for example houses, cannot. At any one time, therefore, some goods and services are likely to be in short supply, with upward pressure on prices, while others are freely available at a constant price.

It is important to remember that pressure on the price of goods in short supply is not always by way of market forces. For example, the Zambian government controls the price of maize to the farmer and of maize meal to the consumer. If the price to the farmer is 'too low' so that supply is less than demand then the government may be persuaded to raise the price for the next agricultural year, in order to try and get increased supplies. This is a bureaucratic process, influenced by market conditions. (In the Zambian case the government has preferred to subsidize consumers rather than allow the price of a staple food to rise, so that the full inflationary impact has not been felt.)[2]

2 DEFINITION: COST INFLATION

There is a third theory of inflation called 'cost inflation'. The theory of cost inflation runs roughly as follows: first there is some autonomous increase in costs, such as a trade union demanding and getting an increase in wages, or a rise in import prices. Second, the rise in cost is passed on by producers in the form of higher prices. Third, the higher prices increase the cost of living, and this causes wages and incomes to rise again, because of trade union pressure, or because of clauses in wage-contracts which tie wages to the cost of living. The whole process then repeats itself.

Now this argument depends on a whole series of assumptions.

Firstly, in order for unions to be able to demand wage rises successfully, without causing unemployment of their members, there must be a fairly high level of demand for labour, or the union must be of fairly highly skilled workers who cannot be replaced. In other words unions, especially unions of the unskilled, are less likely to be able to get wage increases at a time of high unemployment, because at such a time their bargaining power is reduced. In addition, employers are less likely to grant wage increases at a time of low demand for their products, because their profits will be low and they will be less confident of their ability to pass on higher costs in the form of higher prices.

Secondly, wages are not the whole of industrial costs. Firms must also buy raw materials and semi-manufactured goods from other firms; pay rent, rates and fuel costs; set aside profits to pay for existing capital goods (depreciation) and new capital goods (investment); and meet interest and repayment costs on their borrowing. So even if wages do rise, the proportion firms must add to the prices they charge for their own products is less than the proportion by which wages have risen – unless all other costs rise simultaneously, which is only likely to occur in a situation of general excess demand. Where wages are very low initially, a wage increase may cause increased productivity – by reduced labour turnover, better management, better health of the workers – so that wage *costs* may not go up when wage *rates* rise. At the early stages of mining or industrialization in Africa this situation is quite common, a wage rise resulting among other things in a longer average period of employment of migrant labour, with some workers committing themselves to permanent employment. This greatly increases productivity.

Thirdly, in order to be able to pass on increased costs in higher prices, firms must have some control over their prices; or there must be excess demand for their products; or they must be confident that rival firms will also increase their prices so that a competitive position is not ruined. These possibilities are not mutually exclusive; some combination of them is clearly possible.

Finally, the link between price rises and subsequent wage increases is not clear-cut. Certainly there are often delays, especially in the government sector. Civil service and teachers' salaries tend to be the subject of lengthy commissions of enquiry so that salaries are increased months and even years after price rises have occurred. Secondly, there are many types of incomes which are not well protected against rises in the cost of living: for example, people on fixed contracts, people in non-unionized jobs, and so on. Thirdly, workers may not be able to get wage increases (as a result of price rises) if overall demand for their sort of labour is low, and unemployed workers with equivalent skills are available – as already explained.

3 COST INFLATION: WAGE INCREASES

It would appear from this analysis of cost inflation that the various steps in the argument, from cost rises to other price rises to wage rises, depend to some extent on there being *at the same time* a degree of excess demand. Thus it is argued that workers are unlikely to get wage increases unless excess demand exists for labour; employers are unlikely to grant wage increases or be able to pass them on in higher prices unless excess demand exists for their products; finally, workers may not be able to compensate for higher prices unless excess demand exists.

On the other hand, the structure of African economies is such that wage increases *can* occur independently of the aggregate demand and supply situation; in particular wage increases can occur in the modern sector despite there being more people willing to work than there are modern sector jobs.

Firstly, export industries can increase wages when export commodity prices are high – which can occur quite independently of the domestic economic situation. Secondly, import substitution industries can increase wages in the expectation of being granted increased protection by the government. Thirdly, much of industry (especially foreign-owned industry) tends to be very capital-intensive so that higher wages have a relatively small impact on costs. Fourthly, parastatal firms often expect the government to pay if they make a loss and expect the government to lend for investment if they cannot borrow commercially. Fifthly, African governments do not pay unemployment benefit to those out of work, which reduces the government's awareness of unemployment. Sixthly, high urban wages enable the unemployed to live relatively comfortably off their relatives with jobs,[3] thus reducing political agitation for more jobs. Seventhly, the lack of skills of the unemployed prevents them from competing directly with those in jobs.

In countries which depend, like Zambia, very heavily on expatriates, the structure of wages is affected by their salaries which in turn are partly decided by international salaries. Thus the Zambian mineworkers demanded and got a substantial wage increase in 1966 in order to 'narrow the gap' between themselves and the expatriate mineworkers. This wage increase was granted without reference to domestic conditions or needs – except the need to buy industrial peace. In 1967, civil servants got a substantial wage increase and in due course, so did workers in other sectors.[4] This example demonstrates how international salaries can affect wage levels throughout an economy, even among those groups of lower-skilled workers who are not competitive with expatriates.

In a more general sense the level of expatriate salaries creates a target for local workers, and their consumption habits have a demonstration effect. So even when expatriates are replaced by locals, the structure of salaries will remain for a time. In addition, the infrastructure of high expatriate salaries, for example large houses in scattered suburbs requiring a car (or even two cars), will remain.

It is thus possible for high wages to exist, and for wage increases to occur, in the formal sector, *at the same time as* there are more people wanting jobs than can be employed. Those who cannot get formal sector jobs are not usually unemployed in the sense of having nothing to do, but work in the informal sector, where the full impact of an excess supply of labour is felt in the form of low incomes. In the informal sector, workers are not protected by unions nor by government rules (such as minimum wage laws) and there is excessive competition in the provision of services and in small-scale manufacturing (such as the making of buckets and pots and baskets). As a result incomes are very low despite long working hours; these workers have been described as the working poor.

Even in industrial economies there is considerable doubt as to how much effect the level of unemployment has on the rate of increase of wages. At one time it was thought that there was a fairly close and stable link, expressed in the 'Phillips curve' of the type shown in Figure 10.1.

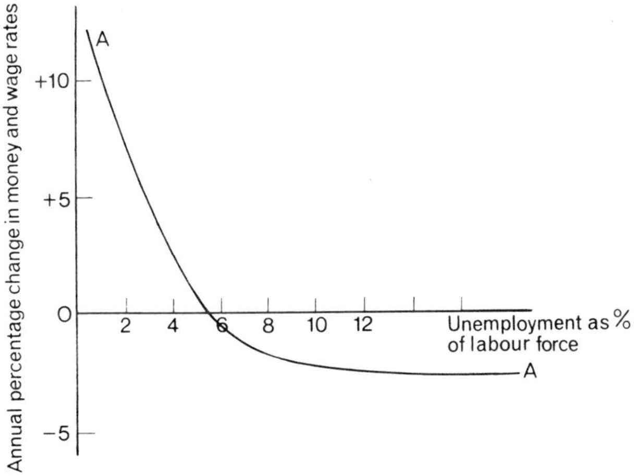

Figure 10.1 The 'Phillips curve'

There is no need to discuss the Phillips curve here,[5] except to point out that in recent years the curve has *not* been a good representation of the relationship between unemployment and the rate of increase in wages, even in industrial countries. It is possible that as the rate of inflation has increased in industrial countries the curve AA has shifted to the right, that is, a higher rate of unemployment is necessary to reduce wage increases to a given level.

In African countries the absence of unemployment statistics makes it impossible anyway to test the Phillips curve relationship. But if the above arguments are correct, then it is not relevant to African conditions. The example of Zambia after Independence certainly suggests that rapid wage rises can occur at the same time as rising urban unemployment. Because income prospects for most farmers are poor, high urban wages tend to attract more people to town than there are formal sector jobs, despite the availability of farming land. The education system also produces more people seeking formal sector (especially office) jobs than are available. At the same time the political influence of those in jobs is fairly effective in preventing the dismissal of workers. So the existence of unemployed workers and of low earnings in the informal sector does not necessarily prevent wage increases in the formal sector.

4 IMPORTED INFLATION

All countries depend to some extent on imports, but small, underdeveloped ones are more import-dependent than large, developed ones. At a time when prices are rising all over the world it becomes impossible for an import-dependent (or 'open') economy to avoid importing other countries' inflation in the form of higher prices for imports. In Zambia's case this has been made worse by the cost of diversifying away from nearby import sources, mainly Rhodesia, and from using the traditional import route from the south.

Even in a very open economy, imports are only a part of total supply, so rising import prices will not necessarily result in inflation at the same rate. Furthermore, if domestic inflation is less than inflation in the rest of the world, the balance of payments effects are not all unfavourable. Of course if import prices rise and export prices do not, then a commodity exporter like Zambia will be worse off in the short run, but no domestic policy can affect this situation. Meanwhile if the prices of domestic goods rise less fast than import prices there will be a tendency for people to avoid buying imports when possible.

Nevertheless, the consequences of inflation are not confined to the balance of payments and a country may wish to avoid the unattractive effects of inflation – on the incentive to save, on income distribution, on the type of investment that is encouraged, and so on. Is there any way a country can insulate itself from other countries' inflation?

If a country has enough foreign exchange then it can indeed avoid importing inflation, but few countries are so fortunate. For example, if Zambia is receiving very high prices for copper, it can revalue the external value of the Kwacha *upwards*, thus offsetting the domestic effect of higher import prices. Thus if import prices rise by 10% in dollar terms, an increase by 10% of the dollar value of the Kwacha will mean that the prices of imports expressed in Kwacha will remain constant.[6] If, on the other hand, the copper price is low at a time of world inflation, revaluing the Kwacha upwards can only go on as long as foreign exchange reserves last. In an industrial economy, the avoidance of domestic inflation should enable exporters to offer very competitive prices in world markets; as a result increased export *volume* may compensate for reduced export *prices*. But commodity exporters do not have this opportunity – supply is usually fixed in the short term and will if anything be reduced as a result of lower export prices.

Commodity exporters can try and bargain for higher prices, as the oil-producing countries have done very successfully, and as the copper producers have also tried to do. The difficulties of achieving international agreement among commodity exporters are very great. The oil producers had a number of unusual circumstances in their favour in 1973: political unity among the all-important Arab producers, created by a common dislike of Israel; a world-wide shortage of oil caused in part by the simultaneous expansion of all the major industrial economies; the ability of several of the Arab producers to cut production, because of having more export earnings than they could use. Even then it has been argued that the oil price was merely restored to its real value of more than 20 years before, having fallen in real terms for all that time.

From Zambia's point of view, a unilateral cut in copper production almost certainly causes a bigger loss in export earnings from lower export *volume* than the gain from a higher price. So only an agreed cut in export sales by the major copper exporters, such as was announced in late 1974, would be likely to have any real impact. Even then, in a situation of falling world demand for copper the move probably only prevented even greater falls in the copper price than would otherwise have occurred, instead of causing an actual rise. Meanwhile the domestic effects of reduced output are severe: either employment must be reduced along with output (both in the copper industry and in industries supplying it) or employment can be maintained while output is reduced with increased costs per tonne of output as a result. A third alternative is to reduce exports but maintain output – stock-piling the unsold output. But this creates an enormous financing problem for the mines which have to pay for output costs without selling part of their output; and creates a lesser financing problem for the balance of payments which has to bear the import costs of mining unsold output; these costs will be offset by a sufficient rise in copper prices, but the strategy remains a gamble which can probably only be attempted after a period of high prices when foreign exchange reserves are high.

The 'openness' of the Zambian economy, that is the very great dependence on imports which it shares with other African economies, does have a *deflationary* effect, as well as making the economy vulnerable to imported inflation. The point is that the availability of imports and the ability of Zambia to pay for them have been an important contribution to supply at times of excess demand. Thus one noted that in the period after Independence 'a country which increases gross domestic expenditure by 150% in 4 years, starts with a very small manufacturing industry, inadequate transport most of which it immediately does its best to stop using, and a very inadequate supply of skilled manpower, has done remarkably well in containing price rises to 30% or so. Looked at in this way one should ask not what caused inflation but what kept it down. The most important factors should by now be clear – the almost complete absence of a foreign exchange constraint which allowed imports to rise, hindered only by physical constraints; and the huge level of capital spending.... Even though a high proportion of government capital spending was on infrastructural projects with a high capital–output ratio, this must have been offset by the number of bottlenecks available to be broken.'[7] Of course, if the country is *not* able to allow demand to be satisfied by rising imports, because foreign exchange is not available (which has been the case more often than not since the above quotation was written in 1970), or if the more obvious supply bottlenecks have been removed so that domestic output cannot increase rapidly, then the economy becomes much more vulnerable to inflationary pressures.

5 THE IMPACT OF COST INCREASES

The dominant sector in industrialized countries is manufacturing, in which firms typically have some control over their prices and can therefore try to pass on cost increases. In Zambia, mining, agriculture and government are more important than manufacturing. Now mining exports most of its production at prices determined externally – by world markets in the case of copper, by OPEC in the case of oil, and so on. So cost increases, from wages or imports, are not reflected in domestic prices.

Wage or import cost increases in agriculture do not affect agricultural prices in the short term where they are market-determined. Where agricultural prices are government-determined, cost increases can only affect prices via a bureaucratic process which is typically quite lengthy.

Government, a major employer, does not generally sell its services but provides them free, so cost increases in this sector do not affect prices.

These three sectors accounted for about half the aggregate increase in the wage bill in Zambia in 1967, for example, when wages throughout the Zambian economy increased very rapidly.[8] The impact of these wage increases was thus *not* on the prices of goods and services of the workers concerned, as suggested by the theory of cost inflation. Instead there was a 'spread' effect to other wages, as workers in other sectors attempted to get comparable wage increases; and there was an important impact on aggregate demand because of the workers' increased spending power.

It is also open to the government to prevent cost increases from reaching consumer prices by subsidizing them. This is especially important for basic items of consumption such as maize meal and cooking oil, and for oil the cost of which affects all commodities that require transport.

Despite all these breaks in the chain of causation, the various links in the cost inflation argument remain important possibilities. Increases in costs have some effect on prices, the cost of living does affect wage demands. Wage increases have some further effect on prices as well as increasing demand via the income of wage earners. In choosing policies, therefore, the government must beware of using only one explanation for an inflationary situation. Before discussing policy, however, it is important to analyse the effects of inflation in order to understand who gains, who loses and what the incentive effects are likely to be on such things as investment, production and savings.

6 THE EFFECTS OF INFLATION

At first sight it might appear that it does not make much difference whether prices go up or not. After all, if all prices doubled, and so did the value of all assets, then nothing would apparently change. In a certain very trivial sense that is what happened in Zambia when the currency was decimalized: everything became worth twice as many Kwacha as it had previously been worth in Zambian pounds. The point is that inflation does not take place in this way.

Some prices increase faster than others; this means that those people *selling* goods or services whose prices rise faster than average have more rapidly rising incomes than those who have to buy such goods and whose incomes rise slower than the average. For example, if the prices of agricultural goods increase faster than the prices of manufactured goods then commercial farmers as a group will tend to gain at the expense of urban workers.

Some groups in society with a strong bargaining position can protect themselves against inflation by negotiating wage and salary increases. Others can not. For example workers in well-organized unions of skilled (and thus irreplaceable) workers are more likely to be able to get wage increases to compensate for inflation than workers without unions and without skills.

Most loans are designated in money terms. As a result, lenders are repaid the amounts of money originally lent which are worth less in real terms if prices have increased in the meantime. For the same reason, borrowers tend to do very well out of inflation because they repay less in real terms than they borrowed. Only if the rate of interest is high enough to compensate for the rate of inflation do borrowers fail to gain at the expense of lenders during an inflation. It seems that in Africa it is unusual for interest rates to be so high in the formal, organized banking sector: for example, the rate of inflation in Zambia in 1973 was something between 8% and 9%, yet the minimum cost of a bank overdraft was only 7½%. The Treasury Bill rate was less than 4% and depositors in the National Savings and Credit Bank got only 3¾%. So those borrowing from the banks for a year, say, paid back their loans with money worth 8% less than what they had borrowed a year earlier, having paid only 7½% for the privilege. The government did even better, paying less than half the rate of inflation for its borrowing. Anyone leaving money on a demand deposit account carrying no interest at all, or holding savings in the form of notes, saw their money lose value without any compensation at all. This applied to most people, since nearly everyone normally has some money for transaction purposes; only those with large borrowings gained more than they lost.

In general, anyone whose income and assets are fixed in money terms (or whose income and assets increase in money value by less than the rate of inflation) loses as a result of inflation. As a result there tends to be a redistribution of income from the weak to the strong. The economically and politically powerful are not only able to get increases in income to compensate for rising prices, they also have better access to credit and so tend to be net borrowers. In particular, the business sector tends to do well out of inflation: most firms have some costs which are fixed in money terms (rates, local taxes on property), are net borrowers and do well when demand is strong, so that profits tend to rise faster than prices. The wealthy, who own businesses, thus gain over the rest of the community.[9]

Another extremely important effect of inflation is on the balance of payments. If the exchange rate is held constant and domestic inflation is faster than in the countries which supply imports, then imported goods become cheaper than domestic goods, thus increasing the demand for imports. Commodity exports, whose price is determined externally, are unaffected in the short term and discouraged in the long term by the higher cost of production. Manufactured exports are rare in Africa – to the extent that they do exist they will be less competitive if higher production costs are passed on in prices. Rather more important is tourism: foreign tourists are discouraged from coming *to* a country by rising domestic prices, local residents find that holidays abroad become cheaper relative to holidays at home. For all these reasons the balance of payments suffers.

Attempts to reduce imports by physical controls reduce aggregate supply and thus tend to make the inflation worse. Import tariffs may reduce the demand for imports but add directly to prices and so worsen the inflation. The addition to prices may also set off demands for wage increases.

Inflation therefore causes a deterioration in the balance of payments unless the country is lucky enough to have the price of its exports rising rapidly. Broadly, this is what happened to Zambia in the five years after Independence. The price of copper fluctuated a lot, but about a rising trend. For a long time, therefore, the country was able to have rapidly increasing imports without having to worry about the balance of payments. Indeed, the price of copper rose so much that in spite of the fact that imports doubled, the foreign exchange reserves also increased. The trouble with this sequence of events, however, was that Zambia became a very high-cost economy. Domestic prices rose much more rapidly than those in, say, Kenya, yet the exchange rate between the Kenyan shilling and the Zambian Kwacha was unchanged. As a result, diversification away from dependence on copper for earning foreign exchange, by developing other export industries, was effectively discouraged; and domestic producers had to compete with relatively cheap imports. As it happened, import substitution in industry was greatly encouraged by UDI and the large increases in transport costs – but it would have been encouraged even more if inflation had been less, or if the rate of exchange of the Kwacha had reflected Zambia's higher rates of inflation. The main damage was probably in agriculture where an 'overvalued' currency discouraged existing export crops, the development of new export crops, and discouraged the use of labour (as opposed to capital). Exchange rate policy was thus a contributory factor to the decline of Virginia tobacco and groundnut exports.

It is perhaps necessary to elaborate a little further: in what sense can a country with a balance of payments surplus be said to have an overvalued currency? International trade theory suggests that such a combination is simply not possible. A balance of payments surplus would suggest that the country derives more benefit from investing in existing exports (copper) than in the alternatives. The point is that high copper prices may be regarded as temporary, and the copper itself is an exhaustible resource so that alternative exports must be developed. Since non-copper exports are so small it is essential that their development be begun a long time before the copper is all mined. Additional reasons for developing alternative *agricultural* exports are the desire for a better balance between rural and urban development and the need for better income distribution.

7 THE EFFECTS OF CONTINUING INFLATION: DIVERGENT AND CONVERGENT INFLATION

Because rising prices create additional income, inflation creates a feedback effect which adds further to demand. So if there is an excess of demand over supply rising prices do not remove this 'inflationary gap'. There are factors which tend to reduce the gap as inflation continues, thus making it a 'convergent' inflation; and factors tending to increase the gap so that the rate of inflation increases, making it a 'divergent' inflation.

Factors making for a convergent inflation are as follows.

(1) Investment should eventually result in more output, so that if

excess demand is caused by increases in investment this should in time result in increases in output and so remove the supply–demand imbalance. Even investment in apparently non-productive items such as primary schools and hospitals should add to national product in the long run, by producing a better-educated and healthier population. Clearly, those investments which produce a large and rapid increase in output are much less inflationary, since supply is more rapidly increased to fill the inflationary gap. One of the most fundamental problems facing underdeveloped countries in drawing up their development plans is the need for improved infrastructure: roads, railways, electricity, government offices, schools and so on. Typically, such investments have a very long life and a yield, in terms of increased output, that is spread over a very long period. The investment spending adds to demand at once, the yield adds to supply only over a long time. Development plans should therefore include a reasonable amount of investment with a low capital/output ratio, in order to mitigate the inflationary pressure of large investments in infrastructure with high capital/output ratios. Of course, some infrastructural investments may break supply bottlenecks and permit rapid increases in output – for example training of some key types of skilled manpower, or the building of transport routes which allow farmers to reach new markets. The building of Zambia's oil pipeline from Dar es Salaam may have been such an investment.

(2) As has been pointed out already, inflation probably increases profits faster than other types of income. Profit earners usually save a higher proportion of income than wage earners and receivers of rent, so this factor should induce higher savings. In so far as profits are paid out as dividends and saved, this is a genuinely disinflationary factor. But most of the higher savings out of profits come from retained profits, which are retained for investment purposes. This type of saving is only disinflationary therefore if there is some delay between earning of profits and spending of them on investment. Such a delay is quite likely, since there is often a time-lag between the earning of profits and firms making up their accounts and *knowing* what their profits are; on the other hand they may not wait for this, but make informed guesses, or simply invest on the evidence of high sales. The other thing that may cause delay is shortage of capacity in the construction industry and the capital goods sector if there is one. Investment spending on imported capital goods creates no new domestic income in itself, but has to be matched by transport capacity on import routes and construction capacity in the domestic economy – which may cause further delays. If profits are earned by foreign companies and remitted abroad then a shift in income distribution in favour of profits will be disinflationary.

(3) Some incomes are temporarily fixed in money terms, and some are not able to increase as fast as prices, as already pointed out in the discussion of cost inflation. When prices rise, therefore, these incomes fall in real terms. The people involved may try to maintain consumption

in real terms by reducing their savings or by borrowing; but in so far as they do not, or cannot do so, excess demand is reduced. In practice many wage increases are subject to delay, while unions negotiate with employers or salaries commissions report to government, so that in the short term this is an important convergent factor, especially when prices first start to rise and workers' reaction is relatively slow. The lower the rate of inflation the less urgent is workers' reaction likely to be.

(4) If the taxation system is income-elastic then inflation will cause taxation receipts to increase faster than the increase in money incomes, reducing real incomes and thus spending in real terms. Clearly this factor gains in importance the more people are affected by the tax system. In Zambia, for example, only a small proportion even of the wage- and salary-earning population pays any income tax; the progressive element in the tax system for non-income-tax payers is thus confined to the higher taxation of luxury commodities. The other condition that is important here is that government spending should increase more slowly than tax revenue. In that a lot of government spending is fixed in the short term (salaries, rents) or immune from domestic inflation (imports) this condition is usually met.

(5) As money income increases, the transactions demand for money also increases. More precisely, as money income increases bank customers draw currency from their banks, causing reduced liquidity in the banking system. Under certain conditions there will be an offsetting *increase* in bank liquidity – for example, if a contributory cause of the inflation is an unfinanced budget deficit. Suppose, however, that inflation is occurring with no offsetting increase in bank liquidity, for example because of a rise in import prices or in government-administered prices, then unless the central bank takes steps to restore bank liquidity, the banks may be forced to reduce their lending, or at least to reduce the rate of increase over what it would otherwise have been. This will reduce spending, consumption or investment, that would have been financed by bank credit, and this is thus apparently a convergent factor. However, to the extent that bank credit is used to finance imports it may reduce short-term supply; and, as was argued in Chapter 8, bank credit often provides the working capital that enables fixed capital to be used, so that credit restraint may reduce domestic supply as well. In general, however, constraints on bank credit tend to dampen demand. It is also possible that if the demand for money increases faster than supply then interest rates will rise. But in Zambia this effect is limited to interest rates on short-term government debt, which is not relevant to private sector borrowing; and in any case it was argued in Chapter 7 that the cost of borrowing has little or no impact on spending. In an economy with widespread foreign ownership of industry there is also a possibility that firms will borrow abroad if they are unable to borrow at home. Indeed, even domestically owned firms may do so,

but it is less likely and more easily controlled. Borrowing abroad enables firms to avoid credit shortages at home.

(6) Balance of payments effects, increasing imports and the increased profitability of selling export goods at home rather than abroad, have the effect of increasing aggregate supply, and thus of damping the inflation; but only so long as foreign exchange reserves last. As already pointed out, one of the likeliest reactions of government to this situation is to impose import restrictions or import taxes, both of which have the effect of increasing inflationary pressure. Another likely reaction, devaluation, is also likely to make inflation worse.

(7) The real balance (or Pigou) effect, such as it is, by reducing the real value of liquid assets expressed in money terms, should reduce consumption. Since by definition the people who have such money balances are able to maintain consumption in real terms by spending their balances, the convergent effect on inflation of the Pigou effect (which is small anyway) is probably negligible.

Most of the factors making for a *divergent* inflation depend on people adjusting their behaviour to take account of expected future inflation. This occurs when inflation is continuous over a long period of time and when price rises are quite large. Both these conditions are rather vaguely stated since it is impossible to be precise about expectations. But clearly an inflation of $\frac{1}{2}\%$ a year, even if continuous over many years, will not cause many people to adjust their behaviour in order to allow for expected future inflation. Equally, if prices sometimes fall or are stationary then expectations of future inflation will be less certain and so less likely to affect people's behaviour. On the other hand, a doubling of prices every month would very quickly cause people to react in any way that would reduce the impact. Divergent factors include the following.

(1) If inflation does in fact produce a shift into profits from other forms of income then high, and rising, profits can be expected to encourage investment. In addition, since changes in dividend payments usually lag behind changes in profits, retained profits will rise even faster, thereby providing part of the finance for this investment. As pointed out in (2) above, this is not necessarily a factor making for a divergent inflation if there is a delay between the earning and spending of profits. One would expect there to be such a delay in the early stages of inflation; but if inflation continues businessmen will be encouraged to spend money as it accrues, in fact to anticipate future increases in prices as far as possible.

(2) Inflation is bad for most forms of personal saving, since these are mainly fixed in money terms, and thus eroded in real terms by rising prices. When inflation begins people do not realize what is happening; and while interest rates are still greater than the rate of inflation, capital values are maintained. But as an inflation continues and accelerates people observe that earlier savings have lost value, and are encouraged

to buy goods rather than financial assets, either for consumption, or for a sort of speculative saving. For example, people will try and buy property during an inflation, since they normally expect property prices to keep pace with other prices, and thus to be a 'hedge' against inflation. In addition people will try and borrow as much as possible and invest in real assets, since their borrowings will have to be repaid in money terms, while their assets maintain or increase their real value. These shifts out of money into physical assets add greatly to inflationary pressure; and tend to divert savings from productive investment to speculative investment.

(3) If an inflation continues and the rate of inflation becomes very high, nobody will hold money for longer than they need. The velocity of circulation of money increases as people try and get rid of money balances as soon as they accrue. Thus the same absolute amount of money can be made to do more 'work', and a tight money policy by the central bank may be frustrated. It has been suggested that this reaction does not begin to occur until the rate of inflation is more than 10% a *month*. That may be too precise a statement, but certainly people do not feel they need to rush out and spend their wages at the beginning rather than the end of the week or month – because of inflation – when prices are increasing at, say, only 1% a month.

(4) If inflation is at a faster rate than the rate of interest then not only are savings discouraged, but borrowing becomes very cheap. Thus if prices rise by 20% a year and the interest rate is only 10%, then the cost of borrowing money is actually negative.[10] Even if investment is not sensitive to interest rates, negative real interest rates make it more likely that people will try and use borrowed money to buy physical assets, the money value of which is expected to keep pace with inflation. This effect only occurs though if people *expect* a rate of inflation higher than the interest rate, since otherwise the *nominal* rate of interest may appear very high.

(5) If inflation continues and accelerates, unions are likely to realize what is happening. They then demand wage increases which not only compensate for past price increases, but anticipate expected future price increases. If firms are making high profits, and have every reason to expect that they can pass on higher wage costs in higher prices, they will have little incentive to resist wage demands.

In summary, divergent factors all depend on what has been called 'inflation psychology', namely, the building of inflationary expectations into economic behaviour. On the other hand convergent factors tend to dominate when an inflation begins and when it is not very rapid. So minor inflations which arrive unexpectedly, or which are expected to be brief and even followed by price falls, are not likely to continue or get worse. Divergent forces, depending as they do on expectations, can only be modified if expectations can somehow be changed towards lower anticipated rates of inflation. Unless there is reason to believe that external forces will reduce inflation, shifting inflationary expectations downwards depends ultimately on an act of collective faith. If unions, government and private sector employers all agree to co-operate in reducing inflation they may all believe that it is possible. In these circumstances divergent forces may indeed be reduced. But it is a difficult thing to achieve and much more difficult if the first attempt fails.

8 INFLATION POLICY: DEVALUATION

From the arguments so far it should be clear that when inflation is more rapid than in other countries and so causes a deterioration in the balance of payments, then devaluation of the currency is a possible policy. Its immediate effect is to make imports more expensive (unless foreign suppliers choose to reduce their prices); and to increase the profits of exporters. Exporters of primary products, like Zambia and most African countries, cannot normally control their export prices as expressed in foreign currency. Thus whether Zambia devalues or not, the number of pounds or dollars or yen earned by copper exports is unchanged. If the Kwacha is devalued, that means that when the foreign earnings are sold (to the Bank of Zambia) the exporter receives more Kwacha than before. Of course the exporter must pay more, in Kwacha, for his imported inputs, but his profits increase nevertheless.

The impact of devaluation on exporters should be spelt out at greater length. Suppose that, using approximate figures for 1970, Zambia is exporting 700,000 tonnes of copper a year at K1,000 per tonne, giving sales of K700 mn. If the exchange rate is US$1·00 = K0·70 then these copper exports are worth $1,000 mn in foreign exchange. Now suppose that the Kwacha is devalued by 10% so that Zambians have to pay K0·77 to buy a dollar. Exports still earn $1,000 mn in a year because they are paid for in foreign currency at a price in foreign currency that is unaffected by Zambia's exchange rate changes. But each dollar is now worth K0·77 so that when the proceeds of copper sales are converted into Kwacha, annual sales become K770 mn, an increase of K70 mn.

Now imports into the mining industry probably ran at about K100 mn a year in 1970, made up of direct imports and the import content of local purchases, so the mines would have to pay an extra 10%, or K10 mn, on their costs. This gives an addition to profits, in local currency, of K60 mn. Of this, the government would get 73%, the marginal tax rate on copper mining profits; so government tax revenue would go up by K44 mn. After-tax profit would rise by K16 mn of which roughly half (49% in fact) would be the companies' share since the takeover. It is not possible to say whether total profit remittances would be more or less in foreign currency. On the one hand profits available for remitting abroad have risen by roughly K8 mn; but an offsetting factor is that all of remittable profits must be turned into dollars at the devalued rate. The figures used in this example correspond very roughly to 1970; at the 1970 level of profit remittance the companies would have gained more from a 10% devaluation in the form of the increase in their Kwacha profits than they would have lost in remitting dividends to overseas shareholders at a lower rate of exchange – but it is perfectly possible for the arithmetic to work in the opposite way.

The impact of devaluation on the agricultural sector would be to make export crops, such as tobacco and groundnuts, more attractive to producers than crops produced for the home market – such as maize – provided that the higher Kwacha price of exports was passed on to producers and provided that the government did not raise the maize price and the prices of other agricultural products sold on the domestic market.

Because the prices of imports increase, devaluation adds directly to inflation. If local industry is in a position to increase output in the short term, devaluation may shift demand from imports to domestic output and result in an output increase which is counter-inflationary. But because devaluation is normally in response to inflation, and inflationary conditions normally mean that domestic output cannot be increased in the short term, the main impact tends to be on import prices rather than domestic output. There is a real danger, then, that devaluation will cause a cost inflation. In a country like Zambia, which produces a relatively narrow range of goods at home, devaluation causes price increases in a wide range of goods including some necessities, so wage earners are particularly likely to try and seek higher incomes to compensate. In addition much of local industry depends on imports of intermediate goods so production costs also rise. Price increases are then likely to spread to locally produced goods, further increasing the probability of wage demands.

The big question in any Zambian devaluation is thus the reaction of the labour force to the resulting higher prices. In particular the mining union would be likely to seek a wage rise and if it were successful there would be a danger of this spreading to other sectors of the economy. On the demand side, the biggest single question would be whether the increase in government revenue from the mining industry was spent or not. On the assumption that most forms of government spending cannot be increased at once, it should be relatively easy for the inflationary impact of a devaluation to be contained. However, the government would be likely to face demands for an increase in civil service wages to compensate for higher import prices, and it *is* possible for them to be increased very quickly – so again the importance of controlling wages is fundamental if devaluation is not to create further inflationary pressure.

Another aspect of devaluation peculiar to the Zambian economy concerns expatriate salaries in general and expatriate remittances in particular. Without compensating salary increases, the Kwacha value of salaries remains the same following devaluation, but their foreign exchange value is reduced. Expatriate workers would also have to pay higher import prices and so would tend to have lower savings to send out of the country. The very high foreign exchange cost of remittances would thus be reduced in the short term; there would be a tendency over time however for expatriate salaries to rise, both as a result of direct pressure from the expatriate workers themselves and because of the need to be competitive when recruiting (and at contract renewal).

Import substitution industries based on the local processing of imported inputs, a category which includes a large part of manufacturing industry, face increased costs as a result of devaluation. All industries use *some* imported inputs, of course, but in Zambia as in most developing countries many new industries are very heavily dependent on imported inputs, with relatively low local value added. The effect of devaluation on such industries is to reduce their profits quite sharply unless they are able (or allowed by the government where prices are controlled) to raise their selling prices. Local industries do, on the other hand, gain a competitive advantage over imports, where competing imports are still allowed into the country.

Essentially what a devaluation does in domestic industry is to increase import costs in relation to local costs (including labour). So industries which use local raw materials, relatively large amounts of labour (especially local labour since expatriate labour may be in a better position to get compensating wage rises) and relatively small amounts of imported raw materials, intermediate goods and capital equipment gain an advantage over other industries. The mining industry gains therefore not only because it exports its products, but because it is based on a local raw material. Thus in 1969, direct imports were only $3\frac{1}{2}\%$ of gross sales in mining, compared with 10% in agriculture and 15% in all other sectors.[11]

In summary, devaluation makes exporting more profitable; makes import substitution industries more competitive but at the same time makes them less profitable unless they are able to offset the increased cost of imports by increasing output; favours industries with a high proportion of local costs (including especially labour) over industries with a high proportion of import costs (including imported capital goods); reduces the volume and foreign exchange costs of expatriate remittances provided expatriate workers are not compensated by higher pay; increases the cost of living because of the increased cost of imports; causes a sharp rise in government revenue because of the high marginal tax rate on copper company profits. There is a considerable danger that a devaluation will set off further inflationary forces unless wage demands are restrained and unless home demand is also restrained (especially government expenditure). If domestic output is able to increase, to meet both the shift in demand from more expensive imports and the increased profitability of exporting, then the danger of further inflation following a devaluation is reduced.

9 INFLATION POLICY: USING INFLATION AS A TAX

By spending money which is not covered by taxation receipts or non-bank borrowing, governments can cause a shift of resources away from the private sector towards the public sector. The government action causes prices to rise if output cannot increase in the short term, some people's real incomes and wealth fall, and the government is able to spend money and command real resources at their expense.

There has been a great deal of discussion in economic writing on development as to whether in fact the governments of underdeveloped countries should use this method of 'taxation' to finance their development plans. The argument runs that because of shortage of administrative staff, and political realities, increased taxation may not be possible. Therefore inflation is the only way of transferring resources to the government. In using this argument, one must be careful to emphasize that such an inflation should be short, and be followed by a period of relative price stability, in order that divergent forces do not get hold of the economy.

My own view on this is that any country attempting development is going to experience *some* inflation, because of the inflexibility of the economy, inelasticities of supply in many sectors, shortages of key goods and skills, etc. Furthermore, even a comparatively mild inflation causes some inequities, for example against those on fixed money incomes, or those too weak to protect their real incomes, and against those who have saved, and perhaps invested in government loans. If, *on top of this*, the government attempts to use inflation as a tax, the rate of inflation will very quickly reach the point where divergent forces could take hold; the government might then find it was no longer able to control the inflation, with the usual serious effects on incentives, allocation of investment, and so on. In short, inflation is a very dangerous weapon, which can easily do more harm than good. At best the government may not wish to try and reduce a 'modest' rate of inflation.

Using inflation as a tax also assumes that the government will make better use of the resources it 'captures' from the private sector than the latter would have done. It also assumes that the greater value of government's use of these resources is enough to offset the distortions caused by inflation. This is true of all forms of taxation, but in using conventional taxes the government has to make a more positive political decision, pass legislation and face up to the political and economic consequences in a more direct way. The costs of inflation are less obvious, being indirect and delayed, so that the danger of excessive use of inflation as a tax are very great.

10 INFLATION POLICY: CONTROLS ON PRICES AND INCOMES

For obvious reasons governments often try and control inflation by direct attack on prices themselves, and on wages when these are believed to be the main cause of inflation. There is also a case for controlling wages on grounds of equity, to prevent strongly organized groups of workers from gaining at the expense of other workers, and to prevent workers in general from gaining at the expense of farmers and the unemployed. To complete the circle of argument, if wages are controlled then it seems fair to control prices in order to prevent profits from rising as a result of wage controls.

Most governments try to keep wages and prices down, at first, by talking. Ministers make speeches about the public interest, the government as a whole lays down 'norms' for price and wage increases which people are asked not to exceed, on a voluntary basis. The trouble with this strategy is that, being difficult to police, it is unlikely to be universally observed. Those who obey the government's requests then lose out to those who do not – any system that makes the 'good guys' look foolish is unlikely to last long.

Compulsory wage and price control is also difficult to enforce, especially when administrative staff are scarce and expensive. Furthermore, it prevents the price mechanism from allocating resources according to scarcity. For example, if the government obeys its own rules and restrains civil service pay, and if other employers disobey the rules or find ways round them, then over time the government will find it difficult to recruit and keep able people who can find better paid employment elsewhere. The same argument applies within the private sector. In the very long run, if pay is not allowed to respond to shifts in the demand and supply of different types of skill, in the different parts of the country and the economy, the government will be forced into *directing* people to jobs. To a small extent this is already done, when those given an expensive university education at government expense are 'bonded' to work where they are placed for a number of years. But it is quite a big step from that to the direction of all workers. So leadership codes, salary reductions for cabinet ministers and the like are essentially political gestures in the context of making wage restraint acceptable and of altering inflationary expectations, rather than ways of effecting a lasting reduction in the differentials between top salaries and average incomes. The latter is only likely to be achieved at all effectively where the government is in direct control of nearly all top salaries, by ownership or participation in the majority of big employers, and where dependence on expatriates does not drive up all top salaries.

Similar arguments apply to trying to control prices. For example, if the government uses its power over agricultural prices to keep down the price of food, farmers have less incentive to produce more, consumers buy more because the price is low, and scarcities of expensive imports are the result. Or else the government is led into using expensive subsidies to keep down the price of food while offering farmers a good price. Another likely result is the creation of unofficial ('black') markets where the price is higher than the official price. All these results of price controls tend to induce yet more controls, more administrators and greater opportunities for administrative delay, mismanagement and corruption.

There is much more to the proper analysis of prices and incomes policies than there is space for here. The main point to make in the context of a chapter on inflation is that a prices and incomes policy may be essential for breaking the vicious circle of divergent forces acting in an inflationary situation. If inflationary expectations create more inflation, which makes people expect yet more inflation with greater certainty, then the government may have to intervene. The government may also have to control prices of key commodities like maize and cooking oil at times of temporary shortage (or temporary excess supply) in order to prevent excessive profits at the expense of the poor.[12] The point is that the case for intervention is essentially one for temporary intervention, not for permanent controls, unless the government wishes to move towards a controlled economy.

NOTES

[1] See C. Young, 'Rural-urban terms of trade' and J. Maimbo and J. Fry, 'An investigation into the change in the terms of trade between the rural and urban sectors in Zambia', both in *African Social Research*, No. 12, 1971. The main reason why agricultural prices may not move with other prices in the economy is that they are mostly government – rather than market-determined. Those that are market-determined can be sharply affected by weather conditions quite independently of aggregate demand and supply.

[2] Price control is further discussed below.

[3] 'Living off' the employed consists not only of direct help, but also making some sort of a living in what is becoming known as the 'informal' urban sector, by providing services such as car-washing, petty retailing, cycle repair, etc.

[4] See J. B. Knight, 'Wages and Zambia's economic development', in Elliott, op. cit.

[5] There is extensive discussion of it in most macroeconomic textbooks based on industrialized economies.

[6] Another effect of an upward revaluation is a reduction in export profits and thus government revenue (the reverse of the devaluation effects described below) but both would be high at a time of high export prices. A reduction in both through revaluation would probably be unimportant, therefore.

[7] See my article 'The control of inflation in a very open economy: Zambia 1964–69', *Eastern African Economic Review*, June 1971, p. 58.

[8] Harvey, 'The control of inflation ...', op. cit., pp. 49–50.

[9] There are, of course, exceptions to this: not all firms are selling goods the prices of which rise faster than costs, and, as is explained below, importers do better than exporters.

[10] This statement assumes that the income of the borrower rises in line with the general rate of inflation.

[11] National Accounts and Input–Output Tables 1969, Lusaka, May 1972, Table 16(a). Among the other sectors, the percentage for industries processing local raw materials (grain mills, brickworks, furniture, etc., columns 3, 4, 5, 6, 7, 8, 9, 11, 15, 16) was 12% and for other manufacturing (columns 10, 12, 13, 14, 17, 18, 19) was 26%. These figures do not give the whole picture because of the import content of current local purchases and of capital goods, but they give some indication of the differences between mining, agriculture and different types of manufacturing.

[12] Agricultural products are a special case because of the variations in supply caused by the weather, disease, etc. Even so, the possibility of imports and exports evens out the effect of these fluctuations for many products.

11 *Theory of Public Finance*

1 INTRODUCTION

The 'theory' of public finance is the theory of the economic functions of government: why they are undertaken, how many should be undertaken, who should perform them and how the resources should be provided. The classic work on this subject[1] identifies three main economic functions of government: allocation of resources between private and public sectors; the distribution of income (for example between rich and poor, or between foreigners and local people); and the stabilization of national income, that is, the prevention of depressions, the control of inflation, and so on. To these three functions most people would now add a fourth, which is the active promotion of economic development; and, although economic development can be defined to include almost anything, most African governments would probably single out the promotion of economic independence as a separate objective.

2 ALLOCATION: COLLECTIVE GOODS AND MERIT GOODS

The most basic reason for governments to interfere in the allocation of resources is the need for collective goods (also known as social wants) which the market economy cannot provide. The classic collective good is defence. Defence services are *indivisible*, that is they are provided to the community as a whole, so nobody can be excluded from the benefits. Indeed everyone must 'consume' collective goods in equal amounts. In addition, they must be *paid for* collectively. Because collective goods are indivisible and so cannot be sold individually, the community must find the necessary resources as a community. No individual will volunteer to pay for collective goods, since he will enjoy the benefits whether he pays for them or not. So collective goods must be paid for by taxation or by some other compulsory method.

Governments also seek to provide some goods, known as merit goods, free or at less than the market price. Examples are education and health services, and, in Zambia, milk which has been supplied at half price to low-income families. Essentially, the government decides that some goods would not be demanded, or not demanded in adequate quantities, or not demanded by those who need them, if the full cost had to be paid by individuals. The reasons are either that people are thought not to appreciate the benefits fully; or that people do not have sufficient income.

An interesting distinction between collective goods and merit wants is that one might expect people to vote for collective goods, provided they are sufficiently well informed to identify their collective needs. Thus although one cannot rationally expect people to volunteer to *pay* for collective goods, one could expect people to want them; so government could respond to the people's wishes in supplying things like defence, police services, flood protection, law courts, and so on.

Almost by definition, however, people do *not* identify their needs for merit wants, since if they did they would buy enough of them, without having to be taxed and have them supplied or subsidized by the government. It may be that some merit goods are desired by people all right, but that they are too poor to afford them. In this case government is acting to redistribute income in supplying the goods free, or more cheaply than the market. The same redistribution effect could in theory be achieved by a transfer from tax revenues to the incomes of the poor, thus allowing them to satisfy their needs. This assumes, however, that everyone has in fact successfully identified his needs. Governments tend not to make this assumption, but to be afraid that income transfers will be spent on beer or betting; so increased consumption of merit goods is usually attempted by direct supply or by direct subsidy.

In principle, the government should only decide to increase its own share of total spending if the additional benefits are greater than the loss of goods and services available in the private sector. This assumes full employment of resources; if the stabilization function of government is being properly performed, then resources should be as fully employed as possible; if not, then the government can increase its own demands on the resources of the economy without reducing the resources available for satisfying private sector demands. *Within* the government's budget, the marginal benefits from the spending of the last Kwacha on each service should be equal; for example, if more benefit accrues from spending an extra Kwacha on health than accrues from the last Kwacha spent on education, then less should be spent on education, and more on health – at least from the economic point of view. Such rules are, however, easy to express on paper, but difficult to put into practice, mainly because the marginal benefits from most types of government spending are difficult if not impossible to evaluate.

In the long run, the total resources used by government tend to be determined to a large extent by available financial resources – mainly taxation, but including borrowing, foreign exchange reserves, money creation and foreign aid. In principle a government has the power to tax people more heavily if it believes that a bigger proportion of total resources should be used to provide government services. However, people do not like paying taxes, so governments need an 'excuse' for imposing heavier taxation. The result seems to be that only in times of crisis, such as a war, are governments able to make big increases in the proportion of income that people pay in taxes.

In more normal times, people tend to regard the existing level of taxation as the maximum tolerable. Research in the UK has shown that after wars the proportion of income paid in taxation falls, *but does not fall* to the pre-war level. The reason suggested is that people quite quickly get used to a higher level of taxation, once it has successfully been imposed, so that governments are not forced to return to the pre-war position.[2] If, on the other hand, taxes are sharply increased *without* adequate political justification, the result is likely to be tax riots, the fall of the government or ignominious removal of the offending taxes. If the country is heavily dependent on internationally recruited labour, heavy increases in income tax may have to be reversed, or compensated by higher wages, because of expatriate workers' ability to leave the country.[3]

The permanent upward shift in the proportion of income which people will pay in taxes has been called the 'displacement effect'. Associated with it is an 'inspection effect'. In times of crisis existing ideas of what needs to be done by government are shaken up and changed. Governments 'inspect' their activities and the people's needs, and discover new spending requirements.

There was a sharp increase in the level of spending by many African governments after Independence – Zambia is an example. In this instance, however, it was not so much the new government being forced by some crisis to discover new needs. The needs were well enough known to the new government; it was simply that they had been badly neglected before Independence. In Zambia's case the period after Independence happened to coincide with very large increases in revenue from copper[4] so there was no need to use the sense of urgency and unity, created by political independence, to increase the overall level of taxation. In short, there has not really been occasion yet to test the concepts of the displacement and inspection effects in a Zambian context.

3 DISTRIBUTION

Governments interfere in the distribution of income because communities seldom believe that market forces distribute income justly. In addition the community may wish to discriminate against certain types of income, such as rent or profits, or against income earned by foreigners.

In a market economy people earn incomes which roughly reflect the scarcity of their skills on the one hand, and their economic and political bargaining power (usually in groups) on the other. The difficulty lies in distinguishing a high income which results from hard work and enterprise, virtues which most societies accept as deserving economic rewards, from a high income which results from luck, or the use of monopoly power or from some other circumstance which the community feels gives 'excessive' rewards. In practice it is not possible to make such a distinction, so high incomes and luxury goods are taxed at higher rates than low incomes and essential goods, regardless of the source of income – at the risk of creating a disincentive to effort and enterprise.

Taxation is discussed at some length in the next chapter. The point to make here is that African governments tend to find it very difficult in practice to redistribute income by means of the tax system – in spite of high marginal rates of tax on high incomes, and heavy taxation of luxury goods. Mainly for practical reasons, governments also rely rather heavily on other forms of taxation which bear disproportionately on the poor. Income tax, also for practical reasons, tends to be very difficult to administer so that it does not have the effect it should have in taxing high incomes heavily. The overall result is therefore that tax systems do *not* succeed in being progressive (by which is meant that the proportion of each person's income paid in tax does *not* rise as income rises).

In Kenya, for example, a recent study found that the overall effect of the tax system on income distribution was more or less negligible.

TABLE 11.1
Combined incidence of direct and indirect taxes in Kenya

Monthly income (in shillings)	*Tax incidence as a percentage of income*	*Monthly income (in shillings)*	*Tax incidence as a percentage of income*
0–199	11·5	700–999	10·5
200–299	11·3	1,000–1,399	9·3
300–399	8·5	1,400–1,999	9·6
400–499	8·3	2,000 and over	12·7
500–699	8·0		

Source: Report of ILO employment mission to Kenya, *Employment, Incomes and Inequality: a strategy for increasing productive employment in Kenya*, ILO, Geneva, 1972, p. 272, quoting M. J. Westlake, 'Tax evasion, tax incidence and the distribution of income in Kenya', University of Nairobi, Institute of Development Studies, 1971, mimeo.

The distributive effects of mineral taxes depend on who, in principle, is really entitled to the profits. This is obviously very important in major mineral-exporting countries where mineral taxes are a large proportion of government revenue (frequently more than half in Zambia, for example). If oil or copper is being exploited by foreign companies, from rich countries and (probably) owned by rich people in those countries, then heavy taxation of the profits is arguably a redistribution of income, via government spending in the country where the minerals are. It is surely much more reasonable to argue however that the most the foreign companies are entitled to is a 'reasonable' payment for their capital and skills and the risks taken (if any). Any remaining profit on copper, say, legitimately belongs to the people of Zambia. If the government spending out of copper revenues benefits all Zambians equally then the overall effect is merely neutral.

If tax systems tend to be ineffective in redistributing income, then it remains to ask whether government spending can be more effective, since clearly it is the overall impact of the fiscal system that really matters.

Many government services are provided free, or at less than cost, in order that they shall be equally available to all. One problem of this form of redistribution is that services provided free may be 'over-consumed' – that is, people may demand more than they need of a service because it is free or cheap. For example, people may use health services which they do not really need because no payment is required and they have nothing to lose. In the case of health, it may be better to risk some over-consumption than to risk a sick person being denied health services because he cannot afford to pay – but this assumes an adequate overall supply.

A much more important problem in providing free services arises when there is not enough for everybody – as is common in poor countries. Even in Zambia, which is relatively rich by African standards, not everyone who needs it can gain access to clinics, doctors, schools, subsidized credit, etc. In these circumstances, distribution must be decided by some administrative process. The result is often that the richer people succeed in gaining access. When some services are of better quality than others, it is again the already privileged who tend to succeed in gaining access to the better services. The reasons are many; rich people are better at filling in forms, are better informed, are better placed (they live in towns, near to good schools and hospitals), or they simply have influence with which to gain access.

If richer people *do* succeed in getting access to government services provided free, then the result is much the same as if the government charged a fee, since under either system poor people are excluded. The only difference is that rich people are subsidized if services are free. In these circumstances it might be better to charge a fee, which if spent on increasing the services available, would result in more people being able to gain access. Alternatively, administrative methods can be changed in order to achieve more egalitarian distribution – but this is extremely difficult.

A special case of a government service provided free is education. On the one hand the community needs highly trained manpower and needs to select as efficiently as possible those who can benefit from each level of education above primary (everyone is assumed to need primary schooling).[5] On the other hand this process means selecting the brightest students, who would be most likely to succeed in earning high incomes anyway, and then spending large sums of government money on further increasing their earning power. Some sacrifice is required of students in that often they have a lower income while studying than they could earn in a job; but the student life is itself often quite pleasant, and the subsequent financial rewards very high in countries where educated people are very scarce, and top salaries are heavily influenced by international salary levels. In addition, the children of richer parents have advantages, not only in gaining access to the better schools, but in passing exams. Children coming from better-off families are well known to have enormous advantages in conventional education, because of parental encouragement, a literate home background, etc. The result is again that an apparently egalitarian policy, the provision of free education, is likely to give great additional advantages to the already privileged – who could afford to pay.[6]

A distinction needs to be made, therefore, between the effect on income distribution of collective goods which are indivisible and *have to* be consumed equally,[7] and the effect on income distribution of government services which are divisible but subsidized. It is the latter which are liable to reinforce unequal income distribution, *even when* governments have the opposite intentions.

Most government policies have some impact, intentional or not, on income distribution. The most important intentional distribution policy, apart from taxation and the provision of government services, is a prices and incomes policy. This has already been discussed in the context of inflation (Chapter 10, Section 10) where it was also mentioned that equity and fairness were involved. It is a reasonable generalization that economic and political power are often cumulative. Thus those who have scarce skills are in a strong position to bargain for even higher incomes than they already receive; those with high and stable incomes are able to borrow and invest in farms and businesses which increase their incomes even further. The rich tend to have influence on the political and administrative process by which their own incomes are decided – whether it be by keeping down urban prices, by influencing the nature of taxation or by deciding their own salaries. So governments try to intervene directly in the determining of prices and incomes, and by legislating to prevent the privileged from having several sources of income (for example, Zambia's Leadership Code), not only in order to control inflation, but in order to redistribute income.

In the context of income distribution, the really important point to make about an incomes policy is that many policies *intended* to introduce greater equity are not as simple in their impact as they seem. For example, increasing the price of maize has been discussed as a way of redistributing income from town to country – but its effect may be to redistribute income from the urban poor (who are the majority of urban consumers and must spend a high proportion of their income on basic food) to the rural rich (who produce the bulk of marketed maize). Similarly, a leadership code may have the effect of redistributing income from those to whom it applies (civil servants) to those who are left out of its provisions (in the private sector). In general, income distribution must be looked at in its entirety, including possession of assets with which to earn income (physical assets, human capital and access to key resources such as credit). It may be that egalitarian asset distribution, especially of land in predominantly rural countries, is a much more powerful way of redistributing income than the whole of fiscal and incomes policy.

4 STABILIZATION

A large part of this book has been about the stabilization function of government, namely the need to prevent the under-utilization of resources on the one hand, and excess demand on the other. Ideally the government should try and use tax, expenditure and monetary policy in such a way that income is as stable as possible around an ideal level.[8] Although that is very difficult, governments should normally be able to prevent extremes of surplus unused capacity and very high levels of excess demand.

The realization that governments can control aggregate demand, (more precisely, the balance between aggregate demand and supply) has been of great benefit in preventing excessive waste of productive capacity, as occurred in the depression of the 1930s. There has been a tendency, however, for governments to pay more attention to the risk of unemployment (whether of people or of other resources) than to the risk of inflation. The result has been steadily rising prices which lead, as explained in Chapter 10, to inflationary expectations, which in turn make inflation worse. Reductions in demand then have progressively less and less impact on prices. Even those countries which may have managed their affairs differently have to 'import' to some extent other countries' inflation. The stabilization function of government has thus shifted in emphasis from the prevention of too little aggregate demand to the control of inflation. And the control of inflation has been made more difficult by past attempts to manage demand.

It would be ironic if the ability to 'manage' the economy, that is the stabilization function, resulted in *either* the destabilizing effects of accelerating inflation *or* the need for much larger reductions in demand (in order to control inflation) than would otherwise have been necessary. In practice, the political constraints on government economic policy lead them to try and fight inflation by controls rather than by reductions in demand so large as to be politically unacceptable.[9]

5 AUTOMATIC STABILIZATION

In Chapter 5 (Section 6) it was explained that receipts from most taxes tend to vary with income and spending, and that this reduces the multiplier effect of changes in demand. Thus the formula for the multiplier without government spending and taxation was

$$k=\frac{1}{1-b}$$

and when G and T were introduced, the formula was

$$k=\frac{1}{1-b+bt}$$

So income fluctuations tend to be smaller as a result of a tax function which depends on income. The major qualification of this formulation is that some income and tax changes have little or no feedback effect on spending. This is allowed for by having a tax function of the form

$$T=\bar{t}+tY$$

where $\bar{t}$ is that part of tax receipts which is independent of income in the short term – $\bar{t}$ tends to be very large in the Zambian case because in the short term receipts from copper taxation are not affected by changes in, say, government spending.

Automatic stabilization, that is the reduction in income fluctuations as a result of the nature of the tax system and government spending, is greater as t is greater. It is thus open to governments to choose taxes for their automatic stabilizing effects.

In effect West African marketing boards did this, in an extreme way, by paying a fixed price to farmers producing export crops such as cocoa, and allowing the entire impact of export price fluctuations to be reflected in marketing board surpluses and deficits. Strictly speaking this amounts to a stabilization scheme and not taxation. Indeed the original intention was purely stabilization with no taxation element, but the price to farmers turned out to be consistently below the world price so that *de facto* the farmers were being taxed – and to add insult to injury the marketing board surpluses were not, by and large, used for investment in agriculture but were spent on industrial development much of which was not successful.[10]

At the other extreme, the income tax in many African countries only applies to a very small proportion of the population so that it has relatively minor automatic stabilizing effects. In Zambia, for example, only about one in six of the wage earners recorded in official statistics pays any income tax, because the 'allowances' exempt the remainder. All wage earners are supposed to pay the 'Personal Levy' but this comes to a maximum of K20 on an annual income of K1,000, so that the 'leakage' from income is only 2%. The employee's contribution to the National Provident Fund also varies with income, but again the amount is very small. As a result, almost all of an increase in wages becomes disposable income and is available to be spent. The same applies to the increase in income from an increase in numbers employed. In reverse, spending is likely to fall by almost the full amount of a fall in wage income.

The main contribution to tax revenue of wage earners is in the form of *indirect* taxes, mainly the taxes on alcohol, cigarettes and imported goods. The contribution to non-copper tax revenue of customs and excise taxes rose from K22 million in 1964/5 to K98 million in 1972 and from 14% to 31% of total revenue. As a result, the marginal propensity for revenue to increase with increases in income (t) was quite large in Zambia (slightly more than 0·25) despite the lack of coverage of the taxes on personal income.

Just as important as tax in providing automatic stabilization is government spending. In African countries there tends to be little or no automatic *increase* in government spending as income falls (there being no payment to the unemployed as in industrialized countries) but government spending is much more stable than private consumption and investment. Basically, as discussed at length in Chapter 5, government spending is independent of short-term changes in income. So the larger is G as a proportion of total spending, the smaller do fluctuations tend to be. Since this proportion has tended to increase slightly over time, there has been a tendency towards greater automatic stabilization.

All the above analysis applies almost exclusively to the monetary economy. The subsistence sector's income fluctuates mainly as a result of the weather and other natural causes. The existence of the public sector affects this sector directly only in extreme circumstances, by providing famine relief, although if a comparison is made with the distant past, the existence of strong government has also reduced cattle and slave raiding and other violent disruptions in supply.

6 GROWTH AND DEVELOPMENT

This book is about short-term changes in macroeconomic aggregates, not about growth and development which involves the longer term. The points to be made here are why governments have become involved in promoting development and just what this additional function implies.

Governments in industrial countries became interested in promoting growth because the elimination of widespread unemployment by demand management enabled them to look to other ways of increasing income. In the rest of the world contact with richer countries awakened governments to the possibilities of growth, as did the gaining of independence in many countries in recent years.

By actively promoting growth, governments are interfering with individual choice in a new way. Firstly, they are deciding that change in social habits, in social relations, in physical surroundings, in traditional values, in the ways in which people work, is worthwhile for the rewards of growth. Secondly, government is deciding, very often, that present sacrifice is worthwhile for future benefit. For example, if government imposes additional taxation to finance some project whose benefit is spread over 25 years starting after 5 years, it is effectively interfering with people's time preferences.

To the extent that governments represent people's wishes in promoting growth, time preference is merely being expressed collectively rather than individually. But it is part of the nature of development that changes are made which are outside the range of understanding and imagination of most of the people, and in any case the amount of interference with time preference, that is the amount of present sacrifice for the sake of future income growth cannot normally be expressed collectively. It is a new type of decision which did not have to be made when governments were concerned only with allocation, distribution and stabilization. People's own private savings, and therefore investment, determined the nation's time preferences between present and future consumption; any government savings were determined by the stabilization function.

Although at one time it was believed that growth was determined by investment, it is now thought that investment as conventionally defined only creates part of economic growth, the remainder coming as a result of improvements in productivity whose causes are much in dispute. Statistical analysis shows typically that less than half of growth can be attributed to physical investment; the remainder is attributed to education, research, better health or nutrition, improved management or any number of other causes according to the prejudice of different writers. The point to make here is that some spending conventionally classified as consumption undoubtedly contributes to income growth: this means that governments must interfere not only with time preferences in the pursuit of income growth but also in the choice of consumption items, both individual and collective.

7 ECONOMIC INDEPENDENCE[11]

Economic independence is a relative concept. All countries depend to some extent on the rest of the world. But some countries (or governments) feel economically dependent because they perceive their relations with the rest of the world as being very unequal. The actual degree of inequality varies according to which variable is under discussion. Politically, dependence is an extremely sensitive subject so that those aspects of economic life in which a country sees itself as being very dependent tend to get more emphasis than others. Furthermore, even in very dependent situations, the 'dependent' government always has *some* bargaining power.

Thus Zambia sees itself as being very dependent, although less so now than at Independence in 1964. Then it was dependent on:

(a) one railway for nearly all its foreign trade, going through countries (Rhodesia, Mozambique, South Africa) to which Zambia was hostile;

(b) foreign manpower to run the modern sector of the economy, because of having only 100 local people with university degrees and 1,000 or so who had been through secondary school;

(c) two 'hostile' countries for 60% of imports (Rhodesia 40%, South Africa 20%) and the former colonial power for another 20%;

(d) foreign technology, especially in mining;

(e) foreign investors in most sectors, including commercial farming;

(f) one commodity, with a very volatile price, foreign-owned and foreign-managed, for nearly all export earnings.

That is a fairly formidable list, yet there are some items on the other side of the argument:

(a) Zambia had more than one potential outlet to the sea and has used them (the Lobito railway) or developed them (the road and railway to Dar es Salaam) since Independence – in this respect the country is substantially better off than, say, Lesotho or Uganda;[12]

(b) Zambia's wealth from copper has given the country great scope for tackling the problems of dependence and in particular for freeing the country from dependence on the south – Malawi, for example, is worse off in this respect;

(c) Zambia is potentially self-sufficient in basic foodstuffs, and, with under-used land, has great potential for increasing food production;

(d) being mainly on a high plateau Zambia has a huge potential for generating hydro-electricity, a 'benign and renewable' source of energy;[13]

(e) English being the official language, Zambia has a much greater range of countries from which it is practical to accept technical assistance than, say, the francophone or Portuguese-speaking countries;

(f) Zambia's hostile neighbours, although economically and militarily more advanced are not overwhelmingly larger, as, for example, India and China are in relation to Nepal.

The second point is that even where economic dependence seems most extreme, Zambia has some bargaining power. Thus Rhodesia gains revenue from Zambian transit trade so that losing that trade is a loss to Rhodesia, even though it caused greater losses to Zambia in the short run. In the longer run, Zambia had everything to gain strategically from diversifying its trading routes. Similarly, Zambia is an important market to its southern neighbours, so that trade dependence on them had some advantages as well as disadvantages. The danger of depending on a few countries for a high proportion of imports is that they might cut off supplies, but they have something important to lose if the trade is large.

Even in Zambia's most extreme areas of dependence, copper and foreign manpower, the sheer size of the copper mines and their expatriate labour force gives some bargaining power.[14] It is possible, though not at the moment probable, that the main copper exporters will combine to control the supply and therefore the price of copper traded internationally. Furthermore, the very great size of the copper mining industry in Zambia means that the mining companies have a great deal to lose and that the large expatriate labour force could not quickly be re-employed elsewhere. At the other extreme, the foreign banks in Tanzania were able to withdraw their expatriate employees when dissatisfied with the terms of nationalization; but Tanzania was able to keep the banks in operation by one means or another, including the hiring of a few foreigners on an *ad hoc* basis. In this case, the smallness of the sector was an advantage to Tanzania.

In one particular way, Zambia has become more rather than less dependent since Independence, and that is in the role of copper in the economy. The very wealth that has enabled the government to spend heavily on education, on new transport routes, on building up administrative capability that had been largely located in Salisbury during Federation (and dominated by whites), and so on, has come from rising amounts of earnings from copper which are still over 90% of visible export earnings. As a result there is a much larger urban sector which is still almost entirely dependent on copper. Further expansion of this urban sector is in turn almost entirely dependent on yet further increases in copper earnings, which would push still further into the future the possibility of diversifying export proceeds. So far, non-copper export earnings have shown little signs of growth and import substitution has had a negligible impact. It is arguable that the government had very little choice after Independence in the way the country developed and that it chose with some skill between the options that did exist,[15] but this analysis does obviously emphasize the great need for developing greater self-sufficiency (especially in food) and for developing alternative exports, notably from agriculture.

8 PUBLICLY PRODUCED GOODS

Should collective goods and merit goods be supplied by governments or supplied by the private sector and paid for by government? What other goods should be produced within the public sector?

In extreme cases the answer is fairly obvious. Hiring out defence services to private contractors is not done very often and is seldom successful when it is done (for example African experience with mercenaries). Defence and police services, law courts and government administration are too vital to be run by any body but the government itself (although some internal security services are provided by private sector security companies and by individual watchmen).

In the less obvious cases, public ownership of the means of production depends as much on the government's political ideology and on historical accident as on whether public ownership is an efficient way of producing goods and services in the public interest. The point is that there are many ways of controlling the private sector – taxation, price control, licensing, exchange control, wage policy, etc. – of which public ownership is only one. What is more, public ownership does not necessarily mean that the government really controls an industry in practice.

In Africa there is a further aspect of public ownership. The primary motive in the Zambian nationalizations has been to lessen *foreign* ownership and control rather than to achieve public ownership itself. Thus where Zambian private sector institutions and private individuals were available to take over from foreigners, they were used – examples are retailers and small-scale building contractors. Where no private sector institutions were able to take over the foreign concerns, the government did so – as in the case of the mines. Similarly, where the government wants new foreign investments to be undertaken in collaboration with local people, the sheer size of the operation usually dictates that the government itself is the only possible partner.

Although localization rather than socialism has been the main motive for nationalizing firms in Zambia, as in some other African countries, there are other reasons. Indeed the railways, airways and electricity supply were all parastatals in the colonial period, when the government was neither particularly nationalistic nor socialist. An important reason usually given for public ownership is that an industry is a 'natural monopoly', by which is meant that competition would be wasteful – for example if two competing railway companies built and ran railway lines between Lusaka and Ndola. Secondly, private ownership of a natural monopoly might lead to exploitation of customers. Thirdly, financial requirements may be too great for private companies to raise.

Logically, these are not very good arguments. American privately owned railways and airways (and telephone companies) are not allowed to exploit their customers by means of their 'natural monopoly' positions, but are controlled by other means. Railways have raised capital privately in the past (the first railway in Zambia was built by private capital). This again makes the point that public ownership is only one way of controlling industry. Secondly, public ownership does not necessarily give control – nor does 100% ownership necessarily give more control than 51% or 25% ownership. Indeed many of the Zambian government's takeovers were to satisfy political aspirations as much as to achieve control, especially in the cases where management contracts had to be given to the former foreign owners.[16] Wholly owned parastatal holding companies, which never did have foreign ownership or management (except for some expatriates on contract), have at times acted in the same if not a more capitalist way than private sector firms – giving rise to the phrase 'state capitalism'.

Public ownership is also of course a way of securing for the public sector the profits of the industries concerned. Again, taxation is a clear alternative method, although it can be objected that discriminatory taxation against particular firms or industries is wrong. In practice, public ownership seldom increases government revenue: either profits are all reinvested or, as is frequently the case, the industry is run at a loss and the government has to cover the cost.

The strongest arguments *against* public ownership are that governments and their civil servants are less efficient at running productive industry than private firms and that governments never allow inefficient firms to fail, thus perpetuating inefficiency and the need for subsidy. These arguments are about matters of fact, however, and should be based on pragmatic appraisal of each situation. There is no *a priori* reason why either private or public management should be more efficient. In Africa, where most countries are rather small and remote and thus at a disadvantage when dealing with large foreign companies, public sector participation is often the *only* way of finding out enough about the way companies are run to exercise effective control in the national interest – but even this is not true in every case.

9 CONCLUSION

Although the problem of paying for government services is very much a part of the theory of public finance, it is such a big subject in itself that it is covered in the next chapter.

NOTES

[1] R. A. Musgrave, *The Theory of Public Finance*, McGraw-Hill, 1959.

[2] See A. T. Peacock and J. Wiseman, *The Growth of Public Expenditure in the United Kingdom*, Oxford University Press, 1961, Introduction and Chapter 1.

[3] This roughly explains what happened in Zambia's 1974 budget when the previous year's income tax increase was reversed, officially instead of wage increases, unofficially because of increasing expatriate labour turnover on the mines. See 1974 Budget Speech.

[4] See Chapter 5, Section 4.

[5] Even this argument needs to be questioned, since it is not certain that governments provide appropriate education which will in fact give the right skills to benefit the community.

[6] Education systems also have the effect of removing the most able from the rural areas by giving them an education which gives them a taste for town life, and because the bulk of jobs requiring education are in towns.

[7] Although it has been argued that rich people, having more to lose, gain more from defence and police services than poor people.

[8] It would be more accurate to say that stabilization should be around a high level of utilization of a *growing* production capacity – however, the additional complication of growth over time is ignored here.

[9] For 'automatic stabilization', see Section 5.

[10] See G. K. Helleiner, 'The fiscal role of the Marketing Boards in Nigerian economic development, 1947–61', *Economic Journal*, September 1964, reprinted in Milton C. Taylor, *Taxation for African Economic Development*, Hutchinson, 1970; and G. K. Helleiner, 'Marketing Boards and domestic stabilisation in Nigeria', *Review of Economics and Statistics*, February 1966.

[11] For a more extended version of the points made in this section see my paper 'International corporations and economic independence: a view from Zambia' in D. P. Ghai (ed.), *Economic Independence in Africa*, East African Literature Bureau, 1973; this book also contains case studies of Kenya, Egypt and the Sudan as well as several general discussions of the subject.

[12] See Zdenek Cervenka (ed.) *Land-locked Countries of Africa*. Uppsala, Scandinavian Institute of African Studies, 1973, especially the paper by Douglas Anglin in which he lists no fewer than 29 routes to the sea from Zambia, of which 21 have actually been used – pp. 122–3.

[13] Benign, because it causes no pollution, renewable because it depends on the waters of the Zambezi and its tributaries, rather than on a finite resource such as coal or oil.

[14] Takeovers, including that of copper, are discussed in the next section.

[15] See my paper 'The structure of Zambian development' in Ukandi Damachi (ed.), *Paths of Development*, Geneva, Institute for International Labour Studies, 1975. See also J. Fry and C. Harvey, 'Copper and Zambia' in J. Cownie and S. Pearson (eds.), *Commodity Exports and African Economic Development*, Lexington, Heath, 1974.

[16] For a detailed description of the way the former management retained control of the copper mining companies after the 1969 takeover, see M. Bostock and C. Harvey (eds.), *Economic Independence and Zambian Copper*, op. cit., Chapter 7.

12 *Paying for Government Spending*

1 INTRODUCTION

There are many ways of meeting the cost of government services – most of them require a degree of compulsion. As already explained, it is irrational to volunteer to pay one's share of the cost of collective goods. Ideally, the community should make a collective decision on how to pay – by taxation, by borrowing from itself or from others, by providing free labour, and so on – but in the end that decision must be enforced since few people are willing to contribute their share unless everyone else does so too. Thus even if a small village community decides to provide itself with a dam or a road or a school building by communal labour, it is necessary that everyone contribute (and be seen to contribute). It may be hard to exclude the shirker once the new facility is built and available and it would be unjust to exclude his children.

In a modern economy, taxation is normally by far the most important way of providing resources to the government, but other methods do exist. This chapter will deal mainly with the principles of taxation, but it is important to remember that governments can choose not only between different types of tax but also between tax and other ways of allocating resources from the private to the public sector.

2 BASIC PRINCIPLES OF TAXATION

Probably the most basic principles of taxation are those of horizontal and vertical equity. Horizontal equity requires that all those with an equal ability to pay should pay the same amount of tax; vertical equity requires that those with a greater ability to pay should pay more. These principles are easy enough to express on paper but extraordinarily difficult to put into practice. What is more, they may conflict with various other criteria. Thus tax systems should be cheap to administer; should be good at controlling private sector expenditure (economic efficiency); should encourage saving, investment, production and the supply of effort (incentive effects); should not distort the allocation of resources *within* the private sector, except where this is a deliberate policy (neutrality); should maintain or even increase the government's share of income as income increases (income elasticity); should provide revenue that is easy to forecast accurately, so as to make planning easier (fiscal marksmanship); should make groups pay for benefits, such as local services, from which they benefit more than others (the benefit principle); should have a high marginal tax rate with respect to short-term changes in income (automatic stabilization).

No tax system can be ideal in the sense of fulfilling all these criteria perfectly. African tax systems, however, are particularly imperfect. Partly this is because African tax systems still reflect the political realities of the colonial period; partly it is because of the structure of African economies; partly it is because tax systems have been heavily influenced by taxes used in industrialized economies. Some examples should make this clear.

One of the first taxes used in Africa was the poll or hut tax. The official justification for this tax was to make Africans contribute to the cost of administering their affairs; the real reason for imposing it was to force Africans to work on European-owned farms and mines in order to earn the money to pay the tax. The poll tax took no account of differing ability to pay, nor of the effect on agricultural production of men being absent from their homes, nor of the social costs of migrant labour, nor of the injustice of making relatively very poor people pay for government services, nor of the inequitable distribution of government services, nor of the political injustice of imposing taxes on people who had no representation.

Royalty on the Zambian mining companies was paid to a foreign company until 1964; and much of the revenue from the income tax on mining profits was spent in Southern Rhodesia during the Federal period. What is more, the royalty was a tax on production not profits, so it had the effect of discouraging high-cost mines and the mining of high-cost ores. The Export Tax, introduced in 1966, was successful in capturing a bigger proportion of the very high profits from a high copper price, but was also a disincentive to produce and invest. There were other things wrong with the system of taxing copper in Zambia before 51% government participation in 1969; the point is that the taxes were a combination of history and convenience (they were very easy to collect) but ignored incentive effects.[1]

Income taxation in English-speaking Africa reflects both political power and the influence of the British income tax system. A comparison of African income tax systems in 1968 showed that white-dominated South Africa had the least burdensome income tax.[2] This is because income tax bears more heavily on the better off while taxes on goods and services bear more heavily on the poor, in relation to their incomes. The 'allowances' in the income tax system are ill-adapted to African conditions. Thus deductions (allowances) are subtracted from salaries for a wife and children, before applying income tax rates. This is intended to make the income tax more equitable, by allowing for the expense of maintaining a family. But in Africa a man with a high-income job is responsible for other members of his family as well. The allowances therefore tend to make the system less rather than more equitable, by reducing the tax payable by a man supporting his wife and children but not reducing the tax payable by a man supporting his brothers, sisters, nephews, nieces, parents, grandparents, etc. Furthermore, the allowances are worth more the higher is the man's income and are worth nothing at all to those whose incomes are too low to pay income tax. It would be possible to make the income tax much simpler, and thus much easier to administer, by abolishing allowances *without* making it less equitable – indeed a simpler income tax would be *more* equitable. Ghana and Tanzania, for example, have done this; Zambia, on the other hand, has not.

The whole tax system is biased against the use of labour and in favour of the use of other inputs, especially capital. Allowances in the company tax based on capital spending make capital cheaper,[3] as do low tariffs on imported capital goods. High tariffs on consumer goods tend to increase the cost of labour (since they are bought by wage earners). Compulsory contributions to provident funds are effectively a tax on labour, thus raising its cost. One should add that low interest rates and overvalued exchange rates also reduce the cost of capital. The overall result is to reduce the rate of growth of employment, by violating the neutrality principle. That is, the tax system interferes in the allocation of resources in the wrong direction. Interference may be justified, but it should make (plentiful) labour cheaper and (scarce, expensive, imported) capital more expensive. There are many other factors pushing African economies into using capital-intensive techniques, and it may be that the tax system is not the most important; but the tax system is something that the government can change so that it is clearly unnecessary for it to be creating the wrong incentive effects.

The taxation effect of marketing boards, which offer a stable price to farmers while export prices fluctuate, has already been discussed (Chapter 11, Section 5). It is also common for agricultural exports to be taxed, thus creating an incentive for farmers to produce other products, for the home market. Even where there are no possibilities for avoiding the tax in this way, a tax based on production is inequitable because it bears more heavily on the smaller producer and because it taxes the exporter but not other producers.[4]

These examples cover some of the major taxes in Africa, suggesting that extensive tax reform is required. But while it is easy to be critical, it is very difficult to devise a better tax system. The next section tries to explain why.

3 THE APPLICATION OF THEORY

Horizontal and vertical equity, or ability-to-pay, would suggest an income tax, backed by a tax on assets (for example, a wealth tax). The latter is necessary because otherwise people with assets which do not yield any (or very much) monetary income – such as owner-occupied houses, under-utilized land – would escape taxation. Alternatively the 'yield' from such assets should be estimated in some way, added to monetary income and taxed. In practice this is seldom done, mainly because of the heavy administrative task of valuing assets or estimating their yield. In Africa, the need to tax capital (wealth) is not as great as in developed economies, simply because less personal wealth has been accumulated. Even so, equity is extremely hard to achieve, even by income taxation.

Income taxation requires an adequate supply of literate and numerate administrators, and literate and numerate taxpayers. Yet both are in particularly short supply in Africa. For example, in Zambia in 1969 the department of income tax had only about 75% of its authorized establishment which itself needed to be increased by 50% – yet there were only 60,000 or so people paying income tax.[5] Many small-scale but prosperous businessmen keep no books – some are even illiterate. For example, the owner of a metal-working shop in Lusaka 'keeps no books but sends large amounts of money home to support several relatives' and still 'manages to put K200 aside each month'[6] – the source does not specify, but he almost certainly paid no income tax. In any case, such a man would have tremendous scope for concealing the extent of his income and for treating personal expenses as business costs and so reducing his tax.

In such conditions, income tax tends to be very inequitable, since the self-employed (and to a lesser extent those who are employed in small-scale businesses) have enormous scope for avoiding tax; those who work for government and for large-scale employers generally, have tax deducted from their wages at source and have almost no scope for avoiding tax. The more the government relies on income taxation, the less equitable does the system become.

Furthermore, with high income tax rates, the incentive to avoid paying tax increases: as a result, rich men find it worthwhile to hire expensive lawyers to find loopholes in the tax law and many also find it worthwhile to devote a lot of energy to tax evasion (illegal tax avoidance) instead of to earning more (legal) income. The government is then forced to counter with more highly paid lawyers, policemen, etc. The end result is likely to be that a significant proportion of the country's scarce highly trained manpower is devoted to the tax fight – lawyers, legislators amending the law, judges hearing tax cases, etc. This is very wasteful. In Africa this process has probably not got much beyond the stage of successful tax evasion and avoidance.

Some improvements can be suggested. If the personal income tax were simplified, getting rid of the rich country complications, more administrative time could be devoted to the really difficult task of taxing businesses. Even small businesses without accounts can be taxed by quite simple methods – *high* rule-of-thumb estimates (based on spot checks of stocks, for example) can be used for assessing tax, throwing the burden on the taxpayer to prove his tax liability is less. But the higher are tax rates (because of heavy reliance on income taxation) the more the system will not be fair, nor be seen to be fair. Furthermore, the incentive to corrupt and the scope for corruption increases the higher are tax rates and the more flexible are the rules (the greater the discretion given to the tax officer, the easier it is for him to bend the rules in response to a bribe without being found out).

Not surprisingly then, in view of this analysis, African governments have relied on ease of collection more than on abstract principles of equity. Poll taxes apart (where the cost and difficulty of collection was considered worthwhile in order to increase the supply of labour) exports and imports are the obvious candidates for taxation. Most countries have only a few ports, border crossing points and international airports so that it is quite easy to 'catch' the goods for taxation.[7] Furthermore, international trade tends to be in the hands of a relatively small number of large-scale businesses – as opposed to internal trade with its multitude of small-scale operators. International trade was in fact the way in which monetary transactions first penetrated African economies on a large scale, so it was the obvious candidate for taxation.

Export taxes on commodities are very certain in their 'incidence', that is, they cannot normally be 'shifted'.[8] Almost all African commodity exports (except oil and possibly cashew nuts and cloves from Zanzibar) are sold at a world price over which individual countries have no influence, so there is no question of forcing prices up to uncompetitive levels, although there is a danger of encouraging some producers to switch to other products. Most export producers have little choice but to accept lower incomes because of taxation, in the short run. In the long run, the value to the economy of export taxes depends on whether governments or exporters invest more out of the proceeds and how productive such investments are.

Import duties serve the double purpose of raising revenue for governments and protecting local industry from competition. Their incidence is partly on importers because demand is reduced, and partly on consumers who pay higher prices. As African economies develop import-substituting industry, the structure of imports shifts away from consumer goods to intermediate and investment goods which are taxed less.[9] Governments must therefore look to other sources of indirect tax revenue. They tend to be unwilling to tax most domestic products however, precisely because these products need protection from overseas competition. The bulk of taxation on locally produced goods is thus on 'demerit' goods – mainly alcohol and tobacco. These have the advantage of fairly inelastic demand – people go on buying when the price is increased by taxation – but the disadvantage of being regressive (they bear disproportionately on poor people) and encouraging illegal production (shebeens). Ministers of finance can also find themselves in the dilemma of wishing to discourage drinking and smoking but being very dependent for revenue on alcohol and tobacco taxes.[10]

4 TAXATION OF FOREIGN FIRMS

There are a number of special problems relating to the taxation of foreign firms. Firstly, they have opportunities for shifting their profits to other countries and so avoiding taxation. For example, if a firm is assembling locally intermediate goods supplied by the same firm in another country, it can pay artificially high prices for the inputs thus reducing its local profits and increasing its profits overseas. This practice, known as transfer pricing, can also occur where firms are not associated, if they agree to collude. Exporters can also undercharge for goods supplied to firms overseas, with the same effect. Transfer pricing can be used to avoid local exchange control rules on the remission abroad of profits. High rates of profits tax increase the incentive to use transfer pricing as do severe constraints on profit remission.

As far as tax is concerned, African countries can do three things about transfer pricing. Firstly, if local tax rates are no higher than rates in the foreign investors' countries of origin then there is no incentive to avoid local taxation. Secondly, governments can negotiate double taxation agreements, whereby they agree that taxes paid in Africa are offset against, say, British tax liability, so that again the firm has no incentive to avoid local taxation.[11] Thirdly, governments can try and secure better information on what international trading prices ought to be, in order to prevent transfer pricing. This is extremely difficult, time-consuming and expensive to do (and sometimes impossible) but nevertheless worth trying. It is almost certainly a situation in which African governments could usefully combine.

Some companies have much better opportunities to use transfer pricing than others. For example, the Zambian mining companies sell their output at a published world price; and generally are horizontally rather than vertically integrated. That is, they have mining enterprises in other parts of the world but are not in general in the business of supplying mining inputs. In any case imports are by now a quite small proportion of total inputs. Firms assembling imported inputs are at the other extreme. Clearly there is an added reason here for encouraging the development of local supplies of inputs as fast as possible.

Another way in which foreign firms can avoid local taxation is by borrowing money from abroad rather than using equity capital (direct investment in the firm). Under 'normal' (that is, foreign-type) tax laws, interest on loans counts as a cost and is deducted from profits before tax is paid. Interest on foreign loans may thus leave the country free of tax. The return to direct investment is in the form of profits, which are taxed. For this reason Zambia, for example, has introduced a withholding tax on interest payments on foreign borrowing. This is an imperfect solution, since the withholding tax is at a lower rate than profits tax and the rate of interest may simply be increased on future loans to offset the tax. Nevertheless, a withholding tax is a step in the right direction. Similar measures are necessary for management fees, licensing payments and other ways of getting money out of the country labelled as costs when they are partly disguised profits.

New foreign investors, that is firms looking to invest in a country for the first time, are frequently offered tax concessions. The commonest of these is a tax holiday – by which is meant that no tax need be paid on profits for the period of the holiday (from two to five years in Zambia's case). As explained in Chapter 7, Section 3, this type of concession is based on a mistaken theory of investment. Most foreign investors are *not* simply looking for opportunities to make a profit on their local production.

Thus if an investor is trying to protect or increase his market share by setting up locally, or to make a profit on the sale of machinery or inputs, then tax concessions will add to his profits but not affect his investment decision very much. Furthermore, if profit on local production is determined by such factors as the degree of protection, price control, monopoly powers granted, etc., then tax concessions become merely a part of the bargaining between the investor and the government, and not necessarily the most important part. Thus the investor who actually needs to make a profit on his local operation (as opposed to making a profit out of some other part of the operation) is primarily concerned to secure guarantees of profitability and permission to remit. At the extreme, if tax concessions are not granted he will simply try and rearrange other concessions to compensate. Most fundamentally of all, most foreign investors are not going to be interested in investing in what they see as small, remote, unstable countries, liable to expropriate investments and prevent remission of profits at any moment, unless they have some other motive than simply a 'normal' rate of return on local production. The only possible exception to this is Nigeria which is large and, since the oil boom, relatively rich.

5 RURAL TAXATION

Most direct taxes reduce income and so give people an incentive to work more and restore their income: this is the 'income effect'. Income taxes also reduce the marginal return to extra work, and so give people an incentive to work less, by substituting leisure for work: the 'substitution effect'. The substitution effect can also be described by saying that an income tax cuts the cost of leisure (by reducing the amount of income foregone in not working) and so induces people to 'consume' more leisure. The poll tax had an income effect, inducing people to work in order to earn income and pay the tax; but had no substitution effect because additional work and income-earning did not attract additional income tax.

The Uganda tax on rural income had a similar effect in a rather more sophisticated way.[12] Essentially it assessed the income-earning *potential* of a farmer's assets – acres of various crops, coffee trees, stores, cattle, etc. – and levied a tax on that basis. This sort of tax reduces income and thus has an income effect; there is no substitution effect because tax liability does not rise with income. A tax based on land value is similar in effect if land value (and thus tax payable) is not affected by short-term changes in yield. Land taxes are impractical in much of Africa, because land is not easily valued. Either there is no market in land at all (as in large parts of Zambia) or the administrative task of valuation is too much for local resources. Furthermore, if such a tax is to give an increasing yield as productivity grows (that is, if it is to be income-elastic) then revaluations must be fairly frequent. An interesting variation has been proposed in India where tax liability would be based on the average value of crops grown in the previous ten years. This proposal has the advantage of continuous upward revision of tax liability in response to growth at the same time as not penalizing success in the short term, that is, an income effect and some income elasticity but no substitution effect.[13]

Clearly the Uganda type of tax can (and should) also adapt to rising income. It is quite likely to do so if it is raised *and spent* within a localized level of government. There is a strong case anyway for devolving some tax-raising responsibility on to local authorites: taxpayers, especially rather unsophisticated taxpayers, are more likely to pay up if the proceeds are spent locally and can be seen and appreciated. There is thus a case for locally based agricultural taxation even in countries like Zambia and Nigeria with adequate central revenues, in order to encourage production and local participation in development. It is difficult to involve people in development except as individual producers if both money and decisions are perceived to come ultimately from the centre. Although the urban wealth of Zambia makes it impossible to think of raising as much from a local tax as from the central 'Western' type of income tax (as was at one time the case in Uganda) enough money could be raised to make a significant contribution at the local level.[14]

It is also argued that locally provided benefits should be paid for locally rather than by taxpayers generally. For example local street lighting mainly benefits local people and so should be paid for by them – the benefit principle. If carried too far, however, this principle would perpetuate and make worse existing inequalities between different parts of a country.

6 ECONOMIC EFFICIENCY

Economic efficiency refers to the effect of taxes on aggregate demand.

A tax is 'efficient' if it reduces private sector spending by the full amount of the tax collected; it is inefficient if a large part of the tax is paid out of money that would not have been spent domestically. For example, a tax on low-income wage earners is likely to reduce consumption by the full amount of the tax since such people have little or nothing in the way of savings; a tax on high-income salary earners is likely to be paid partly out of savings with only a relatively small impact on consumption. Of course if a government wishes to run a surplus and pay off its debts *without* reducing aggregate demand very much, it may choose an 'inefficient' tax.

In general, the economic efficiency of a tax depends on the propensity to spend of the person or institution which actually bears the burden of the tax. At one extreme, increases in the rate of tax on Zambia's copper mines have almost no short-term impact on demand within the Zambian economy. The companies cannot shift the tax onto buyers of copper because Zambia's share of world trade in copper is too small. The incidence of the tax is thus on copper profits. The short-term effect is thus to alter one or more of government revenues, profits remitted abroad and profits retained in Zambia, with almost no effect on demand.[15] Any long-term effect will be on the propensity to invest because of the reduced after-tax profitability of the industry.

At the other extreme, increases in income tax on medium income taxpayers (who save very little) or increases in the tax on beer which is bought by urban wage earners (who save very little and tend to reduce their consumption of other items if the beer price goes up) are extremely efficient in reducing domestic demand.

Somewhere in between is an increase in income tax on high-income salary earners, who are able to maintain part of their consumption out of savings. If a lot of them are foreigners, they may manage to secure salary increases, thus shifting the tax on to their employers and offsetting the immediate impact of the tax on demand. Another intermediate tax increase would be one on luxury consumption items for which demand is sensitive to price. Thus if the tax on luxury consumer durables is increased this will reduce demand for them (thus shifting the incidence onto producers and their employees) and will also be paid partly out of the savings of the high-income buyers of luxuries. Insofar as many luxuries are imported, reduction in demand for them will bear partly on distributors and partly on overseas producers.

A second consideration in choosing between types of tax to change is the political impact on the one hand and the dangers of cost inflation on the other. If people are more aware of direct taxes on their incomes then they are more likely to object to an increase; but indirect taxes are usually added directly to prices (although they can sometimes be absorbed by, that is shifted on to, producers) and so may start off a cost inflation.

The dangers of political reaction and cost inflation are both reduced if tax increases are small. People, whether as voters or as wage earners, are much more likely to react to big increases in tax. This suggests a strategy of tax reform, namely that even when major tax reforms are very desirable, the government should move only gradually towards the ideal system unless a major crisis offers an opportunity for a major shift. This is important even if the government does not wish to alter the total amount of tax, but merely wishes to shift the burden between groups. It is also politically important to combine tax increases with well-publicized increases in relatively popular forms of government spending (education, health, housing) rather than relatively unpopular ones (defence, central administration). It is thus vital that even quite small tax changes be made as part of a long-term strategy of tax reform, rather than being made hastily and without thought, in response to immediate needs and opportunities.

7 TAX EXPECTATIONS

The effects of a tax change which is expected to be permanent and of one which is expected to be temporary can be quite different. For example, if the government announced a temporary sales tax for one year, people would postpone as many purchases as they comfortably could in order to be able to buy at lower prices once the tax was removed. As a result even quite a small tax increase could have a very large effect on consumption. This way of reducing consumption is clearly particularly useful in a temporary crisis, where resources have to be diverted to output of non-consumption goods, such as armaments, or transport routes in Zambia after UDI. A government using this technique must expect to be able to produce additional consumption goods at some time in the near future since demand is only postponed.

In contrast, an increase in income tax that was believed to be temporary would be less effective than one that was believed to be permanent, since people would not bother to readjust their normal consumption patterns for a short period only. A tax surcharge will increasingly appear to taxpayers to be permanent the longer it is continued, so consumption will be reduced over time both for this reason and because people begin to run out of savings and credit out of which to maintain consumption.

Expectations also affect the speed with which tax changes can be implemented. Delays can be considerable because tax changes often take time to legislate for and introduce administratively. Many taxes are also paid in arrears. However, indirect taxes can usually be increased instantly, so that even if the increased revenues do not immediately flow to the government consumers face higher prices with only a small time-lag. Furthermore, even those tax changes, such as in the income tax, which take a lot of time to implement can have an immediate impact on spending if taxpayers start saving for future tax liabilities.

8 FINANCING A DEFICIT – DOMESTIC SOURCES

If government spends more than it collects in tax, it has a budget deficit which must be financed. Some money simply accrues to the government as the economy expands. Thus the public's holdings of currency increase, and this amounts to a loan to the government.[16] Furthermore, as the economy expands, banks and other financial institutions need liquid assets – that is, somewhere to invest their money where it can be quickly recovered when needed. The need of commercial banks for such assets has already been discussed; in their case, the government actually enforces the holding of government debt by legislating for liquidity ratios which exclude other types of investment (except bills of exchange).

Other financial institutions, such as insurance companies, provident funds and so on, also require liquid investments – in Africa, government debt is very often the only possibility *within* the country. In colonial times financial institutions (including banks) invested in liquid assets in places like London, but independent governments have tried to end this practice in two main ways: firstly by providing government debt in which to invest, secondly by legislating that local institutions must have some or all of their investments in local assets.

There is thus a fairly steady flow of lending to the government as the monetary economy expands. Typically, however, there is very little domestic borrowing by African governments from individuals, who hold almost no stock or Treasury Bills.[17] Individual investment is indirect, via financial institutions. Deposits in government savings banks (in Zambia, the National Savings and Credit Bank, formerly the Post Office Savings Bank) are virtually all invested in government debt; deposits in building societies and commercial banks, compulsory savings with pension funds, are partly lent or invested in the private sector and partly lent to the government.

Governments *do* try to encourage individuals to lend money to the public sector. At times quite a lot of money, political energy and administrative time is devoted to 'savings campaigns'. The official justification is twofold: to restrain consumption and to 'put people's savings to work'.

There is very little evidence that savings campaigns have any impact on aggregate consumption which is largely determined by income (as discussed at length in Chapter 4). Some savings may be switched from other savings media (for example from commercial bank savings deposit accounts and building societies) but this does not add to aggregate savings.

If savings are switched from notes and coin, buried in the ground or hidden under the bed, to savings accounts then the individual gains by receiving interest (although he loses liquidity) but again aggregate savings are unaffected. Meanwhile the government pays interest on its debt instead of receiving an interest-free loan, which is what the hoarding of currency amounts to in practice. Governments also press commercial banks to open more branches, especially in the rural areas, to encourage saving and to 'put idle money to work'. If in fact people switch their savings from currency to bank deposits, command over resources is shifted from the government to those who borrow from banks. This only helps the economy to the extent that banks make better use of resources than the government.[18]

In practice, savings campaigns are usually used as an excuse for not cutting expenditure or raising taxes, both of which are unpopular. Their true justification should not be as a short-term policy of restraining consumption, but as a long-term policy of educating people in self-reliance. The amount actually available to the Government of Zambia from the Post Office Savings Bank and its successor was a mere K5 mn in the eight years 1964–72, a negligible contribution.

There are thus two ways in which an African government can try and finance more of its deficit by domestic borrowing: firstly by offering a higher rate of interest on government debt than is available from competing private sector financial institutions, secondly by forcing financial institutions to hold more government debt. If the commercial banks are forced to hold more government debt this tends to be inflationary, as explained in Section 5 of the Appendix to Chapter 8. If the deficit is financed by the central bank, it is money creation, not borrowing, and is highly inflationary unless the domestic economy has spare capacity.[19] If the commercial banks can be prevented from using the additional liquidity created, then the inflationary impact is reduced – this really comes back to forcing the commercial banks to hold government debt instead of lending to the private sector. Forcing insurance companies, say, to hold more government debt transfers resources from the private or parastatal sector to the government, depending on available alternative investments.

Financing a deficit by money creation via the central bank need not be inflationary if the excess demand created can be satisfied by allowing imports to increase. But this requires either that the government has adequate foreign exchange reserves and is prepared to use them, or that the government has other sources of foreign exchange. These are dealt with in the next section.

9 FINANCING A DEFICIT – FOREIGN SOURCES

Government can borrow from abroad, thus using savings from some other economy, or it can use up foreign exchange reserves. There is also aid. Most aid is in fact borrowing on concessionary terms ('soft loans'), the difference between concessionary and commercial terms being the aid element. A small amount of aid is in the form of grants, with no interest or repayment obligations.

Both soft loans and grants tend to have conditions attached, both political and economic. These conditions (or 'strings') can make the aid much less valuable than it at first appears: for example, if a loan is 'tied' to purchases from the lending country whose prices are higher than those of other countries, then the borrowing country could be better off with a commercial loan and freedom to buy at cheaper prices.

From the point of view of short-term management of the economy, foreign sources of finance do add to the resources available to government – *but only* by providing foreign exchange. They do not add to domestic resources. So if shortage of foreign exchange is preventing the government from spending, while at the same time there is spare capacity in the domestic economy so that domestic output can increase rapidly, then foreign finance does enable the government to spend more without creating excess demand. If, however, there is no spare capacity at home, foreign finance will not enable the government to spend more – unless *all* the additional spending is on imports. In practice, most imports require matching domestic resources – skilled labour, transport, construction capacity, etc.

The distinction between government borrowing internally and externally is therefore as follows. Internal borrowing from non-bank sources means that resources are not available for use in the private sector. If private consumption is reduced as a result, then people are worse off, but this may be compensated by future increases in consumption provided that the government invests successfully, or by increases in collective consumption through the provision of current government services. If private sector investment is reduced then people will be better off in the future if the government makes better use of the money than the private sector – and vice versa.

External borrowing enables additional consumption and investment to take place without any reduction in domestic consumption or investment. There is a risk, however, namely that in the future the payment of interest and repayment of the loan will have to be made out of resources that were *not* increased by the borrowing. Furthermore, repayment has to be made in foreign currency which may be scarce – for example if export prices are low.

It is sometimes argued that even internal borrowing imposes a burden on people in the future because of the interest payments (repayment of principal is usually out of new borrowing). The counter argument is that interest on the internal debt is merely a transfer from one section of the community (taxpayers) to another (holders of the national debt). This argument is correct, but the process of payment is not costless – the collecting of taxes and paying of interest requires real resources and the additional taxes needed for this purpose may have additional distorting and disincentive effects of the sort already discussed. But these costs are typically very small; most of the real costs of domestic borrowing are met at the time when the borrowing takes place, when private sector consumption and investment are reduced. The real costs of foreign borrowing are pushed forward to the time of interest payment and repayment of principal (if this is not met from new borrowing). If national income has been increased by the spending of the foreign borrowing then this cost should be easily met. In practice, as mentioned already, foreign exchange may be scarce when payments have to be made.

It has been argued that using foreign finance (loans, aid and foreign investment) reduces domestic saving.[20] On the one hand this might seem reasonable in very poor countries, whose poverty makes it difficult to save. On the other hand, relying on foreign finance creates economic and political dependence, which reduces future freedom of manoeuvre. As a generalization, relatively rich African countries (Zambia, Nigeria) can borrow abroad without becoming dependent; relatively poor ones (Tanzania, Malawi) with stagnant exports create a continuing need for foreign finance by borrowing, and thus a continuing need to please their creditors. Yet it is precisely the poorer countries (in terms of export earnings) that most need to borrow to overcome the foreign exchange constraint. There is no easy way out of this dilemma.

10 OTHER WAYS OF 'PAYING' FOR COLLECTIVE GOODS

Governments can commandeer resources – for example by making it compulsory for all young men (and women in a few countries) to serve in the armed forces or for all university students to do work in rural development. Although conscripts are paid, their income is less than would be required to get the same people to volunteer. The difference between the cost of volunteers and conscripts is the money value of the resources commandeered. Other examples are compulsory labour on public works and the use of prisoners as cheap labour.

Governments can confiscate assets (usually of foreigners) or take over assets with very little compensation, using their political power to pay less than the market price would be under 'free' conditions. Some governments even use the threat of force to induce 'gifts' from the rich – this method was used by English kings in the Middle Ages.

The surpluses (profits) of publicly owned corporations are rather neglected as a source of revenue – the tendency is to hold their prices (and profits) down, because of the political unpopularity of high prices and profits in the public sector. Yet electricity supply to private houses, for example, is a luxury that can and perhaps ought to be 'taxed' as such in poor countries. It may be that politically it is more sensible to impose a tax rather than to impose a high price and make a big profit, even if the financial result (a transfer from the private to the public sector) is the same.

Inflation can provide resources to the government by reducing the real value of privately held money balances – as explained in Chapter 9.

Most significantly, it has been argued that unemployed or under-employed labour is a resource that can be used to create more collective goods. For example, farmers with little to do at certain times of year can get together to improve roads and drainage systems, to build dams and clinics. However there is a limit to what can be produced with labour alone; if other resources are needed as well, then there is a problem of financing their purchase – whether they be skilled labour or tools.

If the government wants to employ surplus labour to produce collective goods, and pays cash wages, then the income of the workers will create demand for private consumption goods, which again must somehow be taxed away from others. It is thus quite difficult to use the resource available in the form of surplus labour unless the government has matching resources. It is clear, however, that the government's financial resources can be made to produce more if they are combined with surplus labour using labour-intensive methods to produce collective goods, than if this resource is neglected.

NOTES

[1] For a more detailed analysis see Chapter 6, 'Tax reform in the mining industry' in M. Bostock and C. Harvey, op. cit., or Chapter 6, 'The fiscal system' in C. M. Elliott, op. cit. The latter contains a description and critique of most of the tax system in Zambia in 1968.

[2] Elliott, op. cit., pp. 175–7.

[3] Strictly speaking, there is only a bias if allowances over the life of an asset are greater than its cost or if allowances are especially generous in the early years. The latter is very common.

[4] An export tax is not inequitable if it merely recovers the extra money spent by government on services to exporters.

[5] See my paper 'Observations on the 1969 Zambian budget and the administrative constraint on further tax reform', *Zambia Law Journal*, 1969.

[6] A. Beveridge and A. Oberschall, 'African businessmen in Lusaka: some initial findings', paper presented to East African Universities Social Science Conference, Dar es Salaam, December 1970.

[7] This is not always true. Quite a lot of smuggling to avoid taxation occurs between some West African states. For example, some 12½% of the Ghanaian cocoa crop was estimated to have been smuggled to neighbouring countries in 1970; see A. Kumar, 'Smuggling in Ghana', *Nigerian Journal of Economic and Social Studies*, July 1973.

[8] Incidence refers to who actually bears the burden of a tax. Some taxpayers can shift the burden on to someone else, by raising the selling price, or in the case of an income tax by securing higher income from their employers.

[9] For example, imports attributed to consumption fell from 30% to 21% in Zambia

between 1965 and 1969: 'National Accounts and Input–Output Tables', 1965 and 1969.

[10] For example 37% of customs and excise duties *combined* came from locally produced beer in Zambia in 1973 and 9% from cigarettes. The only other important excise taxes were on soft drinks (3%) and the general sales tax (3½%). Import duties accounted for the remainder. The relative importance of beer and cigarettes is much less, however, in East Africa.

[11] In the case of ex-British colonies, double taxation agreements have frequently offered *less* advantage to African countries than provisions which *already existed* in British law. See 'Tax treaties between developed and developing countries' (UN publication, Sales no. E69 XVI 2), 5, 1969. The same argument applies to USA, Germany, Italy and France. For the Scandinavian countries, a double taxation agreement is necessary.

[12] For a lengthier description see J. F. Due, *Taxation and Economic Development in East Africa*, Cambridge, Mass., MIT Press, 1963, Chapter 5. This tax has now been abandoned in Uganda, but the same method is used in Tanzania.

[13] See my paper 'Agricultural taxation policy in Africa and the Raj report for India', IDS Discussion Paper No. 20, 1973.

[14] It is unlikely, though, that the theoretical incentive benefits would be greater than the costs. It is also possible to localize decision-making *without* localizing taxation.

[15] If shortage of foreign exchange had been causing the government to restrain demand, then an increase in copper taxation might release that constraint, allowing demand to increase in the short term.

[16] See Chapter 11, Section 3.

[17] For example, the Bank of Zambia's 'Quarterly Statistical Review' for June 1974 shows the results of an issue of stock in May 1974. The issue was of K10 mn. The commercial banks bought K3 mn, other financial institutions K2 mn and the 'household sector' a mere K24,000 (0·2%). The Bank of Zambia was left holding the remainder (just under K5 mn).

[18] See R. C. Porter, 'The promotion of the "banking habit" and economic development', *Journal of Development Studies*, July 1966, Vol. 2, No. 4.

[19] A small increase in borrowing from the central bank, roughly proportionate to income growth, is not inflationary.

[20] Statistical analysis has not on the whole clarified the debate on this point. It is not clear whether countries borrow abroad because they save very little, or save very little because they borrow abroad. One would expect some foreign finance to be used for current consumption since the objective is to optimize consumption patterns over time – and this includes current consumption. Much more important, however, is the *nature* of the investment, public and private sector, that takes place using foreign finance.

Index